THE ONE-BURNER GOURMET

by

Harriett Barker

Contemporary Books, Inc.
Chicago

Cover design by Joseph Mistak, Jr.
Cover photo by Sidney Pivecka
Illustrations by Kent Starr

Published by Contemporary Books, Inc.
180 North Michigan Avenue, Chicago, Illinois 60601
Manufactured in the United States of America
Library of Congress Catalog Card Number: 79-89275
International Standard Book Number: 0-8092-7306-3

Published simultaneously in Canada by
Beaverbooks
953 Dillingham Road
Pickering, Ontario L1W 1Z7
Canada

Here's the latest word from the media on this flavor-saving outdoor cookbook -

" . . . complete, practical, and of a kind not to be found anywhere else." — *Book World, Washington Post*

" . . . could well become a household as well as a campground helper." — *Tent & Trail*

" . . . a very fine book . . . easy and enjoyable reading . . . takes eating out of the canned hash department with gusto." — *Ithaca (N.Y.) Journal*

" . . . Even I could make an edible dish in a short time with the book as guide." — *Hollywood (Fla.) Sun-Tattler*

"For campers, hikers, and backpackers, Harriett Barker's 'One-Burner Gourmet' could be a valuable find." — *Discovery Magazine*

"a handy little book . . ." — *Outdoor People, southwestern Pa.*

" . . . contains so many fine recipes that outdoor cooks are likely to find themselves using it as a standard reference work in their home kitchens." *Sun Journal Publications, Indiana and Illinois*

" . . . goes beyond the simple eggs and beans cooking that prevails on so many camping, hunting and fishing trips . . ." — *Brownsville (Texas) Herald*

ACKNOWLEDGEMENTS

ALASKA MAGAZINE . . .
Box 4-EEE
Anchorage, Alaska
99509
Fruit logs and jerky recipes (Sept., 1970)

SPORTS AFIELD MAGAZINE . . .
Ted Kesting, Almanac Editor
250 West 55 Street
New York, N.Y.
10019
Let the wasps have the cooking pot dregs (May, 1974)

CANOE MAGAZINE . . .
1999 Shepard Road
St. Paul, Minnesota
55116
Uses for soda in the camp (March/April, 1974)

I want to give particular thanks to those who felt this book was worthwhile and contributed favorite camping recipes. Their names go with their suggestions.

I also must thank those who so freely gave opinions on various one-burner stoves. Our discussions produced new friends and renewed acquaintances with the people I feel close to . . . wilderness campers.

Harriett Barker

FOREWORD

In February of 1971, Harriett Barker began her career as a columnist writing "TOOTHPICKS AND PADDLES" for the Valley Canoe Club (of Los Angeles) monthly newsletter "The Gunnel Gazette." She has written under this heading for every issue of the Gazette since then and her expert recipes have reached a wide circle of outdoor cooks.

ONE-BURNER GOURMET combines skill, imagination and a gourmet touch to tempt all palates and save the cook as well!

It is a pleasure for me to introduce you to a style of cooking which you may not have tried before, through this unique collection of recipes.

—**Melba N. Blackstone**
Editor, The Gunnel Gazette 1971-72

INTRODUCTION

If you have planned and packed carefully, outdoor meals should be so simple to prepare that your most difficult task will be to get the camp stove level. Most of the one-burner recipes in this collection are designed to take no more than half an hour. Foil recipes can take longer. Dutch oven cooking depends on the heat in the coals. (Check Dutch oven dishes about 10 minutes ahead of estimated cooking time; the contents may be done to a turn.) Also, the clean-up crew will thank the cook if the menus are kept simple.

If you can cook it from fresh vegetables and meats, you can duplicate or substitute with dry foods. Outdoor equipment catalogs list dry foods. Camping departments and outdoor stores often carry a good supply. Freeze-dried peas smell and taste just like those right off the vine. Canned foods are fine to use when weight is not a consideration.

CONTENTS

Chapter

To my men, Hal and Herb.

CHAPTER ONE

The grub box, packing and other tricks

THE GRUB BOX

Our grub box used to be our ice chest. By carefully figuring out how we wanted it packed, my husband calculated dimensions for a sheet aluminum divider that would accommodate the usual necessities and keep them all easily available. The divider is put together with aluminum angle and pop rivets. It is completely free standing and removable.

A plastic silverware tray holds the small things, such as silverware and kitchen utensils, seasonings, tea bags, clothespins, vitamin pills, soda, a small cutting board, tongs and a pair of pliers to move hot pots.

Another division holds a roll of paper towels and a tall plastic drink and pancake mixer. A folding splatter shield also fits in this section to use as a stove wind screen.

The center area contains our cook kit, dishwashing outfit and heavy-duty cooking foil, carefully folded and slipped into a plastic bag.

The last section can hold eating bowls, cups, the Teflon skillet with folding handle and grub for a weekend trip. Just above is a slot the right size to slip in a plastic tablecloth at the end of the silverware tray.

The grub box travels right side up with the lid on top. At camp it is laid on its side to give the cook two flat clean places to use — the open lid and the side (now top) of the box (see sketch). The silverware tray rides tight along the side when traveling, but when the box is laid on its side, the tray slides out for handy use.

With a tightly latched lid to keep the contents dry, and two handles for easy carrying, our ice box/grub box has proved to be a camping bonus. In fact, improvisation combined with careful, thoughtful, planning can be the key to making your time at the campside more leisurely and enjoyable. For example:

Pots and skillets with wide bottoms and thin skins tend to leave the center of scrambled eggs burnt and the edges raw. Better to use pots of less diameter with your one-burner stove. Small diameter cast iron or heavy aluminum will heat more evenly, but if weight is important, they get left behind. Cast iron also takes longer to cool. The coffee pot that is included with your cook kit works efficiently as a cooking pot. A tall one pound coffee can fits inside to use for an extra pot for heating water for instant coffee or soup. Shape a pouring spout on one side, add a wire bail, then replace it for your next trip.

A well-seasoned cast iron skillet can be cleaned easily *without* soap. Hot water and a pot scratcher or crumpled foil does the work and leaves the seasoning on the pan. DRY THOROUGHLY and slip into a denim bag for travel. Make the bag from the back of cut-off jeans which are usually soft but barely worn.

Jeans legs make good pot holders when padded with old toweling. A comfortable camp cushion can be constructed from jeans, too, but make one side from a naugahyde remnant to render it waterproof next to the ground. If you have several denim colors, you might like to make a patchwork pillow top.

Teflon is a breeze to clean up, and the newer black Teflon is tougher than the brown kind. A Teflon omelet pan may sound like pretty fancy camp cookware, but it will cook a hearty omelet or heat a can of hash. Just flop it over to brown the other side. The hinged cover keeps food warm . . . pancakes, too. Keep the recipe small enough to avoid overflow.

Plastic foam meat trays make excellent heat-retaining, sturdy, non-absorbing plates. The campfire will completely consume them, but DO NOT cook over a fire after they have been thrown in. The fumes are hazardous to your health. Flexible plastic bowls also make good "plates." The higher sides keep food warm longer, and they will hold soup, hash or pancakes with syrup equally well.

Plastic baby bottles make good liquid carriers. Make a gasket from the rubber ring of a nipple. Compress the sides of plastic bottles before putting on the top. This creates a vacuum and they won't be so apt to leak. A plastic "push-pull" topped syrup bottle makes a good cooking-oil container. Because cooking oil has a nasty habit of creeping into everything, make a paper towel collar and fasten it at the base of the lid with a rubber band and slip the bottle into a plastic bag. Repack foods from glass jars and paper bags into plastic containers. They won't break and are lighter in weight. If you do use glass, wrap it in rows of masking tape to prevent shattering. If you use boxes, use masking tape to seal spouts and fasten tops. Never use liquid soap containers for food.

Kitchen tongs should be in your cook kit. Use them to turn a steak or a fish, to hold bread over a flame for toast, or to hold buttered, salted pre-fried tortillas over the flame for a tasty pre-dinner nibble with a cup of soup. They can also be used to pluck foil-cooked food from the camp fire.

A sheet of plastic (slit open a sturdy bag) makes a clean place to lay out gear for food preparation. A dip in the nearest stream gets it clean. A gauze diaper makes a quick drying dish towel. Fels-Naphtha soap will get the dishes squeaky clean and can come in handy for a scrub down if anyone finds poison oak or ivy.

Make a sheath for your sharp knife by folding a piece of shirt cardboard around the knife three times. Score the fold lightly with the dull side of the knife to make a sharper fold. Wrap it generously in masking tape.

Make sure your Halazone tablets are fresh. Shelf life is about six months. A tiny vial of Clorox will be enough for a long trip. A single drop could purify a gallon of water. The strong flavor can be overcome by adding it to the water, stirring several times during the evening, then letting it set overnight.

Aerosol shaving cream can be used for wash-ups in a pinch. It needs very little rinsing. A good camp hand lotion can be made by mixing 1/3 cup baby oil and 2/3 cup hand lotion. It is absorbed by the dry skin, but leaves a thin covering of oil to keep your skin from drying out.

Keeping fresh foods fresh is no problem if you prepare for it. Leave home with meats and pre-cooked one-pot meals frozen VERY HARD. 40-45 degrees is the highest temperature allowable before bacteria begins to take over. Pre-cooked dinners, frozen in milk cartons, should be checked at noon to see if they are melting fast enough for the first night's dinner. A solid block of ice is such a drag to thaw out over a camp stove when everyone is clamoring for food.

For ice, rinse milk cartons with a strong soda water solution, then rinse with clean water. Fill and put in your freezer for several days before needed to allow it to get very hard. Put in the ice chest an hour before leaving to cool the chest. Add food supplies as the last thing before leaving. If you are not taking an icechest, wrap the frozen foods in a plastic bag, then with layers of newspaper. Slip into an insulated grocery bag and then into the middle of a sleeping bag for safe cold keeping. If you are canoeing and the water is cold, make the most of it by placing perishables in an insulated bag on the bottom of the canoe with gear around and over them.

A plastic foam ice chest will be more efficient if you seal the lid with masking tape after filling it. Then wrap with several thicknesses of newspaper secured with masking tape and slip the whole thing into a cardboard box with a lid. Fill the corners and cover the top of the ice box with newspaper before taping shut. If the cardboard box does not have a lid, slip a close fitting box over it. Boat cushions and life jackets laid on top are good insulators from the sun. Cardboard boxes of sturdy construction can be made into food and gear chests if several coats of varnish are applied inside and out. Cut slots for your hands at each end and reinforce with tape. The varnish will make the cardboard water-repellent for a surprisingly long time.

Search the markets for foods that are displayed unrefrigerated. Danish canned ham and bacon, process cheeses and smoked and dry salami are welcome camp fare. Peanuts and peanut butter, cereals, beans and lentils are sources of protein. Eggs will stay fresh for a month if you buy them freshly laid and then grease them with vaseline. Keep them cool.

I prefer to use margarine to cooking oil. There is less mess with basically the same results. It doesn't add noxious odors to your gear as cooking oil does. Melt margarine first in pre-warmed pan, tilt the pan to grease it, then add the melted margarine to your recipe. It will keep better than butter.

It is a good idea to take two days extra food on wilderness trips for use in an emergency. I also include a supply of one-a-day vitamins and separate vitamin C tablets for each day. The vitamin C can be crushed into a glass of water for a breakfast drink or added to a glass of fruit juice or warm tea to give a lemon flavor.

If your first night's camp is only a few hours from home, get a head start on dinner by cooking a casserole and transporting it hot. Use a heavy cooking container. My favorite is a stoneware bean pot. Just before you leave, take the hot food from the oven, wrap it in several layers of newspaper and place in a cardboard box lined on the bottom with many thicknesses of paper. Wad and stuff paper tightly around the pot and put layers of paper on top. Cover with the box flaps and fasten with masking tape. Your food will stay oven-hot for several hours. For bread to go with it, wrap rolls in foil and heat in the oven with your casserole. Place on top of the pot and then wrap both in paper in the cardboard box. This idea is especially useful if your first camp is at a high altitude where it takes longer to cook foods.

If bees, flies, or wasps are giving you a bad time, hang a fresh corn cob, apple core or watermelon rind a little distance from your spot to lure them away. If none of these are available, set your cooking pot (with the dregs) off to one side. They would rather have their own plate than try to steal from yours.

One of the most valuable, yet inexpensive, additions to your camping gear is a box of baking soda. It can be used as a mouth wash, dentifrice, or to settle the stomach. Aspirin will work faster if soda is used as a chaser. Vomiting can be induced (only where safely indicated) by drinking a glass of water with a heaping teaspoon of soda added. Minor burns, sunburn, insect bites, stings, scratches or cuts are relieved by making a paste and putting it on the affected area. Keep it moist with a damp cloth. Weary feet can be revived by soaking in a soda bath. Weary bodies get the same relief. Patted on dry, soda makes an effective deodorant. It will smother small stove flare-ups and sweeten the interior of your grub box when added to your cleaning water. Coffee pots and plastic dishes benefit from the same solution. Damp soda rubbed on the hands will neutralize fish odors so that soap and water will finish the job. Vacuum bottles and jugs can be freshened by adding two tablespoons of soda, partly filling with water and shaking vigorously. Rinse. The cork revives with a dry soda rub.

Packing efficiently can make your wilderness outing a joy. All you need is quiet and a large flat place to sort. The living room floor works very well. Have a pad and pencil handy to jot down "don't forgets."

Ziploc bags make good containers for your pre-measured dry mixes such as pancakes or Dutch oven cake. Pre-mixing saves camp time and space. Don't forget to include any directions you might need.

When packing freeze-dried foods, puncture the plastic bag with a pin at one end of the envelope and force the air out. It will take up much less room. Just make sure you use it as soon as possible to avoid the contents gathering moisture and spoiling. Pack individual meals complete in one bag, including the entree and dessert. Menu decisions are all taken care of ahead of time. Put the LAST DAY'S MEALS on the bottom when packing for the trip.

Arrange your menus to avoid repetition — a pasta entree for three days in a row. Freeze-dried vegetables are delicious. Use them in one-pot recipes. Add according to the directions on the package for the proper cooking time.

Discard as many cardboard boxes as you can when packing food. For instance, remove the Jello envelope from the outer box and reseal in a plastic bag. Don't forget those instructions if you need them.

Pack all lunch material in a separate container so you won't have to go digging. Include a small plastic tablecloth, small cutting board, sharp knife, plastic knives for spreading, cups and drink container, paper towels for napkins.

For a sturdy, light camp line, braid monofilament fishing line (cut from the tangle you made with that duffer's cast). Use also for a clothes line, extra tent guy lines, ties for gear, emergency shoe laces. Use braided line to secure your glasses by drilling small holes in the ends of the frames and knotting the ends of a short length through the holes. Leave the line long enough to slip over your head.

For a small, non-glare light, punch holes with a nail in the sides of a small juice can. Add a candle.

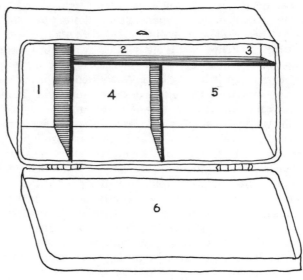

ICE BOX — GRUB BOX

1. Roll of paper towels, tall plastic container, wind screen.
2. Divided silverware tray.
3. Plastic table cloth, hot pad.
4. Cook kit, folded heavy duty foil.
5. Eating bowls, cups, frying pan, grub.
6. Lid of ice box (table space)

Darkened area is the aluminum sheet divider.
Ice box dimensions (outside) 11½" x 26"

Following is a typical weekend menu:

Saturday breakfast:
Canned juice
Granola and milk (Mix dry milk and coffee lightener, half and half into the
    dry granola. Add *hot* water for a delicious hot cereal.)
Poached eggs, or, soft boiled eggs cooked in the coffee water
English muffins, split, buttered and toasted in the frying pan
Coffee or hot chocolate

Saturday dinner:
Hot bouillon
Beans Hawaiian (Chapter 7)
Green salad, washed and trimmed at home and put in a plastic bag
Rolls heated over the pot of beans on an inverted lid or foil pan, covered
Instant pudding and cookies
Hot tea

Sunday breakfast:
Juice crystals mixed with warm water (Tang or Start)
Bacon
Pancakes and honey or marmalade
One fried egg apiece
Coffee or hot chocolate

Lunches:
Drink mix with sugar added. (include a plastic container and cups)
Honey spread
Peanut butter
Cheese spread
Dry salami (include a sharp knife and a cutting board)
Crackers: Wheat Thins, Ritz, Waverly's, Rye Crisp, etc.
Cinnamon graham crackers
Dried fruits (raisins, prunes, apples)
Fresh fruit (apples, oranges)
Toasted sunflower seeds for cracker spreads (Chapter 11)
Fruit logs for mid-meal snacks (Chapter 11)
Gorp bags for mid-meal snacks (Chapter 11)
Several plastic spreading knives, paper towels, tablecloth

For lunch on a cold day, hot instant bouillon or the individual cups of
soup are easily heated in Sierra metal cups on your one-burner stove.
Two boxes of Wheat Thins can be stacked into the Tupperware plastic
box called Pak-N-Stor.

CHAPTER TWO

In The Beginning . . .
Breakfast

Breakfast is the fuel that gets you started. Whether you are canoeing 500 miles of the Yukon River, backpacking Midwest trails or fishing in the stream behind your Vermont camp, you need energy to get you through the day. A hearty, rib-sticking breakfast will see you on your way.

Pancake variations are seemingly endless:
- Substitute cherry or strawberry flavored soft drinks for the liquid.
- Use the syrup from a can of fruit for the batter liquid. Add water, if necessary, to meet the liquid requirement.
- Add diced fried bacon or bacon bar (sparingly) to batter.
- Add pared, diced apples, drained blueberries, fresh strawberries, drained pineapple, mashed banana, thin-sliced fresh peaches. Also add 2 tbls. sugar to 2 cups of mix.
- Add coconut or chopped nuts.
- Add 2 tbls. cocoa to each cup of dry mix.
- Substitute beer for the liquid.
- Drop raisins on uncooked side before turning.
- Add 2 tbls. molasses to the batter.
- Add chocolate or butterscotch chips and 1 tbls. sugar to dry mix.
- Add Granola cereal to the dry ingredients.
- Grind piñon nuts in a food chopper and mix half and half with mix.
- Add wild berries; raspberries, strawberries, huckleberries, blueberries, salmon or thimble berries.
- Dandelion Pancakes: Wash and drop blossoms, either whole or cut up, on uncooked side of pancakes. When turned the blossom is cooked.
- Add a few chopped pitted prunes.
- Try grated orange rind with chopped pecans.
- Mix cranberry sauce with the batter.
- Add toasted sesame seeds or toasted coconut. (To toast: spread on a flat pan and bake at 350 degrees for 5-10 min. Stir a couple of times.
- Chop a few slices of Spam and add to uncooked side.
- Add wheat germ to the batter, ¼ cup to 2 cups of mix.
- Add cooked rice to pancake mix.

PANCAKES WITH FRUIT

BANANA FRITTERS

2 ripe bananas
1 egg, beaten
2 tbls. flour

Mash bananas well with a fork. Add egg and flour to make a batter. Drop by spoonfuls onto a hot, greased griddle. Turn.
When browned, sprinkle with cinnamon sugar or powdered sugar.

ORANGE FRITTERS

Peel 2 oranges and separate into sections.

Remove seeds from each section, making the smallest slit necessary. Use a knife or toothpick.

Dip each section in pancake batter and fry.

Variation: Add orange sections to the pancake batter and scoop out each section to fry separately.

PINEAPPLE FRITTERS

Combine: Pancake mix, liquid, and egg (if needed). Add: 1 small can drained pineapple.

Drop by spoonfuls onto a hot greased griddle. Brown both sides.

Add the pineapple syrup to an equal amount of maple flavored pancake syrup for a topping.

Boil the pineapple juice and a little sugar until thickened.

APPLE PANCAKES

¼ cup apple juice
⅔ cup applesauce
1 egg
3 tbls. melted margarine
⅓ cup water
⅓ cup dry milk
1 tbls. sugar
1 cup pancake mix

Melt margarine in the frying pan and add to the other ingredients.

Drop by spoonfuls onto hot skillet. Brown both sides.

Serve with sausages and applesauce.

CEREAL PANCAKES

GRANOLA PANCAKES

Combine:
1 cup granola
½ cup flour
2 tsp. baking powder
¾ cup dry milk
Stir in:
2 tbls. melted margarine
1½ cups water
1 egg

Spoon batter on lightly greased frying pan or griddle.

Brown both sides.

Top with a fried or poached egg.

BREAD CRUMB PANCAKES

Combine:
1 cup dry milk
2 cups fine bread crumbs
1 tbls. sugar
¾ tsp. salt
1 cup unsifted flour
3 tsp. baking powder
Add:
2 cups warm water
3 tbls. melted margarine (melted in frying pan)
2 eggs
　Beat thoroughly and bake on a hot frying pan or griddle.

ROMAN MEAL PANCAKES

Combine:
⅓ cup dry milk
½ cup flour
1 tsp. baking powder
½ tsp. salt
1 tbls. sugar
⅓ cup Roman Meal cereal
Combine and add:
1 egg
1 tbls. melted margarine
⅔ cup water
　Stir until batter is smooth. Bake by spoonfuls on a hot greased griddle.
　OR, add ⅓ to ½ cup Roman Meal cereal to 1 cup pancake mix.

CORN CAKES

　Cut up three slices of bacon and fry until crisp. Drain and save fat.
Combine bacon with:
1 can (1 lb.) creamed corn
3 eggs
½ cup flour
½ tsp. salt
Dash of pepper
　Drop by spoonfuls onto hot greased griddle.
　Brown both sides.
　Top with a fruit jam.

CORN PANCAKES
Use a box of JIFFY CORN MUFFIN MIX, but add more milk to make a thinner batter.

Variation: Add a small can of whole drained corn and a little bacon bar. Add ¼ cup wheat germ.

CORN GRIDDLE CAKES
Combine:
2 cups biscuit mix
1 cup dry milk
Add:
2 eggs, beaten
2 cups water
¼ cup melted margarine
1 small can whole corn, drained
Drop by large spoonfuls on hot greased griddle. Brown both sides.

POTATO CAKES
Cook instant potato according to directions, but use double the amount of dry milk needed to make up the recipe. Drop mixture by spoonfuls onto hot margarine or bacon drippings in a hot frying pan. Brown five minutes on each side. Serve with catsup.

Chef's secret: Save bacon fat in a 7 oz. metal baking powder can with a plastic lid. Use this in place of margarine for frying.

PANCAKE TOPPINGS
CINNAMON BUTTER
Cream together:
2 tbls. margarine
⅓ cup powdered sugar
½ tsp. cinnamon
Sit near heat or over hot water to melt slightly.

HONEY BUTTER
Heat ¼ lb. (½ cup) soft margarine with ¼ cup honey and stir until blended.

MOLASSES BUTTER
Cream ½ cup margarine and add 1 tsp. sugar, 1 tbls. molasses. Blend.

MAPLE BUTTER
Cream ½ cup soft margarine. Add 1 cup syrup gradually. Beat until smooth.

ORANGE HONEY BUTTER
Beat ½ cup honey with ½ cup margarine. Add 1 tsp. grated orange rind.

PINEAPPLE BUTTER
Mix 1 can (1 lb. 4 oz.) crushed pineapple, ¼ cup packed brown sugar, 2 tbls. margarine. Simmer 3 minutes.

APPLE SYRUP
Simmer together 10 to 15 min. until thickened:
1 cup packed brown sugar
1 cup apple juice
1 tbls. margarine
Dash of cinnamon or nutmeg

CLOVER BLOSSOM SYRUP
Simmer until sugar is dissolved:
1 cup water
2 cups sugar
Handful of fresh, washed, shredded clover blossoms
   Variations: Use fragrant violets instead of clover.

HONEY-ORANGE SYRUP
Heat until blended:
1 cup honey
⅓ cup orange juice (or reconstituted orange crystals)
1 tbls. margarine
   Variation: Use orange marmalade instead of orange juice.

JELLY SYRUP
In a small saucepan, combine:
½ cup jelly (apple, grape, etc.)
2 tbls. margarine
   Stir and heat until melted and smooth.

MAPLE SYRUP VARIATIONS
To one cup of maple flavored syrup add:
¼ cup apricot nectar, 1 tbls. margarine. Heat.
¼ cup chopped pecans or toasted almonds.
½ tsp. cinnamon
Grated rind of orange
   (Maple flavored syrup has only 6% maple syrup in it)
   Heat together Karo Syrup and jam. (Strawberry, cherry, etc.)

SUGAR SYRUP

Combine:
1 pound dark brown sugar
1 cup water
Dash of cinnamon (optional)
    Simmer until sugar is dissolved.
Variation:
½ cup white sugar
½ cup brown sugar
1 cup water
    Simmer until sugar is dissolved.

WILD BERRY SYRUP

Measure washed berries and add *half* the amount of sugar. Stir together over the heat, mashing the fruit with a fork. Add water to make a syrup.
    Sprinkle powdered, granulated, or brown sugar over buttered pancakes.

HOT TOASTS

HOT DOUGHNUTS

Slice plain doughnuts in half lengthwise.
Butter each half and place butter side down in a hot skillet.
    When browned sprinkle buttered side with cinnamon sugar or drizzle with honey.

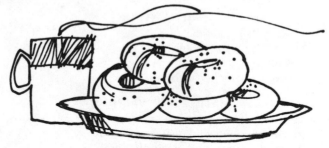

FRENCH TOAST

For 8 slices of stale bread combine:
2 eggs, slightly beaten
¾ to 1 cup milk
¼ tsp. salt
2 tsp. sugar
    Heat margarine in a frying pan.
    Dip bread, one slice at a time, in the egg mixture.
    Place in hot frying pan and brown on both sides.
    Variations: Add 2 tbls. molasses to egg mixture.
    Chef's secret: Sprinkle a little bacon bar over uncooked side of toast before turning.

HOT PEACH CRUMBLE
(Serves 2)
4 Shredded Wheat biscuits
1 can (17 oz.) sliced peaches, drained
½ cup brown sugar, firmly packed
¼ cup margarine, melted
¼ cup chopped nuts
1 tbls. lemon juice
½ tsp. cinnamon

Melt margarine in a frying pan. Combine brown sugar, nuts, lemon juice and cinnamon.

Place biscuits in a single layer in skillet and arrange peach slices on top.
Spoon margarine mixture over the top.
Heat in a covered skillet until hot.
Add peach juice if too dry.
Chef's secret: Add a drizzle of Karo syrup to a cut grapefruit instead of sugar.

WARMED ROLLS
Place sweet rolls on a foil pie pan. Cover with an inverted foil pan and fasten with wooden clothespins around the edges. Use as a lid on the pot used to soft boil eggs.

PEANUT BUTTER FRENCH TOAST
Make a peanut butter sandwich.
Dip in beaten egg and milk.
Fry as you would French toast.
Top with:
Apple jelly heated until it melts.
Heated cherry pie filling.
Hot apple sauce.

ASPARAGUS TOAST
Stand washed and trimmed asparagus stalks in the coffee pot with about
one inch of salted water or less.
Put a lid on the pot and cook for 10 min.
Arrange a handful of croutons, plain or flavored, in a bowl.
Lay cooked asparagus over the croutons and pour cooking water over all.
Chef's secret: To get tender stalks, snap off the bottom end and discard. If the stalks are too long, cut to fit. Lay the stems on the bottom of the pot, but have the tips out of the water to steam.

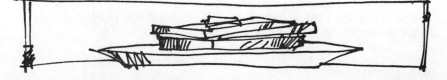

ALL IN ONE BREAKFAST

Butter one side of a slice of bread.
Cut out a hole about the size of an egg yolk in the center.
Place buttered side down in a hot, greased skillet.
Break an egg into the hole.
Cover the skillet and cook slowly on one side till egg white is set.
Turn and cook for a few seconds more.
Salt and pepper to taste.
Fry the "hole" too, and spread with jam.

SKILLET CORN BREAD

Combine corn muffin mix as directed on package.
Drop by large spoonfuls on hot greased griddle.
Cook over low heat, turning to brown both sides.
Serve with margarine and jam.

CORNY EGGS
(Serves 2-3)

4 slices of bacon, cut into pieces
1 can creamed corn
4 eggs

Fry bacon pieces and drain fat.
Add corn. When hot add eggs and stir until set.
Salt and pepper to taste.

FRUIT FOR BREAKFAST

FRIED BANANAS

Slice bananas lengthwise.
Dip in flour
Fry slowly in margarine until light brown, turning often.
Sprinkle with sugar.
   Variation: Fry with the breakfast bacon.

FRIED APPLE RINGS

   When the sausage links are nearly cooked, push them to the edges of the frying pan. Add cored, sliced apple rings (1/2" thick) and sauté in the sausage fat until tender, turning once to brown both sides.

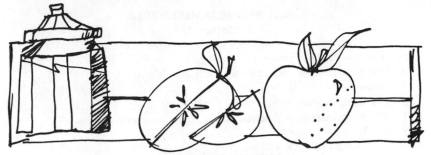

SHREDDED PEACHES

Cover shredded wheat biscuits with canned peach slices and juice, brown sugar, and a dash of cinnamon.

Add milk, or reconstituted dry milk and coffee lightener, measured half and half.

BACON AND PRUNES

Using pitted prunes, wrap each one in a half slice of bacon.

Arrange on skewers and hold over hot coals, turning often, until bacon is crisp.

Variation: Alternate with other dried fruit on a long skewer.

MUSHROOM EGGS
(Serves 2)

1 pkg. (2¾ oz.) freeze dried eggs with butter
2-3 tbls. onion soup mix
Salt and pepper

Combine eggs and liquid according to package directions.

Add soup mix, salt and pepper.

Cook as directed on package.

SWISS SCRAMBLED EGGS
(Serves 3-4)

2 tbls. margarine or bacon drippings
1 tbls. dry onion flakes
¼ cup water
2 tbls. dry milk
½ cup cubed Swiss cheese
1 tsp. Worcestershire Sauce
6 eggs, lightly beaten
Salt and pepper

Add dry onion flakes to the melted fat.

Combine water, dry milk, Worcestershire Sauce and cheese, and add to eggs.

Pour into frying pan and cook over low heat, stirring until set.

Season with salt and pepper.

RICE AND SCRAMBLED EGGS
(Serves 3)
(Bob Minnick — Los Angeles, Calif.)

Heat ¾ cup salted water to boiling.
Add ¾ cup minute rice. Stir and let set 5 min.
Combine:
3 eggs with ¼ cup milk
½ tsp. Worcestershire Sauce
1 tsp. dry onion flakes
½ cup shredded Jack cheese
  Add to rice and stir — cook until set.

DEVILED HAM AND EGGS
(Serves 3)

6 English muffin halves spread with butter and deviled ham spread
2 tbls. margarine
6 eggs
¼ cup evaporated milk
¼ cup water
½ lb. Jack cheese, shredded
Salt and pepper
¼ tsp. prepared mustard
  Melt margarine in a skillet over low heat.
  Beat eggs with milk and water and add to skillet.
  Add cheese, salt and pepper and mustard. Stir until cooked and cheese is melted.
  Spoon over muffins.

SCRAMBLED POTATOES
  Cook a package of hash brown potatoes as directed. Break in several eggs, add salt and pepper and stir gently until cooked.
  Serve with a catsup topping.
  Chef's secret: Add freeze-dried rehydrated meats or bacon bar to dry scrambled egg mixes.

MEXICAN OMELET
(Serves 3)

2 bacon strips, cut up
5 eggs, lightly beaten
1 can (2 oz.) diced green chilis
1 tsp. Worcestershire Sauce
¼ cup dry milk
¼ cup water
Salt and pepper
Sliced Jack cheese

  Fry bacon until crisp. Drain fat.
  Combine eggs, chilis, seasonings, milk and water.
  Pour into heated pan. Stir often until cooked.
  Top each serving with a slice of Jack cheese.

NOPOLITOS OMELET
(CACTUS PAD OMELET)
(Serves 2-3)

1 can (15 oz.) nopolitos (Shop in Mexican food section)
1 large onion diced (or 2 tbls. dry flakes soaked in water)
4 eggs
2 tbls. milk

  Rinse and drain nopolitos.
  Fry nopolitos and onion in a little margarine until lightly browned.
  Add beaten egg and milk, and salt and pepper to taste.
  Stir-cook until eggs are set.
  Nopolitos have a green-bean taste.

JOHN'S OMELET
(Serves 6)
(John Apuan — Acton, Calif.)

12 eggs, beaten
1 can zucchini squash with tomato sauce
1 small can sliced mushrooms
1½ cups finely chopped cooked pork or salami

  Heat a *large griddle* over a campfire (or use a two-burner stove). Pour eggs to thinly cover griddle.
  When eggs just begin to set, add the other ingredients in the center.
  Fold sides toward center. Cook long enough to heat through.

COTTAGE CHEESE OMELET
(Serves 2-3)
4 eggs
½ cup milk
½ tsp. salt, dash of pepper
1 pkg. freeze dried cottage cheese, re-hydrated (or use fresh)
1 tsp. parsley flakes
Combine eggs, milk, salt and pepper, using a wire whip.
Pour into greased skillet.
When eggs begin to set, add cottage cheese and parsley flakes. Stir.
Cook until eggs are set to suit.

CRAB OMELET
(Serves 2-3)
1 tbls. margarine
1 small can crab meat
1 tsp. dry onion flakes
¼ tsp. each dry parsley and celery flakes
1 small can mushrooms, drained
3-4 eggs, well beaten
Slices of sharp cheddar cheese
Sliced fresh tomato (or well-drained canned tomato)
Melt margarine in a frying pan. Sauté crab meat, seasonings and mushrooms until lightly browned. Add eggs, salt and pepper. Top with cheese slices and tomato. Cook, covered, on low heat until eggs are set.

PADDLERS BREAKFAST
(Serves 4-5)
¼ cup margarine
1 tbls. dry onion flakes
3 medium potatoes, boiled, peeled and cut into cubes
1 can (12 oz.) luncheon meat, cubed
6 eggs
½ tsp. salt, dash of pepper
¼ cup shredded sharp cheddar cheese
Melt margarine and sauté onion, potatoes, and luncheon meat.
Beat eggs with salt and pepper and pour over potatoes.
Lift edges as it cooks to let egg flow underneath.
When eggs are set, top with cheese to serve.

EGG DEVILS
Spread pan-toasted bread with deviled ham. Top with a poached egg and a dollop of American cheese spread. (See CAMP TOAST suggestions at end of chapter.)

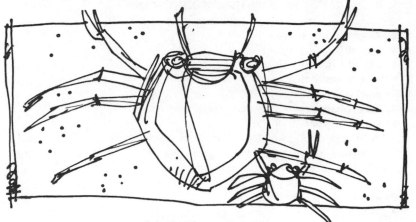

OMELETS TO SERVE 3-4

Combine 5 eggs with:

CHEESE: ⅓ cup milk, 1 cup diced sharp cheese, ½ tsp. Worcestershire Sauce.

HAM: ⅓ cup milk, 1 cup diced cooked ham, 1 tsp. prepared mustard.

CHICKEN: ⅓ cup milk, 1 cup diced chicken, 1 tsp. each celery and parsley leaves.

SHRIMP: ⅓ cup milk, 1 cup cut-up cooked shrimp, ¼ tsp. Worcestershire Sauce.

MEXICAN: ⅓ cup chili *salsa*, 2 strips crisp-cooked bacon, 1 tbls. onion flakes.

ITALIAN: ⅓ cup catsup, 2 tbls. water, ¼ tsp. salt, ½ cup sliced dry salami, ¼ cup sliced ripe olives.

NATURE: ½ cup washed, chopped dandelion blossoms, ⅓ cup milk, ⅓ cup dandelion leaves.

JAM: ⅓ cup milk, salt and pepper, top each serving with a spoonful of apricot or strawberry jam.

CUSTOM POACHED EGGS

Fashion individual poaching cups by shaping a strip of foil, doubled, around the bottom of a small can or cup. Stand in a frying pan with 1 tsp. margarine in each. Break one egg into each cup. Sprinkle with salt and pepper. Pour water ½" deep in the pan, cover tightly and steam until eggs are set, 5-6 min. Eat from the cup.

COFFEE WATER EGGS
(Melba Blackstone — Los Angeles, Calif.)

Boil your breakfast eggs in the coffee pot. Use the hot water for instant coffee, hot chocolate, or hot citrus juice from crystals.

FRIED RICE AND EGGS
(Serves 4-5)
3 slices bacon, diced
1 tbls. dry onion flakes
1 tbls. dry parsley flakes
¾ cup minute rice
¾ cup water
5 eggs, beaten
Salt and pepper
   Fry bacon until crisp. Drain fat. Add onion, parsley, rice and water.
   Reheat to a boil and remove from heat. Cover and let set 5 min.
   Add beaten eggs, salt and pepper. Stir-cook until set.

Pre-cooked Rice Variations:
Add ¼ cup slivered almonds, or other nuts.
Add ¼ cup raisins before bringing to a boil.
Add 2 tbls. chopped fresh mint, ½ tsp. sugar.
Add dash of cinnamon, blob of margarine, 1 tsp. sugar.

HURRY BREAKFAST
(1 serving)
Blend with a wire whip:
2 tbls. orange juice crystals
½ cup water
1 tbls. honey
1 egg

FRY PAN POTATOES
(Serves 3-4)
The night before: in a saucepan, simmer
2 cups diced dehydrated potatoes
1 tsp. salt
6 cups water
   Cook for 25 min. Drain. Keep in cool place.
Next morning:
Fry bacon strips
Add potatoes and brown, stirring often.

HASH AND EGGS
(Serves 2)

1 can corned beef hash
2 eggs
Salt and pepper
Catsup

Melt some margarine in a small frying pan.

Crumble the hash into the pan. Stir and heat, then spread evenly on the pan bottom.

Make two depressions with the back of a spoon. Break an egg into each. Sprinkle with salt and pepper. Circle the eggs with catsup.

Cover and steam until the eggs are set, about 15 min.

CEREALS: HOT
LAZY BREAKFAST

Before crawling into your sleeping bag, fill a wide mouth Thermos half full of any quick cooking cereal, 1/2 tsp. salt, a few raisins.

Add boiling water to 1" from the top. Replace the stopper and cap. Cooked cereal is waiting next morning.

QUICK BREAKFAST

AT HOME: Carefully open the top of an Instant Quaker Oats package. Add 2-3 tbls. coffee lightener. Reseal with masking tape or cellophane tape. AT CAMP: Place cereal in a bowl, add hot water until right consistency.

ROMAN OATMEAL
(Serves 2-3)

In a saucepan combine:
1/2 cup quick cooking oatmeal
1/2 cup instant Roman Meal cereal
1/2 tsp. salt
2 cups water
1/4 cup raisins

Bring to a boil and stir until starting to thicken.

Cover and remove from heat. Let set 5 min.

Serve with reconstituted dry milk to which has been added 1 tbls. of molasses, Karo syrup, or pancake syrup.

Chef's secrets:
- *Add ½ fresh banana or some dry banana flakes to hot cereal.*
- *Try pancake syrup as a topping on hot cereal.*
- *Use brown sugar or granular honey instead of white sugar.*
- *Look for quick-cooking cereals for breakfast. Try Malt-O-Meal, Roman Meal, Cream of Wheat, as well as oatmeal.*
- *Instant oatmeal with a few raisins and a sniff of spice costs almost three times as much as plain quick oatmeal that you can doctor up yourself.*
- *Quart and half gallon milk cartons make sturdy camping canisters. Wash well with soap and water. Rinse thoroughly, drain and dry completely. The pour spout makes measuring easy and is easily closed. Store flour, sugar, pancake mix, biscuit mix, rice, etc. Metal cans with plastic lids also make good canisters for traveling.*

GRANOLAS YOU CAN MAKE: One cup makes a very generous serving.

GRANOLA COLORADO
(8 cups)
3 Shredded Wheat biscuits, crushed
2 cups Grape Nuts
1 cup All-Bran
1 cup broken, slivered almonds
½ cup toasted coconut
½ cup brown sugar
⅓ cup wheat germ
16 small or 8 large figs, cut up and rolled in ½ cup powdered sugar
Combine all ingredients and store in a tightly closed container.

GRANOLA YUKON
(8 cups)
¾ cup chopped filberts
¾ cup chopped almonds
3 cups quick cooking oats
¾ cup wheat germ
1 cup raisins
⅔ cup finely chopped prunes
¾ cup firm packed brown sugar
Combine all ingredients and spread on cookie sheets.
Bake 350 degrees for 15-20 min. Stir once or twice.
Cool and store in air tight container.

GRANOLA SKAGIT
(8 cups)
Combine:
4 cups quick cooking oatmeal
1 cup wheat germ
1 cup chopped nuts
1 cup shredded coconut, cut up, or use flaked coconut
Combine:
⅓ cup melted margarine
⅓ cup honey
Combine both mixtures thoroughly. Spread on cookie sheets.
Bake at 300 degrees, 15 min. Stir every 5 min.
Add:
1 cup diced prunes
and
1 cup chopped dates which have been rolled in powdered sugar so they
don't stick together.
Store in closed container. *Use within a few weeks.*

GRANOLA ATHABASCA
(12 cups)
Combine:
3 cups quick rolled oats
¾ cup wheat germ
2 cups corn flakes or Wheat Chex
2 cups Grape Nuts
½ cup sesame seeds
1 cup chopped pecans, almonds or filberts
¾ cup firm pakced brown sugar
2 tsp. cinnamon
Spread out in large flat pans. Bake at 350 degrees for 15-20 min. or until
golden brown. Remove to a large bowl and sprinkle with 2 tsp. vanilla. Stir
well and cool completely. Store in air tight containers.

To Serve Cranola: For each cup of cereal add ¼ cup each of dry milk and
coffee lightener. Combine thoroughly. Add cut-up fruit if desired. Sprinkle
with dry cherry or strawberry Jello if desired. Moisten with either hot or
cold water and stir. The addition of *hot* water makes a delicious cereal.

DOUBLE BOILER BREAKFAST

Boil your breakfast eggs in the bottom of a double boiler. Place coffee cake squares, sweet rolls, or slices of nut bread in the top half. Cover and warm the bread as the eggs are cooking. Lift the eggs from the water when done and replace the top half with the bread to keep warm over the hot water.

Reconstituted powdered eggs may be used in place of fresh eggs. Measure egg powder and water carefully.

For 1 egg: Use 2½ level tbls. egg powder plus 2½ tbls. water.

2 eggs: Use 5 tbls. egg powder and 5 tbls. water.

3 eggs: Use ½ cup each.

Method: Put lukewarm water in a bowl. Sprinkle powdered egg on top. Use a wire whip to beat until smooth.

Add dry egg powder to dry ingredients in recipes calling for eggs. Increase liquid accordingly.

Chef's secrets:

- *Perk up powdered eggs with dry onion flakes, parmesan cheese, pinch of marjoram or oregano, or a little bacon bar.*
- *Fresh eggs will keep without refrigeration for a couple of weeks if greased well with shortening. Keep as cool as possible.*
- *If you drop a piece of egg shell into the egg in the pan, scoop it out with . . a piece of egg shell.*
- *Use your finger to scoop out the raw egg that clings to the shell. You will be surprised at the amount of egg you have been throwing away.*

BREAKFAST RICE

APRICOT-RICE CEREAL
(Serves 2-3)

½ cup chopped dried apricots
3 cups water
½ tsp. salt
1 cup dry milk
½ cup rice cereal (for making hot rice cereal)
¼ cup brown sugar

Combine apricots and water and bring to a boil.
Stir in the other ingredients and cook, stirring for 1 min.
Cover, remove from heat, and let stand 5 min.
Any dried fruit can be used in this recipe.

FRUITY RICE
(Serves 2)

1 cup minute rice
1 can fruit cocktail, drained
½ tsp. cinnamon
½ tsp. salt
1-2 tbls. brown sugar
¼ cup raisins

Drain liquid from fruit cocktail into measuring cup.
Add water to make 1 cup liquid.
Put the liquid in a saucepan and add the drained fruit and other ingredients.
Heat quickly, stir often, until bubbly.
Cover and remove from heat. Let set 5 min.
Serve with milk.

APPLE RICE
(Serves 2)

1 cup minute rice
1 cup water
½ tsp. salt
1½ cups finely diced, unpeeled apple

Add apple to the water before bringing it to a boil.
Simmer 2-3 minutes.
Add rice and salt, reheat until bubbly.
Cover, remove from heat, and let set 5 min.

SKILLET SCONES
RAISIN SCONES
(Makes 12)

2 cups biscuit mix
½ cup raisins
2 tbls. sugar
¼ tsp. orange drink crystals
½ to ⅔ cup milk to make soft dough

Combine biscuit mix, raisins, sugar and orange crystals.
Stir in milk. When dough gathers into a ball, dust hands with flour and lift out to a floured cutting board. Shape into a 9" round. Cut dough with a sharp knife to make 12 triangles. Bake 10 min. on an *ungreased* heavy skillet at medium heat. Turn and bake 10 min. longer.

SHORT CAKE SCONES

Combine:
2⅓ cups biscuit mix
3 tbls. sugar
3 tbls. melted margarine
¼ cup dry milk
½ cup water
Flour hands and shape wads of dough into flat rounds.

Bake on a hot, lightly greased griddle or skillet, about 7 min. on each side.

Top with prepared freeze-dried fruit or heated canned pie filling.

Chef's secret: Stretch refrigerator rolls into scones and fry in the grease left over from sausage or bacon. Turn once to brown both sides.

CAMP TOAST

SKILLET MUFFINS

Split and butter English muffins
Heat, cut side down, on a griddle or frying pan.

FRYING PAN TOAST

Sprinkle a coating of salt in a hot frying pan.
Lay in a slice or two of bread. Turn when brown.
With salt, the bread won't stick and it leaves no taste.

FLAME-TAMER TOAST

Place a heat-spreader on your camp stove flame. When the spreader is hot, use it to toast your bread.

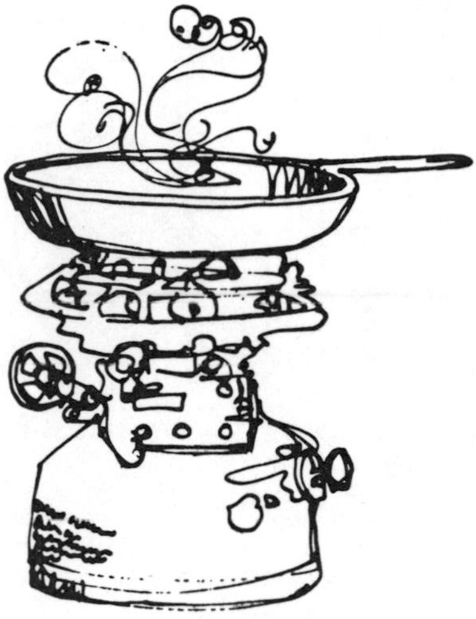

CHAPTER THREE

Snacks

It doesn't take a seasoned outdoorsperson to realize that a combination of fresh air and strenuous exercise creates hearty appetites. After a long day in the field, on the water or engaged in activities around the campsite, many ravenous campers — especially the younger ones — can barely wait until dinner is ready. Snacks help the cook by providing a "back-up system" to keep the crew from getting underfoot.

Many of these recipes have a high salt content which helps to rehydrate the members of an active group after a long day. Most are prepared at home.

DRY CEREAL SNACK

Measure 6 cups each:
Miniature Shredded Wheat
Rice Chex
Corn Chex
1 jar dry roasted mixed nuts
1 envelope onion soup mix
6 tbls. melted margarine

In a large bowl, combine cereals, nuts and dry onion soup mix.
Add melted margarine and mix thoroughly.
Spread in a shallow pan. Bake 300 degrees for 10 min., stirring at least once.
Store in an airtight container.

NUTS AND BOLTS

1 cup Cheerios
1½ cup Kix
2 cups cheese crackers
2 cups thin pretzels
½ lb. mixed nuts
¼ cup melted margarine
½ tsp. Worcestershire Sauce
¼ tsp. each garlic and onion salt

Combine cereals, crackers, pretzels and nuts in an oblong flat pan.
Mix margarine and seasonings and pour over ingredients. Mix well.
Bake in 250 degree oven, 30 min. Stir gently after 15 min.
Store in an airtight container.

TOASTED PUMPKIN OR SUNFLOWER SEEDS

2 cups of shelled seed (found in health food stores)
2 tbls. Worcestershire or Soy Sauce
2 tbls. melted margarine
2 tbls. grated Parmesan or Romano cheese
Salt to taste, regular or garlic.

Mix all ingredients in a bowl, then put in an oblong flat pan.
Toast in 375 degree oven, stirring every 5 min. for 15 min. or until browned.

TO USE: Spread crackers or bread with peanut butter, cheese spread, honey, or any sticky topping. Press cracker or bread upside down on the toasted seeds. These seeds are also delicious on ripe bananas, apples, mixed with scrambled eggs or cooked in macaroni and cheese, to name but a few uses.

SALTED SOYBEANS

Wash and soak raw soybeans in warm water overnight. Drain and place on paper towels to dry. (To speed drying, place on cookie sheet with shallow sides in a slow oven a few minutes.)

Deep-fry in hot oil for 10 min. or until golden brown.

Drain on paper towels and sprinkle with salt.

Store in an airtight container.

TOASTED RAW PEANUTS

Melt 2 tbls. margarine in a large flat pan.

Add raw peanuts and stir until coated.

Sprinkle with seasoned, garlic or onion salt.

Toast in 350 degree oven, stirring every 5 min. for 15-20 min.

Cool on paper towels.

MUNCHIES

In a small plastic bag combine the following for each person:

1/4 cup shelled salted peanuts

1/4 cup M and M's

1/4 cup raisins

Strip of beef jerky (Chapter 11)

1 stick of gum

2 tbls. unhulled sunflower seeds, toasted.

TOASTED SUNFLOWER SEEDS
—from your garden—

Rub the ripe seeds from the sunflower head, spread out on a flat surface and dry in the sun.

Mix one gallon of water with 1/4 cup salt.

Add up to 4 cups sunflower seeds (unhulled).

Soak overnight, drain. Spread out to dry.

Coat two baking sheets with 2 tbls. melted margarine for each.

Add sunflower seeds, sprinkle with salt.

Bake at 400 degrees for 15 min., stirring every 5 min.

Spread out on paper towels, and dry overnight.

Store in airtight containers.

CANDIED BACON

Cut bacon strips into thirds. Place in a flat pan, not touching.
Sprinkle brown sugar over bacon pieces.
Bake 300 degrees for 25-30 min. until sugar carmelizes.
Lift out of pan with tongs and drain on wire racks over paper towels.
(Do not drain directly on paper towels. The sugar sticks to them.)
Provide paper towels or napkins. It is messy, but good.

The following are "at camp" recipes:

TORTILLA WEDGES

Spread fresh tortillas lightly with margarine taking care to cover surface.

Place margarine side down in a hot frying pan. When hot, turn to other
side and sprinkle with salt. Cut in wedges with scissors.

Variation: Spread pre-fried tortillas or taco shells (from the market) with a
thin layer of margarine. Hold with tongs over flame of camp stove or fire,
rotating to melt margarine and to keep from burning. It takes only half a
minute. Sprinkle with salt, or leave it plain and use as a scoop for the following:

FRY PAN FONDUE

Slice thin or shred any cheese that melts readily, and place in a ½" thick
layer in a shallow pan. Use Jack, Cheddar, Swiss, processed, or cheese
spreads, or a combination of two or more. Place over low heat until cheese
melts.

Variations are endless. Top melting cheese with chopped green chilis, a
sprinkle of taco sauce, caraway seed or Worcestershire Sauce. Marjoram,
oregano, taco or spaghetti sauce mixes also can be added, *sparingly.*

Scoop up cheese with your own tortilla wedges, or commercial tortilla
chips or corn chips.

FANCY CAMPFIRE POPCORN

½ cup corn makes about 8 cups popped.
To hot buttered pop corn add any of the following:
1 tsp. paprika
Onion or garlic salt
Grated parmesan cheese
2-3 tbls. dry Jello powder
Tiny pinch of chili powder
1 tsp. Worcestershire Sauce added to melted margarine.

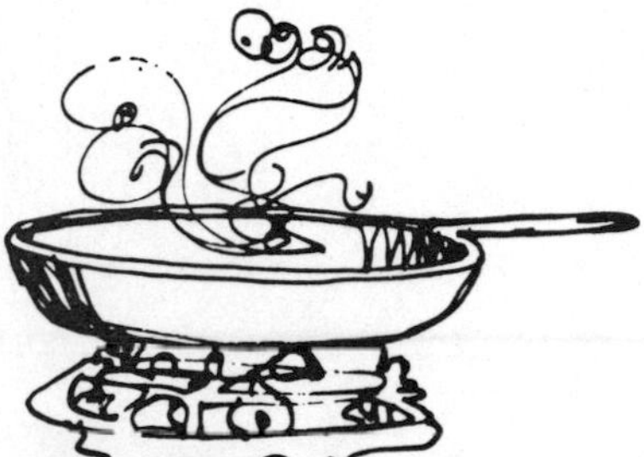

CHAPTER FOUR

Lunch Time!

WHAT TIME IS IT?
. . . LUNCH TIME!

Lunch usually is anticipated with much "relish." The basic preparation can be done at home to make serving it much quicker and easier.

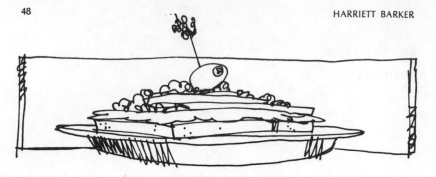

SANDWICH IDEAS
GRILLED SANDWICHES
Make extra pancakes to use for lunch sandwiches. Spread margarine on the "outside" of each pancake and grill in a frying pan, with shredded cheddar or Jack cheese sprinkled over.

Tuna mixed with chopped celery and mayonnaise.

Cheese, both sliced and spreadable.

Avocado, mayonnaise, garlic and onion salt.

Commercial meat spreads mixed with mayonnaise.

BANANA SANDWICH
Slice banana lengthwise and place on buttered bread. Spread mayonnaise on other slice. Sprinkle with cinnamon sugar.

Mash ripe banana and combine with crunchy peanut butter.

RAW CARROT
Put raw carrot and salted peanuts through the fine blade of a food grinder. Moisten with mayonnaise or salad dressing.

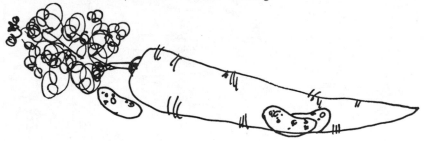

DRIED BEEF SPREAD
2 tbls. mayonnaise
1 pkg. (3 oz.) cream cheese, cut up
1 tsp. prepared horseradish
½ cup shredded dried beef

Place all ingredients in a blender and whirl until smooth. Chill and keep cold.

HAM SPREAD

2 tbls. milk
1/3 cup mayonnaise
1/4 tsp. dry onion flakes
1/3 cup pickle relish
1 cup cooked ham, cut up
   Put milk, mayonnaise, onion and relish in blender. Mix well.
   Add ham, a little at a time, and blend.
   Chill and keep cold.

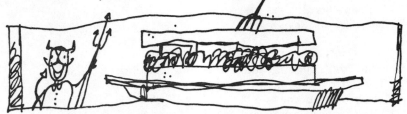

DEVILED HAM SPREADS

To commercial spreads add one of the following:
   Sweet pickle relish
   Chopped hard-boiled egg, salt and pepper.
   Top with a slice of cheese.

PEANUT AND JELLY SPREAD

1/2 cup peanuts
1 1/2 tbls. soft margarine
1/2 cup orange marmalade
   Chop peanuts in a blender, add to other ingredients, mix well.

FIG FILLING

1 cup figs
1/2 cup nuts
2 tbls. fruit juice
   Put figs and nuts through fine blade of food chopper.
   Blend with fruit juice.
   (Especially good on graham crackers or Waverly's.)

CHEESE SPREAD

Combine:
1 jar (5 oz.) sharp process cheese
1/2 cup (1/4 lb.) soft margarine
Variation: Add one of the following:
1/2 cup finely chopped pecans
1/4 cup toasted sesame seeds
1/2 tsp. caraway seed

PEANUT BUTTER SPREADS

Combine any one of the following with peanut butter:
Chopped raisins and nuts, honey
Bacon bar, sparingly
Shredded apple
Honey and a dash of cinnamon
Marshmallow spread
Grated cheese
Orange marmalade
Chopped nuts
Fruit jellies and jams

FLAVORED BUTTERS

To 6 tbls. soft margarine add one of the following:
2 tbls. lemon juice
1½ tbls. minced chives
1½ tbls. minced watercress
1½ tbls. minced parsley or celery flakes
1½ tbls. minced mint
1 tsp. Worcestershire Sauce
1 tsp. dry onion flakes
1½ tbls. prepared mustard
1-2 tbls. finely minced plain or stuffed olives
1 tsp. prepared horseradish

*Chef's secret: To spread a large loaf of sliced French bread, blend 1 pkg.
onion soup mix with ½ lb. (1 cup) margarine. This makes about 1¼ cups.
Try other soup mixes such as beef-mushroom or split pea. Onion-based dip
mixes make good spreads, too.*

ONE-BURNER FONDUE
(Serves 3-4)

2 cups plain croutons
¾ lb. sharp cheddar cheese, shredded
1 small can evaporated milk plus water to make ¾ cup
1 tsp. dry mustard
¼ tsp. salt, dash of pepper
1 egg, slightly beaten
1 tbls. margarine
French bread, sliced

Place croutons in top of a double boiler with cheese, milk, seasonings.
Place over hot water. Stir constantly until cheese melts and the mixture thickens.

Whip egg and add with margarine. Cook, stirring about 5 min.
Dip up mixture with French bread.

FILLINGS FOR GRAHAM CRACKERS AND WAVERLY'S
ALMOND-APRICOT

Combine 1½ cups dried, cut up apricots and 1 cup water in a saucepan. Simmer, covered, for 25-30 min. Uncover last few minutes if water is not mainly evaporated. Mash and stir in ½ cup firm packed brown sugar and ½ cup chopped almonds.

NUT-DATE

Combine 2 cups pitted dates, ⅔ cup water, 1 tsp grated lemon peel and 3 tbls. lemon juice in a saucepan. Simmer, covered, 25-30 min. until most of water is evaporated. Mash and stir in ⅓ cup firm packed brown sugar and add ½ cup chopped walnuts.

PRUNE-NUT

Combine 2 cups pitted prunes, ⅔ cup water, 1 tsp. grated lemon peel and 3 tbls. lemon juice in a saucepan. Simmer, covered, 25-30 min. until most of water is evaporated. Mash and add ⅓ cup brown sugar, packed, and ½ cup chopped filberts.

CINNAMON HONEY

Warm ½ cup honey over hot water. Add 1 tbls. margarine and 1 tsp. cinnamon. Use wire whip to blend well. (This is especially good sprinkled with Toasted Sunflower Seeds — Chapter 3.)

RAW VEGETABLES TO MUNCH

Carrot, celery, zucchini, cauliflower, cucumber, tomato, asparagus tips, Jerusalem artichoke (Chapter 13) and Jicama. Jicama (hee-cah-mah) is a popular Mexican root vegetable. It looks like a giant tan turnip. Wash, cut in wedges, peel and slice. Keep in a plastic container with a tight lid. Add a tbls. of water to keep moist. Keep cool. It has a sweet refreshing taste and is crunchy.

Lunch can include a wide variety of foods. The following suggestions travel well if packed carefully, and need no refrigeration:

Canned brown bread
Canned date bread
Pumpernickel bread
Rye rounds
Melba toast
Wheat thins
Ritz Crackers (stak pak)
Waverly's
Pilot biscuits
Triscuits
Rye Crisp
Pre-fried tortillas (taco shells)

Dry Fruits:
    Prunes
    Dates
    Figs
    Raisins
    Dry banana flakes
    Dry pineapple

Fresh fruit:
  Apples
  Oranges

Cookies packed in cans with plastic lids.
Fruit logs (Chapter 11)
Beef Jerky (Chapter 11)
Dry Salami
Canned meat spreads
Cheeses; sliced and spreads
Peanut butter
Honey
Jam

Toasted Sunflower Seeds (Chapter 3)
Dry roasted mixed nuts
Peanuts (Chapter 3)
Tropical chocolate candy

Cold Drinks:
  Pre-packaged with sugar
  Instant iced tea
  Solar tea (Chapter 5)

Hot drinks:
  Bouillon, cubes or instant
  Flavored Jello
  Lemonade mix
  Instant soup pkgs

Search the supermarkets for cheeses and dry sausages sold at room temperature. They will keep safely for the length of your trip.

Chef's secrets:
- *Include a serrated, unflexing steak knife to cut breads and dry salami. Don't forget a small cutting board and some plastic knives for spreading.*
- *Going light? Cheese, fruit, and a candy bar make a high energy lunch.*
- *Use up the stale bread by making croutons. (Chapter 10).*
- *In your lunch box include paper towels and a "tablecloth" made by cutting open a large plastic bag. A few towelettes come in handy, too.*

CHAPTER FIVE

Liquid Energy

OLD DUTCH PROVERB: Coffee is a drink that has two virtues; it is wet and warm.

BOILED COFFEE
Start with cold water. Add fresh coffee. Allow to come to a boil. Remove from heat and let stand a few minutes to let the grounds settle.

DRINKS FROM TANG OR START
Use hot water to reconstitute. It dissolves much quicker and is delicious.

Float dry banana slices and a pinch of dried mint leaves in orange juice made from crystals.

Add a crushed Vitamin C tablet to hot water or orange juice for flavor and extra vitamins.

Lemonade mix, dissolved in hot water, is a good pick-me-up.

DRY MILK CAN TASTE GOOD
If you don't like plain powdered milk as a drink, try adding it to hot chocolate, instant puddings, and other recipes calling for milk. Be very generous in measuring.

The addition of a coffee lightener makes dry milk more palatable.

To improve the taste add 1 tablespoon of molasses, chocolate syrup or ice cream topping.

To cool mixed dry milk, place the container in the shade wrapped in a damp towel. Or, build a box of rocks in the stream and provide some kind of shade. A damp towel will wick cold water over the top of the container for more cooling.

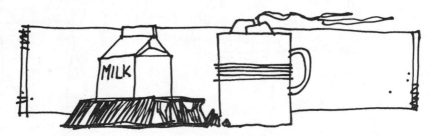

HOT CHOCOLATE
Make your own cocoa mix. Into a sturdy plastic bag mix the following:

1 cup dry milk
½ cup coffee lightener
¼ cup cocoa
4 tbls. sugar
⅛ tsp. salt

At camp: Add 3 cups water, stir with a wire whip and heat just to boiling. Turn heat very low and keep cocoa warm for a few minutes to blend flavors before serving. Makes about 4 cups.

Chef's secret: Add ½ tsp. molasses to coffee or hot chocolate for a new taste.

COCOA MIX FOR A CROWD
10-15 cups

Combine:
½ cup cocoa
6 tbls. sugar
¼ tsp. salt
2 cups dry milk
Use 3-4 tbls. mix for each cup. Add hot water and stir vigorously.

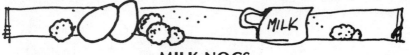

MILK NOGS
WILD BERRY NOG

Mix up one quart of dry milk.
Beat 2 eggs well and stir into milk.
Add 4 tbls. sugar and stir well.
Add 1 cup mashed wild berries and stir.
Set in a cool creek to chill before serving.

Variation: Mix one quart of dry milk and add about ¼ cup coffee lightener. Add a cup mashed sweet berries. Put 1 tbls. sugar to each glass and add berry mixture. Sprinkle with cinnamon.

DRY MILK NOGS

To a cup of milk add:
Orange: Add orange crystals and a little sugar.
Banana: Mash half a banana in the cup with a fork.
Add milk and a drop of vanilla if available.
Apricot: Add apricot juice, some sugar, dash of salt.
Eggnog: Add 1 beaten egg, 2 tbls. honey, dash of salt, nutmeg or
     cinnamon.
Fruit: Combine a half cup of fruit juice and a half cup milk.
Add sugar if desired.
For making one cup of milk use:
½ cup dry milk powder
2 tbls. coffee lightener
1 cup water

Carob Drink, Hot or Cold: (Carob is an acceptable substitue for chocolate.)
For each cup, combine:
3 tbls. dry milk
3-4 tsp. Carob drink mix (instant)
ADD: hot or cold water. Stir often while drinking.
Chef's secret: Add 1 tsp. instant Carob drink mix to instant coffee before adding hot water.

COFFEE LIGHTENER

Pream, Coffee Mate, etc., dissolves instantly in hot liquid and can be used in any recipe that calls for milk or cream. Mix it dry with other ingredients beforehand, or dissolve in hot liquid at camp before using.

LIGHTENER	HOT WATER	EQUIVALENT
¼ cup	1 cup	1 cup milk
½ cup	1 cup	1 cup light cream
¾ cup	1 cup	1 cup heavy cream

Chef's secret: In cooking, substitute ½ cup evaporated milk and ½ cup water for 1 cup fresh milk.

TEAS

There are a number of herb teas in health food stores, such as nettle, mint, rose hip, sassafras, and many others.

- CONSTANT COMMENT tea comes loose, bagged or instant. It contains orange peel and spices and is a delicious pick-me-up. It goes well with desserts.
- Specialty shops have loose tea. Try several small packets in different blends. (Don't forget a tea strainer)
- Oriental sections of markets have exotic blends to try.
  Make your own exotic tea: Dissolve striped peppermint candies in hot tea for a campfire drink.
- Dry your own orange peel in the sun by cutting it into thin strips. At camp, pour hot tea over a few strips. Add honey to taste.
- Though hot tea is delicious and refreshing just as it is, you might like to vary it by adding one of the following:

Honey
Lemon juice
Strawberry jam
Orange marmalade
Flavored Jello powder
Crushed wild mint leaves (fresh or dried)
Whole cloves
Orange peel (fresh)
Lemon peel (fresh)

SOLAR TEA
You will need: Glass jar with a lid.
Tea bags
Cold water

For each quart of cold water you will need 2-3 tea bags. Set the jar in full sun in the morning. About an hour before dinner, set the jar in a cool stream, or in the shade wrapped in a damp towel. Serve with ice from your cooler if possible.

CITRUS-SPICE TEA
(Melba Blackstone — Los Angeles, Calif.)

Combine:
1 cup instant tea
1 cup orange crystals (Tang or Start)
1 pkg. lemonade mix
½ cup sugar
1 tsp cinnamon
½ tsp. ground cloves

Use 2 heaping tsp. for each cup of boiling water.

SOUPS

Save the liquid from canned vegetables or fresh cooked vegetables. Season with instant or cubed bouillon, add water and heat for a before-dinner pick-me-up. Or add to V-8 juice for an extender.

Look in the soup section of your market for various bouillons. They are full of energy, and good for lunch or before dinner. For lunch, heat bouillon and water in a metal Sierra cup over the flame of your stove until warmed to your liking.

Lipton Cup-a-Soup is handy for a hot lunch drink.

A delicious hot drink can be found in the Oriental section. Look for Kikkoman Instant Miso-Shiru. It is a soy bean soup mix in individual packets. Open into your cup, add hot water.

Look in foreign specialty markets for unusual soups.

Chef's secret: To go with your soup, spread ready-fried tortillas or taco shells with a thin film of margarine. Sprinkle with salt. Hold with tongs over the flame of your camp stove until the margarine melts. Don't hold too close or the tortilla will burn. It takes only a few seconds.

HOT MULLED DRINKS

COFFEE POT APPLE JUICE
(Serves 6-8)

In a *clean* camp coffee pot, heat:
1 quart apple juice
1 three inch stick of cinnamon
12 whole cloves
½ tsp. nutmeg
Simmer 10 min.

HOT BUTTERED CIDER

For each serving:
Drop ¼ of an orange slice and ½ of a lemon slice into cup.
Add one- to two-inch cinnamon stick.
Add 1 tsp. margarine.
Heat apple juice or apple cider to boiling.
Pour into individual cups.
Let steep until cool enough to sip.

MULLED CRANBERRY TEA
5 tea bags
2½ cups boiling water
¼ tsp. cinnamon
¼ tsp. nutmeg
¾ cup sugar
1 pint cranberry juice cocktail
1½ cups water
½ cup each orange and lemon juice. (Use fresh or reconstituted frozen, or dry crystals, reconstituted.)

Pour the boiling water over the tea bags and spices. Cover and steep 5 min. Add sugar and stir until dissolved. Add juices and serve hot.

MULLED FRUIT DRINKS

Combine Wyler's or Lipton fruit drink powder or lemonade with hot water. Add a couple of whole cloves and a dash of cinnamon to each serving.

Chef's secret: Add cloves and cinnamon to any heated canned juice. Heated grapefruit juice is an eye-opener.

TAKE-ALONG LUNCH DRINK
At home combine and simmer 5 min.:
Rind of 2 lemons and 2 oranges
  (remove white pulp)
12 whole cloves
¼ cup sugar
2 cups water
  Strain and cool.
Add:
2 cups water
½ cup lemon juice
1 cup orange juice
½ cup molasses (optional)

Variation: Add Karo syrup instead of sugar, to taste. Add honey instead of molasses.

Don't forget to squeeze the oranges and lemons before removing the rind.

Chef's secret: No need to chill Jello to enjoy it. Try drinking it hot. Just put a heaping teaspoon full in a cup, add boiling water and stir until dissolved.

CHAPTER SIX

Vitamin Corner: Getting the most from fruit and vegetables

Fresh vegetables are loaded with vitamins, and they may be taken along on an outdoor expedition, especially if you are traveling over water. Here's how:

SALADS AND RELISHES

Make a simple evaporating cooler by folding a "well-furred" old towel in half and sewing up the sides. Fold over the top, leaving holes for a shoelace drawstring, and stitch. To keep perishables such as lettuce and other *fresh* vegetables, wrap them in a *damp* towel, place in a plastic bag and fasten the top securely with a rubber band. Place in the towel bag. Immerse the whole thing in cool water and hang in a shady spot. In a canoe, drain and place in the shade on the bottom of the canoe next to the cold (hopefully) water. You can keep cheeses, margarine, beer, etc. in this cooler, also. Fresh greens and vegetables to take along include:

Squashes
Potatoes
Onions
Egg Plant
Cabbage
Carrots
Celery Root (Celeriac)
Romaine and Iceberg Lettuce
Cauliflower
Tomatoes
Celery
Parsley
Watercress
Cucumbers
Radishes
Alfalfa Sprouts
Green Pepper

SALAD DRESSINGS:

Chef's secrets:
- *An oil and vinegar dressing made from a mix will not spoil.*
- *Melt a tablespoon of jelly (your choice) and add to bottled French Dressing for a change.*

TAKE ALONG FRENCH DRESSING

¼ **cup each of vinegar, catsup, salad oil, sugar**
½ **tsp. dry onion flakes**
½ **tsp. each dry parsley and celery flakes**
¼ **tsp. dry garlic chips**
    Shake well and allow to set several hours so flavors will mingle.

CABBAGE SALAD

Chop cabbage into a bowl. Sprinkle with salt.
Add ¼ cup raisins, mix lightly. Add dressing and stir again.
Dressing:
1 tsp. lemon juice
2 tbls. sugar
2 tbls. milk (2 tbls. dry milk, 2 tbls. water)
Combine thoroughly.
This dressing is also good on wild greens.

CABBAGE 'N PINEAPPLE SALAD
(Serves 4-5)

Slice very fine: 2 cups cabbage
Add:
1 can diced pineapple, drained
Salt and pepper.
Moisten with salad dressing.

CABBAGE SLAW

1 small cabbage, shredded
1 small green pepper, chopped
1 small onion, sliced into rings (or use soaked dry flakes)
Combine:
2 tbls. sugar
1 tsp. salt
3 tbls. vinegar
2 tbls. salad oil
Stir to dissolve sugar.
Pour dressing over cabbage mixture and toss.
Chill in the nearest stream until dinner.

PIMIENTO SLAW
(Serves 5-6)

Combine in a large bowl:
5 cups finely shredded cabbage
1 can (4 oz.) chopped pimiento
½ cup chopped green pepper
Combine:
2 tbls. milk
¾ cup mayonnaise
2 tsp. celery seed
Pour over salad, mixing well.
Chef's secret: Add cubed Jack cheese for a light, hot weather supper.

WILTED GREENS

Wash and dry greens on a towel. Chop or cut with scissors into a bowl.
Fry several slices of chopped bacon until crisp.
Add 1 tbls. vinegar. Pour the hot mixture over greens and toss.
Add flavored croutons (See Chapter 10) or drained canned vegetables.

RICE SALAD
(Serves 3-4)

3 cups cooked rice, flavored or plain
1 jar artichoke hearts, drained
1 jar pimiento, chopped
French dressing
Combine and mix well. Serve on lettuce leaves.

COTTAGE CHEESE SALAD

Use the liquid from a small can of fruit plus water to reconstitute freeze-
dried cottage cheese. Top with the drained fruit. Serve on greens.

FRUIT NOODLE SALAD
(Serves 3-4)

Combine:
3 medium oranges, peeled and cut into chunks
¾ cup canned, drained grapefruit sections
1 cup pineapple chunks, drained
1 can (3 oz.) Chinese noodles
¼ cup French dressing
*Chef's secret: Save the drained fruit juices and add to your breakfast
orange juice crystals.*

BANANA SALAD
(Serves 3)

2 bananas, cubed
1 tbls. lemon juice (optional)
½ cup peanuts
½ cup cut up celery
½ tsp. salt
½ cup salad dressing or mayonnaise
Mix cut up bananas and lemon juice. Add rest of ingredients and mix
lightly with a fork.

APPLE-BACON SALAD
(Serves 4-5)
Combine:
½ cup diced apple
½ cup diced celery
¼ cup mayonnaise
Set aside while you:
Shred 3-4 cups lettuce
Add ½ cup cold cooked bacon, crumbled, or ½" of a bacon bar.
   Combine lettuce and apple mixtures, toss lightly.
   Chef's secret: Cook extra bacon while making breakfast.

VEGETABLE SALAD
Combine:
Flowerettes of raw cauliflower
Shredded raw carrots
Small can of peas, drained and mashed
French dressing
   Serve on a heated tortilla while waiting for dinner.

SUMMER SALAD
1 small head cabbage, shredded or sliced fine.
Combine with:
1 cup grated raw carrot
1 cup chopped tart apple, unpeeled
½ cup chopped celery
1 tbls. dry onion flakes
Salt and pepper
   Moisten with salad dressing and let bowl set a few minutes in a cold
stream or wrapped in a damp towel in the shade.
   *Chef's secret: Soak onion flakes in a small amount of cold water. Drain
before adding.*

SUPPER SALAD
(Serves 2)
1 can peas and carrots, drained
1 cup canned ham, cut into cubes
2 tbls. mayonnaise
   Combine and serve on salad greens.
   Chef's secret: Add chopped celery or chopped nuts for "crunch".

CELERY ROOT (CELERIAC) MARINADE
Peel and cut one celery root into strips. Cook in boiling salted water with 1 tbls. vinegar added. Cook until barely fork tender.

Drain (save liquid for soup). Place celery root in a container with a tight lid. Cover with Italian or French dressing.

Cover securely and refrigerate. Flop the dish upside down occasionally to distribute dressing.

Include lettuce and tomatoes in your towel "cooler" for salad and use the dressing from the marinade. Sharpen the flavor with a little vinegar.

Chef's secret: To peel tomatoes: Insert a fork into the stem end of the tomato. Hold over the lighted burner turning constantly. When the skin wrinkles or bursts remove from heat. The skin should slip off easily.

MARINATED ARTICHOKES
Boil one large globe artichoke approximately one hour in salted water. Drain and chill in the refrigerator overnight.

Separate leaves and place in a plastic bowl with a tight lid. Remove the choke and discard. Slice the heart and stem and add to the leaves.

Mix 1 pkg. Good Season's oil and vinegar dressing (I like Italian) and pour over artichoke.

Marinate 5-6 hours or overnight, turning occasionally to coat leaves.

Substitute crisp-cooked cauliflower, cooked green beans, drained lima beans.

ALFALFA SPROUTS
(Get seed at health food store)
Sterilize a 3 lb. peanut butter jar or the equivalent size.

Put 1 tbls. alfalfa seed in the jar. Add a couple of inches of slightly warm water. Cover jar with cheesecloth fastened tight with a rubber band.

Let set overnight. Next morning drain off water through cheesecloth.

Lay jar on its side on a towel on a dark shelf until the seeds sprout, about 24 hours. Don't let the seeds dry out. Rinse and drain several times a day.

When the seeds start to sprout, place on a north facing window sill and turn the jar to get light to the sprouts. Keep the jar on its side.

In 4-5 days the jar will be full of greens. Don't forget to rinse while they are growing.

Place sprouts in a plastic bag and keep cool.

Use on sandwiches, as a garnish for soups and vegetables, or in a salad.

BANANA-CRANBERRY RELISH

Combine:

2 bananas, mashed

1/2 cup fresh cranberry relish (recipe follows)

Chopped salted peanuts

CRANBERRY RELISH

In a food chopper, alternate fresh cleaned cranberries and two oranges, peeled, quartered and seeded. Use a medium blade.

Add 1 1/2 cups sugar. Mix well and chill.

CRANBERRY SAUCE
(Makes 4 cups)

Combine:

2 cups sugar

2 cups water

Stir and bring to a boil, simmering for 5 min.

Add 1 pound of fresh cranberries (4 cups) washed and sorted.

Cook until skins pop, about 5 min.

CARROT TOPPING
(Mildred King — San Fernando, Calif.)

Combine and cook until soft:

4 lbs. carrots

4 lemons, washed and put through a food grinder

Small amount of water to cook

Add: 6 cups sugar. Boil till thick.

Add: 3/4 lb. blanched almonds, whirled in blender until fine.

To keep: Pour into sterilized jars and seal with melted parafin.

Use as topping on puddings or Dutch oven cakes, or on pancakes.

CHAPTER SEVEN

Dinner Is Served:
In Half An Hour

Contents . . .

The following recipes are calibrated
to be HEARTY complete one-pot meals.

DINNER IS SERVED
In Half An Hour

When dinner is over and all you have left is a well-scraped pot, you know
you have concocted a winner. Learn to adapt recipes. Don't be afraid to
substitute.

Freeze-dried vegetables often are easier to take along than fresh or
canned ones. Add them when your meal is almost ready, "cooking" them
only as long as suggested on the package.

Why pay for something you can do yourself? It is easy to dry your own
celery and parsley flakes. Wash, then strip leaflets from the stem. Lay on a
paper towel on a cookie sheet and place in an unlit oven. A gas pilot light is
enough heat to dry them overnight. If your oven is electric, turn it to the
lowest setting and leave the door ajar. When the leaves are dry enough to
crumble easily, store them in an airtight container.

Green pepper strips and minced onion also can be dried at home. Wash,
then cut up into ¼" cubes. Spread on a paper towel and proceed in the
same way as for celery leaves.

You might like to try drying your seasonings in the sun. Place them on
foil, shiny side up, and cover with a layer of cheesecloth. Leave in the *hot*
sun to dry. (Take them in at night to prevent them from absorbing moisture.) Store in a tight container.

Mayonnaise can be substituted for sour cream in Stroganoff dishes. Try
adding a large spoonful to a hamburger and bean combination.

Cracker meal or bread crumbs are easily made at home. Dry the bread in
a 350 degree oven. A food blender will cut up the dry bread as fine as you
like. Crush dry crackers into a blender for cracker meal. Combine a variety
of crackers for something different. At camp make a coarse cracker meal by
crushing crackers by hand into a bowl, then use the bottom of a can or bottle to break them up finer.

If you are using dehydrated foods, presoaking will speed up the cooking
time.

One tablespoon of instant minced onion is equal to a small fresh onion
when rehydrated.

Add cornstarch or a few grains of rice to salt in shakers to keep it dry.

If you boil water to purify it, let it stand for 10 minutes, stirring occasionally, to improve the taste.

Herbs can brighten the flavor of your camp meals. Following are suggestions to experiment with. Begin with a light touch of seasoning until you
please your own taste:

SOUPS
To *Tomato soup* add a pinch or two of sage and garlic salt.
Chicken soup: add rosemary or a dash of paprika.
Beef soup is pepped up with a little basil.
Vegetable soup and marjoram go well together.

VEGETABLES
Potatoes are more interesting with dill seed or rosemary.
Corn — season with chili powder.
Green beans — add garlic salt or thyme.
Peas — cook with savory or mint (fresh if you can find it)

MEATS
Pork — sage or thyme.
Meatballs — savory, mustard or garlic salt.
Chicken — thyme or marjoram.
Hamburger — sweet basil.
Beef stew — add basil.
Fish — tarragon or marjoram.

Other combinations to try:
Carrots, zucchini, broccoli, beets, lima beans — dillseed, oregano.
Broccoli, carrots, onions, cauliflower — chili powder, paprika.

Meats will accept a variety of spices and herbs:
Beef — thyme, rosemary, basil, marjoram, savory.
Pork — thyme, sage, basil, chives, rosemary, marjoram.
Fish — parsley, sage, thyme, basil, fennel, chives, dill.
Poultry — savory, sage, tarragon, thyme.

CAN CONTENTS

Size	Cups
No. 300	1¾ cups
No. 1 (tall)	2 cups
No. 303	2 cups
No. 2	2½ cups
No. 2½	3½ cups
No. 3	4 cups
No. 10	12-13 cups

The first meal at camp is always the most difficult. Make it as simple as possible. Pierce the top of the can to allow steam to escape. Place the can in a pot filled with water. Heat while camp is being set up. Serve with split English muffins, pre-buttered and wrapped in foil. Use the hot water from the heating pot for hand washing before dinner.

Try canned beef stew, pork and beans, chili and beans, spaghetti.

Another quick dinner is to open a can of beef stew into a pot. When it is bubbling, add about a quarter of a cup of pre-cooked rice to absorb some of the liquid. Let it stand, covered, off the heat for about five minutes. To give it some zip, add a bay leaf to the stew when you dump it in the pot.

Put hamburger meat between waxed paper, roll flat with a bottle or can, and cut out patties with the can which has had top and bottom removed. Or, shape at home, wrap in foil, separating the patties with a flattened paper cupcake cup. Freeze.

You might like to use this method to shape dumplings for the stew. Have the dough well floured before placing it between the waxed paper.

If grease catches fire throw some flour on it. Flour sprinkled in a frying pan will stop the spattering of the fat.

Heating a frying pan before adding oil or shortening will help prevent sticking.

Following are recipes combining hamburger and beans:

CHILI BURGERS
(Serves 3-4)

1 pound hamburger
1 can bean and bacon soup
½ cup catsup
1 tsp. Worcestershire sauce
3-4 buns

Brown beef in a skillet, stirring often to break up the pieces. Add soup, catsup, Worcestershire sauce. Simmer 5-10 min. Serve on open, buttered buns.

SKILLET CHILI
(Serves 3-4)

1 pound hamburger
1 medium onion, chopped
1 tbls. chili powder
1 can tomato soup
2 cans (15½ oz. each) kidney beans, undrained
1 can (20 oz.) garbanzo beans, drained

Brown beef in a skillet with onion, stirring often. Add chili powder, soup and beans. Simmer, stirring occasionally, 10-15 min. Serve with crackers.

BEANS AND DUMPLINGS
(Serves 6-8)
3 cans (15 oz. each) kidney beans
2 cans meat balls
½ cup water
1 pkg. corn muffin mix
½ cup shredded cheddar cheese

Heat beans, meat balls and water in a large pot. Prepare muffin mix, except decrease milk and stir in cheese. (It needs to be thick). Drop by spoonfuls onto the boiling mixture. Cook uncovered 10 min., cover and cook 10 min. longer.

KIDNEY BEAN MIX-UP
(Serves 2-3)
½ lb. hamburger
1 small onion, chopped
2 stalks celery, cut up
1 pkg. Lipton Beef Mushroom Soup Mix
1 can kidney beans, undrained (15 oz. can)

Brown hamburger with onion and celery. Drain fat if necessary. Add rest of ingredients with enough water to make a gravy. Simmer until celery is tender.

SKILLET LOAF
At home: make up your favorite meat loaf and freeze or keep chilled. At camp: Combine 1 can tomato sauce, 1 can mushrooms, drained, 1 can kidney beans.

Place thawed meat loaf in a heavy skillet, flatten and score into wedges. Pour tomato sauce and bean combination over the meat loaf. Simmer, covered about 20 min., then uncover for 10-15 min. Serve with large slices of French bread.

KIDNEY BEAN CARNE
(Serves 2-3)
½ pound hamburger
½ large onion, sliced
1 stalk celery, diced
1 can (1 lb. 14 oz.) kidney beans
Salt, pepper, oregano

Sauté meat, onion and celery together until meat is cooked. Add kidney beans. Sprinkle with seasonings. Simmer covered 10 min., and uncovered 5-10 min.

BEANS N MUFFINS
(Serves 3-4)
Butter English muffins and toast upside down in a frying pan.
Remove and keep warm wrapped in foil and then wrapped in a towel.
Combine and brown:
1 lb. hamburger
½ cup chopped green pepper
¼ cup chopped onion
Drain fat and add:
1 can (1 lb.) kidney beans and juice
½ tsp. chili powder
½ cup mayonnaise
    Heat slowly just until hot.
    Spoon over the toasted muffins and top with grated sharp cheese.

RANCH BEANS
(Serves 6-8)
In a large pot brown 1 lb. hamburger
Add:
1 envelope onion soup mix
2 1-lb. cans pork and beans
1 1-lb. can kidney beans
½ cup catsup
¼ cup water
2 tbls. prepared mustard
2 tsp. cider vinegar
    Simmer 15-20 min.

BEEF N BEANS
(Serves 3-4)
1½ lbs. hamburger
2 tbls. instant onion flakes or 1 medium sized fresh onion, chopped
1 envelope spaghetti sauce mix
1 can (1 lb. 12 oz.) pork and beans
1 can (1 lb.) whole tomatoes
¼ cup firm packed brown sugar
    Brown beef and add onions. Cook until onions are opaque.
    Drain fat and add spaghetti sauce mix, beans, tomatoes and sugar.
    Cover and simmer 15-20 min.

RIVERSIDE BEANS
(Serves 6-8)

1 lb. hamburger
1 envelope onion soup mix
2 cans (1 lb.each) pork and beans
1 can (1 lb.) kidney beans
1 can tomato sauce
1 can water
2 tbls. prepared mustard
2 tsp. cider vinegar (optional)

Brown the hamburger and drain fat. Add remaining ingredients and simmer 15-20 minutes, stirring occasionally.

BEAN BURGERS
(Serves 8-10)

Brown 1 lb. hamburger, drain fat.
Add:
1 lb. weiners, cut in ½" slices
2¼ cups water
1 6-oz. can tomato paste
1 envelope spaghetti sauce mix
1 tbls. prepared mustard
2 tsp. instant minced onion
¼ cup pickle relish
¼ tsp. salt

Simmer 10 min.

Add 2 1-lb. cans pork and beans. Heat thoroughly.

Spoon over buns, bread, English muffins, crushed corn chips, Chinese noodles or shredded wheat biscuits.

Chef's secret: Enrich the flavor of hamburger by adding a heaping teaspoon of instant beef bouillon to each pound of meat.

HAMBURGER AND VEGETABLES

LIGHTWEIGHT GOULASH
(Serves 3-4)
1 cup uncooked macaroni
1 can (15 oz.) meatballs
1 can green beans (Save juice)
Combine:
1 envelope stew mix
1 envelope sour cream sauce mix
1 tbls. coffee lightener
1 tbls. dry celery leaves
1 tbls. dried parsley
1 tsp. sugar
Water

Cook macaroni in 2 qts. boiling salted water about 10 min.; drain. Add meatballs and beans.

Add enough water to the bean liquid to make 2 cups and add the combined sauce mixes. Stir with a wire whip until blended.

Stir sauce into pan and heat thoroughly.

Chef's secret: Substitute freeze dried meatballs and green beans; reconstitute first in hot water.

STEW AND DUMPLINGS
(Serves two generously)
1 8-oz. can whole potatoes, drained and rinsed
1 8-oz. can green beans, drained (save liquid)
1 8-oz. can diced carrots, drained (save liquid)
1 15-oz. can meatballs in gravy
1 8-oz. can tomato sauce
2 tbls. minced dry onion
1 cup biscuit mix
¼ cup dry milk
⅓ cup water

Reserve ¾ cup total liquid from vegetables.

In a large pot, combine vegetables, liquid, meatballs, tomato sauce and onion. Bring to a boil.

Combine biscuit mix, milk and water.

Drop by spoonfuls onto boiling stew.

Cook uncovered 10 min., covered 10 min.

Chef's secret: Add ½ tsp. instant bouillon to biscuit mix for more flavor.

GROUND BEEF STEW

1 pound hamburger
1-2 cans mixed vegetables with juice
Garlic and onion flakes
1 can tomato sauce (or small can tomatoes)
Shape hamburger into small balls and brown in hot fat in a pot.
Add rest of ingredients and simmer, covered, 15 min.
Chef's secret: Add a dash of sugar to tomato dishes to reduce the sharp flavor.

FIRST NIGHT MEAT LOAF
(Serves 2-3)

At home: Combine the following ingredients and form into a loaf. Keep chilled and use the first night.
1 lb. hamburger
1 egg
1 small onion, chopped
1 small potato, shredded
¼ tsp. oregano
1 tsp. instant bouillon
Dash of pepper
At camp: Heat 1 tbls. fat in a heavy skillet with a tight lid.
Flatten the loaf and brown on all sides. Reduce heat.
Combine a can of tomato sauce and water to make 1½ cups.
Add ½ cup to pan, cover, and simmer 15 min.
Turn the loaf (may need to cut it) and add celery stalks, small carrots cut in half lengthwise.
Add remaining tomato liquid. Cover and simmer 30-40 min. or until vegetables are tender.

CHEESE STEW

4 strips bacon, cut into small pieces
1 large onion, chopped
1 pound hamburger
2 cans (No. 303 — 2 cups each) whole tomatoes
1 tsp. sugar
Salt and pepper
Fry bacon and chopped onion until onion is opaque.
Add crumbled hamburger and brown. Drain fat.
Add tomatoes and seasonings.
Simmer 15 min. Add to hot stew ½ pound processed American cheese cut into ½" cubes. Stir just until cheese is soft.
Spoon over buns or bread.

HAMBURGER AND DUMPLINGS
Crumble 1 lb. hamburger into frying pan.
Add salt and pepper. Stir and brown. Drain fat.
Add 1 small onion, chopped; two stalks celery, chopped.
Add 1 can tomato soup; 1 can vegetables, undrained (your choice)
Top with biscuit mix dumplings and cook as directed on pkg.

CABBAGE STEW
(Serves 2-3)
½ pound hamburger
1 tbls. instant minced onion
4 cups chopped cabbage
½ tsp. celery seed
½ tsp. salt
1 can cream of celery soup
¼ cup milk
Sauté meat and drain fat.
Add onion and cabbage and stir fry over low heat until cabbage is soft.
Add other ingredients. Simmer 10-15 min.
Chef's secret: Use dry milk and water or diluted canned milk.

BONANZA STEW
(Serves 3-4)
1 pound hamburger
1 can cream of mushroom soup
2 tbls. catsup
1 8-oz. can whole potatoes, drained and quartered
1 small onion, chopped
⅓ cup water
1 tsp. Worcestershire sauce
1 8-oz. can peas, drained
Brown hamburger. Add rest of ingredients. Heat, stirring occasionally.

SKILLET STEW
1 lb. hamburger
1 can mixed vegetables
1 onion, chopped
1 can soup (minestrone, vegetable-beef, celery)
Salt and pepper.
Sprinkle salt in the bottom of a heavy skillet. Add crumbled meat and brown. Drain fat.
Add onion, soup and vegetables, stir and heat.
Simmer 15-20 min.

ZUCCHINI STEW
(Serves 2-3)

1 pound hamburger
1 egg
4 tbls. dry bread crumbs
¼ tsp. salt, dash of pepper
1 can mushroom gravy
1 lb. zucchini, cut into 2 inch slices
½ tsp. basil
1 large tomato, cut into chunks

Combine meat, egg, crumbs, salt and pepper. Shape into small balls.
Brown meatballs in a skillet, drain fat. Add soup, zucchini, basil.
Cook over a low flame 15-20 min.
Add tomato chunks and simmer 5 min. longer.

FRY PAN CASSEROLE
(Serves 3-4)

1½ pounds hamburger
1 medium onion, chopped
½ cup celery, chopped
½ green pepper, chopped
1 cup pre-cooked rice
1 pkg. onion soup mix
1-2 tsp. instant bouillon
1½ cups water
1-2 medium carrots, sliced thin

Brown hamburger with onion, celery, pepper. Drain excess fat.
Add rice, soup mix and water, add bouillon and sliced carrots.
Simmer 20-30 min.
Add more water if necessary toward end of cooking time.

Sloppy Joes and Stroganoff
SLOPPY JOE TOSTADAS
(Serves 3-4)

Lightly butter 6-8 corn tortillas on one side. Place buttered side down in a medium hot heavy fry pan. When butter is melted, turn and crisp other side.

Wrap in a well-furred towel and put in a kettle with a lid to keep warm.

In the skillet sauté 1 pound of hamburger with one large onion, chopped. Stir until browned. Drain fat.

Sprinkle 1 pkg. Sloppy Joe seasoning mix over meat.

Add 1 can (6 oz.) tomato paste and 1½ cups water.

Stir and cook until mixture thickens, about 5 min.

Add some chopped ripe olives and simmer 10 min. more.

Spoon some of the meat mixture over a tortilla, add another tortilla and add some more meat mixture.

Top with a slice of sharp cheese.

SLOPPY JOE'S
(Serves 2)

½ **pound hamburger**
1 **small onion, chopped**
2 **stalks celery, chopped**
1 **pkg. beef gravy mix, combined per directions.**
¼ **cup catsup**
Dash of salt and pepper

Simmer over low heat 15 min., stirring occasionally.

Serve over split rolls or buns, or bread slices.

Chef's secret: Add a can of beans to make more.

SLOPPY JOE STROGANOFF
(Serves 3-4)

1 pound ground beef
1 stalk celery, sliced
1 small onion, quartered and sliced
1 can (1 lb. 14 oz.) kidney beans, undrained
½ cup mayonnaise
Shredded cheddar cheese

Brown hamburger with celery and onion. Drain fat.
Add beans and simmer until well blended, 10-15 min.
Just before serving, add the mayonnaise and mix well.
Spoon over hamburger buns, top with cheese.

CAMPERS STROGANOFF

Make a Stroganoff sauce using Wilson's dry meat patties, crumbled, and
Lipton Beef Mushroom soup mix thickened with 2 tbls. flour. For the sour
cream, mix 1 tbls. vinegar into 1 cup evaporated milk. Let stand for 5 min.
and then add to Stroganoff. (Don't expect it to taste like the real thing. It is
a good substitute.)

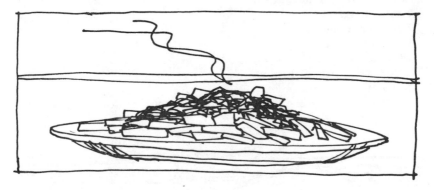

OUTDOOR STROGANOFF
(Serves 2)

To 1 pkg. sour cream sauce mix add ¼ cup dry milk, stir well and reseal
with masking tape (Or combine in a plastic bag).

To 1 pkg. Lipton Beef Flavored Mushroom soup mix add 2 tbls. flour, 2
tbls. dry onion flakes, combine and reseal.

AT CAMP . . . Mix up sour cream mix with ½ cup cold water. Stir with a
wire whip and let stand.

In a sauce pan place Wilson's beef patties, crumbled. Add 2 cups water,
blend in soup mix. Simmer 10 min.

Serve over cooked noodles, rice or mashed potatoes.

Place a generous dollop of sour cream on each serving.

15 MINUTE STROGANOFF
(Serves 2-3)
1 pound hamburger
1 can (3 oz.) mushroom pieces (Save liquid)
⅔ cup water
2 tbls. flour
1 envelope dry onion soup
1 envelope sour cream mix
Stir up sour cream mix and set aside.
Brown meat with drained mushroom pieces.
Add water and mushroom liquid.
Add flour to onion soup mix envelope and stir to combine.
Add to meat mixture. Cook until it thickens, simmer a few minutes.
Add sour cream and stir.
Serve over pre-cooked rice, cooked noodles or packaged mashed potatoes.
Chef's secret: Substitue a can of beef slices in gravy for hamburger

MAKE-AHEAD TOMATO SAUCE
Brown 1 pound of hamburger, drain fat
Add 2 cans tomato sauce
2 tbls. margarine
2 tbls. chopped onion
1 tsp. sweet basil
1½ tbls. molasses
½ tsp. salt, dash of pepper
Simmer 30 minutes.
AT CAMP: Reheat and serve over spaghetti, meat patties or an omelette.

SKILLET SPAGHETTI
(Serves 2)
1 can (16 oz.) spaghetti sauce with mushrooms
1¾ cups water
4 oz. spaghetti, broken
1 can meat balls
In a skillet combine sauce and water. Heat to boiling.
Add broken spaghetti, stirring to separate.
Simmer covered for 20 min. stirring once or twice.
Add meat balls and heat for 10 min. more.
Serve with parmesan cheese.

SPEEDY SPAGHETTI NO. 1
(Serves 2-3)
½ pound ground beef
1 med. onion, chopped
Pinch of oregano
Salt and pepper
2 cans spaghetti
1 can (4 oz.) mushroom pieces, drained
Parmesan cheese
   Brown the beef and onion. Drain fat.
   Add seasonings, spaghetti, mushrooms.
   Simmer, covered, stirring occasionally, for 15 min.
   Top each serving with grated cheese.

SPEEDY SPAGHETTI NO. 2
(Serves 2)
1 pound ground beef
1 medium onion, chopped
1 can tomato soup
Pinch of oregano
1 can (15 oz.) spaghetti
Cheddar cheese, cubed
   Brown beef with onion. Drain fat.
   Add soup and spaghetti, oregano.
   Heat, stirring occasionally, until bubbly.
   Add cubed cheese and stir until cheese gets soft.

ALL-AT-ONCE SPAGHETTI NO. 1
(Serves 2-4)
1 lb. ground beef
I large onion, sliced thin
1 stalk celery, sliced thin
1 pkg. spaghetti sauce mix
2 cans tomato sauce
1½ cups water
1 8 oz. pkg. spaghetti, broken
Parmesan/Romano grated cheese
In a large pot:
   Crumble beef, add onion and celery and cook until beef is browned.
Drain fat.
   Add sauce mix, tomato sauce, water and heat to boiling.
   Add broken spaghetti and stir into sauce.
   Cover and simmer 20-30 min. Stir occasionally.
   Serve with grated cheese.

ALL-AT-ONCE SPAGHETTI NO. 2
(Serves 2-4)

1 pound ground beef
1 medium onion, chopped
1 tsp. sweet basil
1 can tomato soup
1 can tomato sauce
1 soup can water
¼ lb. thin spaghetti, broken

Brown beef with onion. Drain fat.
Add remaining ingredients through the water. Bring to a boil.
Add spaghetti, stirring into sauce.
Cover and simmer 20 min., stirring occasionally.
Serve with grated cheese.

Chef's secret: Allow all-at-once spaghetti to set 5 min. without flame after cooking so any spaghetti stuck to the pan will loosen. Add water during cooking if it is getting too dry.

ONE SKILLET SPAGHETTI
(Serves 2-3)

In a large skillet: brown 1 lb. hamburger. Drain and set aside in a foil packet.

In the same skillet combine 1 pkg. (8 oz.) spaghetti which you have broken into small pieces, 1 envelope onion soup mix, 1½ qts. water.
Cook 20-25 min. until liquid is reduced. Do not drain.
Add the cooked meat, 1 can tomato sauce, 1 can tomato paste, 1 tbls. parsley flakes, 1 tsp. oregano, ½ tsp. sweet basil.
Simmer 10 min.

Chef's secret: Other uses for spaghetti sauce mix: Add a few tbls. or the whole package to a pot of stew. Combine with canned tomatoes for a delicious spaghetti or macaroni topping. Add to canned beans for more zip.

PRONTO MACARONI
(Serves 3-4)

½ pound hamburger
2 tbls. minced onion
salt and pepper
1 can (I lb.) tomatoes
2 cans Franco American Macaroni and Cheese

Brown hamburger. Drain fat.
Add onion, tomatoes, seasonings and bring to a boil.
Add macaroni and heat until bubbly.

MACARONI BEEF SAUTÉ
(Serves 2)

½ lb. hamburger
½ cup uncooked macaroni
¼ cup chopped onion
¼ cup chopped green pepper
½ garlic clove, minced
¼ cup salad oil or margarine
1 can (12 oz.) tomato juice
1 can (8 oz.) whole tomatoes, cut up
1 tsp. salt, dash of pepper
1 tbls. Worcestershire sauce

Heat oil or margarine in skillet.

Sauté beef, macaroni, onion, green pepper and garlic until macaroni turns yellow. Drain fat.

Add tomatoes, juice and seasonings.

Bring to boil, simmer, covered for 20 min. Uncover and simmer until sauce thickens.

ONION-BEEF MACARONI
(Serves 3)

1 cup uncooked macaroni
1 can beef and gravy
1 env. onion soup mix
1 tbls. flour added to soup mix
1 can tomato sauce
2 cups water
Grated cheddar cheese

Cook macaroni in salted water until tender. Drain.

Add beef, soup mix with flour stirred into it, tomato sauce and water. Heat until bubbly. Sprinkle each serving with grated cheese.

SKILLET MACARONI AND BEEF
(Serves 3-4)

1½ pounds hamburger
½ lb. (2 cups) uncooked macaroni
1 medium onion, chopped
½ cup green pepper, chopped
2 cans (8 oz.) tomato sauce
1 cup water
1 tsp. salt, dash of pepper
1 tbls. Worcestershire sauce

Brown hamburger in skillet. Include macaroni, onion, green pepper, and sauté until onion is soft.

Add tomato sauce, water, seasonings.

Cover and simmer 20-25 min. until macaroni is cooked and tender.

Chef's secret: Substitute canned meat balls and gravy for hamburger. Sauté vegetables in vegetable oil.

SKILLET MACARONI AND CHEESE
(Serves 3-4)

1 pound hamburger
Salt and pepper
4 cups water
1 can (13 oz.) evaporated milk
1 tsp. salt
2 cups uncooked macaroni
8 oz. process American cheese, sliced
3 tbls. prepared mustard

Brown crumbled hamburger in a skillet. Drain fat and remove to foil. Combine seasonings, water, milk, and bring to a boil. Add macaroni. Cook covered, 15 min. Add cheese and mustard and browned hamburger. Stir until cheese is melted. Top each serving with snipped parsley. Serve with carrot sticks.

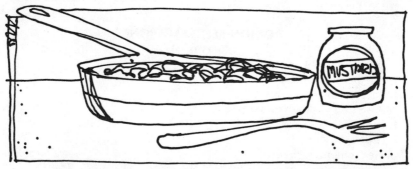

HAMBURGER AND NOODLES
NOODLE CASSEROLE
(Serves 3-4)

1 pound ground beef
1 medium onion, chopped
1 can tomato soup
1 cup water
2 cups uncooked noodles
2 tbls. margarine
1 can creamed corn
1 small can chopped ripe olives
1 cup shredded sharp cheese

Brown the meat and onion. Drain fat. Add soup, water and noodles. Simmer 5 min. Add corn, olives and margarine and cook until noodles are done, about 15 min. Top each serving with cheese.

NOODLE-ONION BURGER
(Serves 3-4)

1 pound ground beef
1 medium onion, chopped
1 can onion soup
1 can water, approximately
3 cups uncooked noodles
¼ cup barbeque sauce

Brown beef with onion until onion is tender. Drain fat. Add remaining ingredients, cover and simmer until noodles are done. Stir occasionally.

Chef's secret: Substitute dry onion soup mix for canned soup and onion. Add water recommended on soup packet.

FIESTA NOODLES
(Serves 2-3)

1 pound ground beef
1 med. onion, chopped
½ cup chopped green pepper
1 can (1 lb. 12 oz.) tomatoes, cut up
¼ cup chili sauce
1 tsp. salt
4 oz. (3 cups) noodles
  In a large skillet, brown beef with onion until tender. Add rest of ingredients. Cook, covered, over low heat 30 min. or until noodles are tender, stirring often. Add water if necessary.

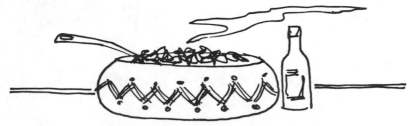

HAMBURGER AND RICE
RICE MEDLEY
(Serves 2-3)

1 pkg. dry onion soup
3 cups water
Meat balls, canned or freeze-dried and soaked
2½ cups pre-cooked rice
  Combine all and simmer 10-15 min. or until liquid is absorbed.

BEEF-MUSHROOM MIX

  Combine freeze-dried beef patties and dry mushrooms. Soak to rehydrate. Add to brown gravy mix with water called for. Simmer until all ingredients are cooked. Serve over cooked rice, mashed potatoes or bread.

CRUNCHY HAMBURGER RICE
(Serves 3-4)

In a skillet:
Brown 1 lb. hamburger (drain fat).
Add 1 can tomato soup plus water to make 2 cups.
Bring to a boil.
Add 1⅓ cups pre-cooked rice (minute rice).
Reduce heat, cover and *simmer* 5 min.
Add ¼ cup sliced onion and ¼ cup chopped celery.
Stir and simmer 5 min. longer.

TOMATO-RICE SKILLET
(Serves 3-4)

1 pound ground beef
1 medium onion, chopped
1 tsp. crushed basil
1 can tomato soup
1 can water to which you have added a heaping tsp. instant
beef bouillon.
1 cup water
2 cups pre-cooked rice (uncooked)

Brown hamburger with onion. Drain fat. Add remaining ingredients and bring to a boil. Cover and simmer 10 minutes. Stir often.

SPANISH RICE
(Serves 2)

½ cup cut-up fresh or canned tomatoes, drained
2 tbls. dry onion flakes
1½ tsp. salt, dash of pepper
3½ cups water (use juice from canned tomatoes for part of liquid)
1 cup pre-cooked rice (minute)
1 can (15¼ oz.) meatballs (or use dried, rehydrated)

Combine all ingredients except meatballs, if canned. Bring to a boil, cover and simmer 10 minutes. Add canned meatballs and heat thoroughly.

RICE CASSEROLE
(Serves 3-4)

1 lb. ground beef
1 cup raw rice
1 tsp. salt
1 small onion, chopped
¼ cup catsup
1 can green beans, drained
1½ cups water (include bean juice)

Brown meat with onion. Drain fat. Add rest of ingredients and bring to a boil. Lower heat, cover and simmer for 15 min. or until rice is done. Optional: Add chopped celery and snipped parsley.

BEEF RICE-A-RONI
(Serves 3)

In a cooking pot:

Brown ½ lb. hamburger with the rice-vermicelli.

Drain fat, if necessary.

Measure the liquid from a can of green beans. Add water to measure
to pkg. directions.

Add liquid to hamburger mixture. Top with contents of flavor envelope,
beans. Stir. Cover.

Simmer over low flame 15 min. or until liquid is absorbed.

*Chef's secret: Brown ground beef. Drain fat. Add a can of spaghetti, a can
of macaroni and cheese or add it to canned soups or packaged dry soups.*
(Lois Pitzer)

HAMBURGER AND EGGS
SCRAMBLED HAMBURGER
(Serves 2)

¼ lb. ground beef
2 tbls. finely chopped onion
1 tsp. salt, dash of pepper
4 eggs
¼ cup milk

Brown the meat and onion together. Drain fat. With a fork or wire whip,
beat eggs, milk, salt and pepper together. Pour eggs over meat mixture.
Cook slowly, stirring gently. Do not brown. Serve with English muffins.

CREAMED HAMBURGER
(Serves 2)

½ lb. hamburger
1 can cream of celery soup
1 cup milk
4 hard-cooked eggs
Split buns or bread slices, toasted or plain

Brown hamburger. Drain fat. Add soup, milk and heat. Stir in sliced eggs.
Spoon over bread.

*Chef's secret: To make the recipe to serve more, add a small can of
drained peas or carrots.*

HAMBURGER QUICKIES
BEEF AND SOUP
(Serves 3-4)
Brown 1½ pounds of ground beef (drain fat)
Add 1 can tomato soup
⅓ cup chopped onion
1 tbls. prepared mustard
1 tbls. Worcestershire sauce
1 tsp. salt

Heat, stirring constantly. Spoon over weiner buns. Top with sliced tomatoes and sharp cheese, shredded.

BURGER MUFFINS
Split English muffins, butter and spoon tomato sauce on each.
Sprinkle with crushed oregano.
Brown hamburger and drain fat.
Spoon over muffins.
Top with shredded Jack cheese.

QUICK HASH
(Serves 2-3)
At Home: Boil 2 medium sized potatoes. Do not peel.
At Camp: Brown 1 lb. hamburger with ¼ cup chopped onion. Drain fat. Add peeled, diced cooked potatoes and 2 tsp. salt, dash of pepper, 1 tbls. Worcestershire sauce. Brown, turning often. Serve with catsup.

SMOTHERED BURGERS
(Serves 3-4)
Sauté 2 cups sliced onion in margarine until soft.
Add 2 cans hamburgers in gravy
1 can cream of mushroom soup.
Heat until bubbly and serve over split buns.
Variation: Add chopped celery and mushroom pieces, drained.

HAMBURGER MEXICAN STYLE

CHILI RICE
(Serves 3-4)
Brown 1 pound ground beef. Drain fat.
Add 1 envelope chili mix
1⅓ cups precooked rice
1 can tomato sauce
3 cups water
Bring to boil, reduce heat and simmer 10 min.

SPANISH RICE
(Serves 3-4)
1 pound ground beef
2 tbls. chopped onion
3 tbls. chopped celery
1 can (1 lb. 12 oz.) tomatoes
1-2 tsp. salt
1 cup bouillon (1 cup water, 1 tsp. instant bouillon)
1 tsp. sugar
¾ cup Minute Rice
Brown hamburger with onion and celery. Drain fat. Add tomatoes, salt, bouillon, sugar and simmer, covered, 15 min. Add rice, cover and set off heat for five minutes.

RAINBOW RICE
(Serves 3-4)
1 lb. ground beef
¼ cup diced onion
2 tsp. salt
1 tsp. chili powder
¼ tsp. pepper
1 can (1 lb.) tomatoes
1 can (12 oz.) whole kernel corn
1¼ cups bouillon
½ cup green pepper cut in strips
1⅓ cups Minute Rice
Brown meat, drain fat. Add onion and cook until tender. Add seasonings, tomatoes, corn and bouillon. Bring to a boil. Stir in green pepper and rice. Cover and remove from heat. Let stand 5 min. Fluff before serving. Note: To make bouillon, dissolve 1 rounded tsp. instant bouillon in 1¼ cups hot water.

SKILLET TAMALES
(Serves 3-4)

1 onion, chopped
½ green pepper, chopped
2 tbls. margarine
2 cans (15 oz. each) tamales, cut up into pieces
2 cans (1 lb. each) creamed corn
Cheddar cheese, sliced

Sauté onion and green pepper in margarine until tender. Add cut tamales and corn. Heat until bubbly. Cover with slices of cheese, replace lid and cook five minutes longer.

FIESTA TAMALES
(Serves 2-3)

1 can (14 oz.) tamales
1 can (1 lb.) chile and beans
1 can (7 oz.) whole kernel corn, drained

Empty tamales into a large greased frying pan. Remove outer husks if any. Cover tamales with chili and corn. Cover pan and heat slowly. Do not stir.

CAMPERS TAMALE PIE
(Serves 4)

1 lb. ground beef
1 can (1 lb. 12 oz.) tomatoes
½ tsp. garlic salt, pepper
¾ cup yellow corn meal
¾ cup water
1 can (1 lb.) whole kernel corn
1 small can minced olives, drained

Brown beef in skillet. Drain fat. Add tomatoes, seasonings. Combine corn meal and water and add to mixture. Simmer 20 min. Mixture will thicken while cooking. Stir occasionally. Add olives and corn just before serving. Reheat until bubbly.

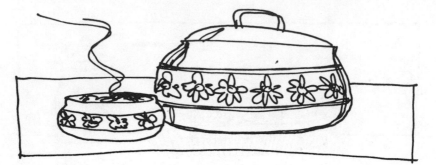

CARNE CORN
(Serves 2)

½ lb. hamburger
1 stalk celery, cut up
1 can (1 lb.) whole kernel corn
½ pkg. taco seasoning mix
¼ cup water

Brown hamburger with celery. Drain fat. Add corn, taco seasoning mix. Stir well. Add ¼ cup water. Cover. Simmer 10-15 min.
Variation: Add sliced pimiento.

CHEAP CHILI
(Serves 2-3)

1 lb. ground beef
1 medium onion, chopped
1 can (1 lb.) stewed tomatoes
1 can (1 lb. 14 oz.) kidney beans
Chili powder to taste
Salt and pepper

Brown beef with onion. Drain fat. Add rest of ingredients and simmer, covered, 15-20 min.

CHILI BEAN CORN CHIPS
(Serves 3-4)

1 lb. hamburger
1 small onion, chopped
1 can (1 lb. 14 oz.) chili beans
1 small can sliced olives, drained
½ tsp. salt

Brown hamburger and onion. Drain fat. Add rest of ingredients and simmer 10 min. Cut a small slit at one end of a bag of corn chips to allow air to escape. Crush chips in the bag with your hand. For each serving, put a mound of corn chips on the plate, cover with mixture. Top with shredded sharp cheese.

CORN CHIP TOSTADAS
(Serves 3-4)
1 lb. ground beef
1 pkg. taco seasoning mix
1 cup water
1 stalk celery, cut up fine
½ medium onion, chopped
Brown beef. Drain fat. Add rest of ingredients, bring to a boil, then simmer 15-20 min., stirring occasionally.

Crush corn chips according to preceding recipe. Place ½ cup corn chip pieces on each plate. Cover with beef mixture.

Top with grated Jack cheese, shredded lettuce and chopped tomatoes.

Variation: Add sliced ripe olives and sliced avocado to the top.

MEXICAN SANDWICH
(TACOS)
(Serves 4)
Thinly spread one side of a tortilla with margarine.

Place spread side down in a hot skillet leaving only until margarine sizzles . . . a few seconds.

Turn with tongs. When tortilla starts to puff remove to a paper towel in a turkish towel. Wrap to keep warm.

Cook 2-3 tortillas for each person keeping them wrapped.

Place the cooked tortillas in the towel in a covered pot while you prepare the meat filling.
1 lb. ground beef
½ onion, sliced
1 stalk celery, cut up
1 pkg. taco seasoning mix
1 cup water
Brown meat with onion and celery. Drain fat. Add seasoning mix and water. Bring to boil and simmer, uncovered 15-20 min.

Spoon 3 tbls. meat filling on bottom of each taco shell. Top with grated cheese (Jack, cheddar or both). Add shredded lettuce, chopped tomatoes, olives, avocado slices. Roll up and eat from the end.

Variation: Top with mayonnaise or sour cream.

TOSTADOS
To assemble a tostado, make alternating layers of meat filling and two cooked tortillas. Top with shredded lettuce, grated cheese, sliced ripe olives and tomatoes. Avocado slices also are good.

NOPOLITOS STEW
(Serves 4)

1 lb. ground beef
1 small green pepper, chopped
1 large onion, chopped
1 tsp parsley (or ¼ tsp. dry crushed flakes)
1 can (1 lb.) stewed tomatoes
1 cup nopolitos (diced cactus)
½ tsp. chili powder
Salt and pepper
¾ cup minute rice

Brown hamburger with onion and pepper, stirring often. Drain fat. Add remaining ingredients *except rice.* Simmer 25-30 min. Add rice, cover and let set 5 min.

ORIENTAL HAMBURGER
CHINESE STEW

1 lb. hamburger
1 small onion, chopped
1 stalk celery, sliced diagonally, ¼" wide
1 can (1 lb.) carrots, drained
1 can (1 lb.) potatoes, drained and rinsed with clear water
Undiluted vegetable soup
Chow mein noodles

Brown hamburger with onion and celery. Drain fat. Add vegetables and soup. Heat and simmer 10 min. Serve over chow mein noodles.

HAMBURGER FOO YOUNG
(Serves 3)

½ lb. hamburger
1 medium onion, chopped
1 stalk celery, cut in thin diagonal slices
1 can bean sprouts, drained
6 eggs, well beaten
1 tsp. salt, dash of pepper

Brown hamburger with onion and celery. Drain fat and save to grease skillet.

In a bowl put the eggs and salt and pepper. Beat with a wire whip until light and fluffy. Add sprouts which have been cut up finer. Add hamburger mixture and stir to coat with the egg.

Drop by large spoonfuls into hot frying pan, shaping patties by pushing egg back into the patties. Brown on both sides.

Serve with gravy made from a beef gravy mix, or sprinkle with soy sauce.

CHOW MEIN #1
(Serves 2-3)

1 lb. ground beef
1 medium onion, chopped
4 stalks celery, cut in ¼" slices
1 can mushroom pieces, drained
1 can cream of mushroom soup
Salt and pepper
1 can chow mein noodles

Brown meat with onion and celery and mushrooms. Drain fat. Add soup and seasonings and heat thoroughly, 10-15 min. Add chow mein noodles and stir into mixture.

CHOW MEIN #2
(Serves 3-4)

1 lb. hamburger
1 large onion, sliced
1 cup celery chunks
1 can bean sprouts, drained
1½ cups water
1 heaping tsp. instant bouillon
½ cup sliced fresh mushrooms
1 tbls. cornstarch
1 tsp. salt
¼ cup soy sauce
Canned chow mein noodles

Brown meat with onion and celery. Drain fat. Add bean sprouts, water, bouillon and mushrooms. Reheat until bubbly. Mix cornstarch with ¼ cup water and add to hot mixture, stirring constantly. Season with salt and soy sauce. Serve over noodles.

CANNED ROAST BEEF

BEEF 'N PANCAKE DINNER

Open a can of roast beef and gravy and heat in a small pot. Set small pot in a larger pot of hot water to keep warm.

Drain the liquid from a can of whole kernel corn and use as part of the liquid to mix pancakes.

Add drained corn to batter and fry like pancakes.

Spoon hot beef and gravy over corncakes.

Chef's secret: Add canned roast beef to canned spaghetti. Add a pinch of basil. (Lois Pitzer)

BEEF SPECIAL
(Serves 2)

Combine:
1 can roast beef in gravy
1 can mushroom soup
1 can water
1 tbls. dry minced onion
1 tbls. A-1 sauce

Simmer until well blended and hot, about 15 min. Add more water if necessary. Serve with thick chunks of French bread.

BEEF CURRY
(Serves 2-3)

1 tsp. curry powder
2 tbls. margarine
1 cup chopped onion
1 can roast beef and gravy
1 can (1 lb.) corn, drained
1 tsp. instant beef bouillon
Water

Sauté curry powder and onion in margarine until onion is tender. Add water to corn juice to make one cup liquid. Add bouillon to liquid and stir to dissolve. Add corn, roast beef and liquid and simmer until hot, about 10 min.

Chef's secret: Make dumplings from biscuit mix (recipe on box) and add to dinners that have large amounts of liquid in the pot. Add 20 minutes to cooking time.

RAVIOLI SUPPER
(Serves 4-5)

1 small onion, chopped
margarine to sauté
3 cans (1 lb. each) beef ravioli
2 cans (1 lb. each) meat balls
1 can (3-4 oz.) mushroom pieces, drained
1 can (1 lb.) green beans, drained

In a skillet, sauté onions in margarine until tender. Combine rest of ingredients, cover and simmer 15 minutes.

CHICKEN

Chicken and pork are often inter-changeable in recipes. If you don't have one, substitute the other. Combining chicken broth or bouillon with pork is delicious.

Add sage to poultry dishes for more flavor.

Substitute turkey for chicken. If you can refrigerate cooked poultry use it in the recipes instead of the canned.

Freeze-dried chicken is available if weight is a consideration.

For something different, simmer canned chicken in cranberry jelly.

CHICKEN GRAVY

Boil 3 cups of water to which you have added 1 tbls. margarine and half cup of dry milk.

Combine 3 level tsp. instant chicken bouillon with 2-3 level tsp. flour. Add to the boiling water stirring constantly with a wire whip until thick. Simmer over low heat 5 min. stirring often.

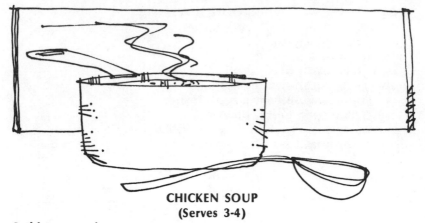

CHICKEN SOUP
(Serves 3-4)
2 tbls. margarine
2 medium sized tomatoes, diced
2 medium sized green peppers, cut in thin strips
1½ cups water
2 level tsp. instant chicken bouillon or 2 cubes
1 can chicken
1 can (14½ oz.) evaporated milk
Salt and pepper to taste
¼ lb. Jack cheese, diced

Heat margarine in a skillet, add tomatoes and peppers and cook until peppers are limp. Add broth (water and bouillon) and simmer 10 min. Add chicken, milk, seasonings and cheese. Stir briefly. Do not boil.

CHICKEN CORN CHOWDER
(Serves 5-6)
1 can cream of chicken soup
2 soup cans milk (or 2 cans water and 1 cup dry milk)
1 can condensed chicken noodle soup
1 can (1 lb.) cream style corn
1 can (5 oz.) boned chicken

Blend soups and milk. Add remaining ingredients. Heat; *do not boil.*

HIKERS CHICKEN CHOWDER
(Serves 2-3)
1 pkg. chicken soup mix
4 cups water
1 cup dry milk
¼ cup dried corn
1 pkg. freeze-dried, diced chicken
1 pkg. chicken gravy mix

Blend ingredients. Simmer until all are done.

CHICKEN STEW
(Serves 3-4)
1 can (1 lb.) stewed tomatoes
1 can (10½ oz.) chicken a la king
1 can (1 lb.) peas and carrots, undrained
1 5-oz. can chicken, cut into pieces
1 tsp. instant chicken bouillon or 1 cube
1 tsp. parsley flakes

In a saucepan, combine all ingredients and bring to a boil. Simmer, uncovered, stirring occasionally for 10 min.

Chef's secret: Dress up canned chicken stew by adding Worcestershire sauce to taste.

CAN-OPENER CHICKEN
(Serves 3-4)
(Lois Pitzer — Long Beach, Calif.)
1 can green beans, drained. Save juice
1 can cream of mushroom soup
2 cans (5 oz. each) boned chicken, cut up
1 large can chow mein noodles

Stir beans, soup and chicken together in a saucepan. Add drained bean juice to thin the mixture. Heat until bubbly. Serve over noodles.

ORIENTAL CHICKEN
(Serves 2-3)
1 can (10½ oz.) chicken a la king
1 can (5 oz.) boned chicken, diced
¼ cup evaporated milk
1 can peas, drained

Combine and simmer uncovered 5 min., stirring occasionally. Serve over Chinese noodles. Add diced hard cooked eggs and chopped pimiento for a colorful entree.

SAUCED PEAS N' CHICKEN
(Serves 3-4)
In a skillet combine 1⅓ cups water (part juice from the peas), salt, margarine and 1⅓ cups minute rice. Heat to a boil, cover and remove from heat for 5 min.

Add:
1 can cream of celery soup
½ cup milk
1 can (1 lb.) drained peas
1 can diced boned chicken

Heat to boiling. Use freeze-dried peas and chicken cubes instead of the canned.

CHICKEN N' RICE
(Serves 2-3)

In a saucepan combine:
1 cup water
1 cup minute rice
½ tsp. salt
Heat to a boil, cover and set off flame for 5 min.
Add:
1-1½ cups cubed cooked chicken (or canned)
1 can (10½ oz.) chicken gravy
1 tbls. chopped pimiento
¼ tsp. celery salt
1 tsp. dry onion flakes
1 can (2 oz.) mushroom pieces
Heat and simmer 10-15 min.

SPEEDY CHICKEN AND RICE

Prepare instant rice. Add 1 can (14 oz.) boneless chicken fricassee, salt and pepper, and heat thoroughly.

To cooked rice add a can of chicken, mushroom or celery soup and a can (14 oz.) of boneless chicken fricassee. Reheat and sprinkle with parmesan cheese.

CAST IRON CURRY
(Melba Blackstone — Los Angeles, Calif.)

8 chicken bouillon cubes
2 oz. dried apples
1 oz. raisins (¼ cup)
⅔ cup minute rice
2 tbls. green pepper flakes
2 tbls. onion flakes
canned chicken
1 tbls. curry powder
¼ tsp. garlic powder
1 piece of chopped candied ginger
1 tbls. dried lemon peel

Combine all ingredients in a skillet and add ⅓ cup water. Cook until apples are tender.

CHICKEN MANDARIN
(Serves 2-3)
1 stalk celery, chopped
⅓ cup onion, chopped
¼ tsp. marjoram
2 tbls. margarine
1 can (10½ oz.) chicken gravy
1½ cups cooked diced chicken (2 jars)
1 small can mandarin oranges, drained

In a saucepan sauté celery, onion, marjoram in margarine. Add remaining ingredients and heat. Simmer 10-15 min. Serve over shredded wheat biscuits.

CHICKEN BACON SANDWICHES
(4 sandwiches)
8 slices bacon
1 small can mushroom pieces, drained
1 tsp. dry onion
1 tsp. instant chicken bouillon or 1 cube
1 can (10½ oz.) chicken gravy
1 tsp. parsley flakes
1 can (5 oz.) chicken, slivered
4 hamburger rolls, split
4 slices tomato
Olives and sweet pickle

Cook bacon and drain off fat, reserving 2 tbls. Sauté mushrooms and onion until tender. Add bouillon, gravy, parsley and chicken. Heat, stirring occasionally. Spoon over buns, top with tomato and top half of the bun. Serve with olives and pickle.

CHICKEN N' DUMPLINGS
(Serves 2-3)
1 can (14 oz.) boneless chicken fricassee
1 small onion, chopped
1 carrot, sliced
1 stalk celery, sliced
Pepper and salt

Combine and heat to boiling.
Make dumplings:
1 cup biscuit mix
⅓ cup milk
½ tsp. parsley flakes

Mix with a fork and drop by spoonfuls on boiling stew. Simmer 10 min. uncovered, then cover and simmer 10 min. more. Makes 5-6 dumplings.

Chef's secret: To serve 4-5 add 1 can peas and carrots, drained.

FANCY CHICKEN N' DUMPLINGS
(Serves 3-4)
1 can mixed vegetables, drained
1 can cream of celery soup
1 can cream of chicken soup
½ cup water
⅛ tsp. celery seed
1 can (14 oz.) boneless chicken, cut up
Salt and pepper
¼ cup biscuit mix
¼ cup water

Combine all ingredients through salt and pepper. Heat to boiling. Combine biscuit mix and water, then add gradually, stirring constantly until thickened.

Make dumplings:
Combine 1 cup biscuit mix
⅓ cup milk
½ tsp. dry celery flakes
¼ tsp. sage

Drop by spoonfuls on hot mixture. Cook uncovered 10 min., and covered 10 min. at a simmer.

CHICKEN STROGANOFF

Steam minute rice in a saucepan using the liquid from a can of drained peas as part of the liquid.

Add canned chicken, drained peas, and a can of undiluted cream of chicken soup. Heat.

CHICKEN PILAF NO. 1
(Serves 3-4)
2 tbls. margarine
¾ cup uncooked rice
1 pkg. onion soup mix
2 cups water
2 cans cooked chicken

In a medium sized skillet sauté rice in the margarine until golden. Add soup mix and water, stir, cover and simmer 20-25 minutes or until water is absorbed. Add chicken and heat thoroughly.

Chef's secret: Top with slivered almonds.

CHICKEN PILAF NO. 2
(Serves 2-3)

Sauté 1⅓ cups minute rice and ½ cup chopped onion in 3 tbls. margarine.

Gradually add 1⅓ cups water to which you have added 2 cubes chicken bouillon or 2 tsp. instant bouillon.

Add
1 jar or can of chicken
¾ tsp. salt, dash of pepper
½ tsp. sage.

Bring to a boil, cover, remove from heat and let set 5 min.

CHICKEN PAELLA
(Serves 2)

1⅓ cups minute rice
2 tbls. minced onion
1½ cups bouillon (1½ cups water, 2 level tsp. instant bouillon)
1 can (6 oz.) boned chicken
½ tsp. salt
small jar chopped pimiento

Combine all ingredients in a pot. Cover and bring to a boil. Simmer 5 min.

CHICKEN RICE-A-RONI
(Serves 3-4)

In a sauce pan or a skillet with a tight lid:

Combine: 1-2 jars of boned chicken with the rice-vermicelli mixture in the package. Brown in 2 tbls. margarine, stirring often.

Measure the liquid from a can of peas. Add water to measure to package directions.

Add liquid slowly to the chicken mixture. Top with the contents of the flavor envelope and the drained peas. Stir and cover.

Simmer over a low flame 15 min. or until liquid is absorbed.

SKILLET TAMALES
(Serves 3-4)

In a skillet combine:
1 can cheddar cheese soup
1 can tomato sauce
2 cans (5 oz. each) boned chicken
¾ cup minute rice
Several sliced ripe olives

Cover and simmer 5 min. Add 2 cans (15 oz. each) tamales. Lay on top of mixture. Cover and simmer 10-15 min.

CHILAQUILES
(Serves 3-4)
4-5 corn tortillas, cut in narrow strips.
3 tbls. margarine
½ medium onion, diced
1 can (4 oz.) diced green chilis
½ tsp. salt
4 eggs, lightly beaten
1 cup shredded Jack or cheddar cheese
2 cans (5 oz. each) boned chicken
Chili salsa

Fry the strips of corn tortillas in margarine, stirring until crisp. Add onion, chilis, salt and eggs. Stir and cook until partially set. Add cheese and chicken, stirring lightly until eggs are set. Served topped with chili salsa.

CHILIS N' CHICKEN
(Serves 3-4)
1 can cream of chicken soup
⅓ cup water
1 jar chicken pieces
½ of a 4 oz. can diced green chilis

Combine soup and water and mix well with a wire whip. Add chicken and chilis. Heat and simmer 10 min. Serve over shredded wheat biscuit, or cooked rice. Use the rest of the diced chilis in scrambled eggs for breakfast.

EGG FOO CANOE
(Makes 7-8 patties)
1 can bean sprouts, drained, or use fresh sprouts.
1 can (5 oz.) chicken, diced
½ cup onion, diced
3 eggs
½ tsp. salt, dash of pepper
Fat for frying

Chop bean sprouts, add onion, chicken and seasonings. Mix well. Break eggs over mixture and stir well. Fry by spoonfuls, browning both sides. Make a package of chicken gravy to serve over patties.

FRIED RICE CASSEROLE
(Serves 4-5)

4-5 slices bacon, diced
1½ cups minute rice
4 eggs, slightly beaten
1 tbls. onion flakes
½ tsp. salt, dash of pepper
1 can (8 oz.) peas, drained (save liquid)
Combine liquid from peas and water to make 1½ cups.
2 cans (5 oz. each) boned chicken.

Fry bacon until crisp. Drain fat leaving 2 tbls. Add rice and brown lightly. Add eggs, onion, salt and pepper. Cook until eggs are set and water is absorbed. Add peas and chicken and heat thoroughly, stirring often.

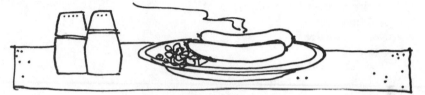

DINNER IS SERVED
WIENERS AND SAUSAGE

CORN N' FRANKS
(Serves 3-4)

Combine in a pot:
1 can cream of celery soup
1 can niblets corn, not drained
A few green pepper strips, cut up
½ tsp. mustard
1 tsp. Worcestershire Sauce
1 pkg. wieners, sliced

Simmer 15 min. Spoon over minute rice or bread slices.

QUICK SUPPER
(Serves 3)

½ lb. wieners
1 can (1 lb.) kidney beans
1 small can garbanzo beans, drained
1 stalk celery, chopped
1 tsp. dry onion flakes
Salt to taste

Cut franks into 1" slices. Add to rest of ingredients. Simmer, covered — 15 min.

LIMAS AND FRANKS
(Serves 3-4)

1 lb. wieners, cut up
1 can (1 lb.) corn and juice
1 can kidney beans and juice
1 can limas and juice
2 tsp. prepared mustard
Pinch of basil

Combine and heat 15-20 min. uncovered. Stir often.

BEAN STEW
(Serves 4-5)

3 tbls. margarine
1 medium onion, chopped
1 lb. weiners, sliced ½″ pieces
1 tbls. flour
1 tsp. chili powder
1 tsp. salt
2—15 oz. cans kidney beans
1 can (1 lb.) stewed tomatoes
1 can (12 oz.) whole kernel corn

In a large pot, sauté onion and franks in margarine until browned. Blend in flour, chili powder and salt. Add beans, tomatoes and corn. Simmer, covered, 15-20 min.

FRY PAN FRANKS AND BEANS
(Serves 2-3)
(Mildred Howell—Granada Hills, Calif.)

6 weiners, sliced
2 tsp. dry onion flakes
¼ tsp. oregano
1 tbls. margarine
1 can (28 oz.) New England baked beans
1 tomato, cut in wedges.

Sauté weiners, onion and oregano in margarine until browned. Add beans and simmer 10 min.
Add tomato wedges and heat gently.

SOUPED SANDWICHES
Combine:
1 can bean and bacon soup
⅓ cup water
¼ cup catsup
pinch of chili powder
6-8 weiners, thin sliced
Heat, stirring constantly.
Spoon on weiner buns.
Serve with sweet pickle relish.

WEINERS HAWAIIAN
(Serves 4-5)
Combine in a skillet:
1 can (8½ oz.) crushed pineapple
½ cup finely chopped green pepper
¼ cup firm packed brown sugar
2 tbls. margarine
1 tbls. soy sauce
1 tbls. dry onion flakes
Simmer 5 minutes, stirring occasionally.
Add large can pork and beans
6-8 weiners
Heat another 10 min.
Top weiner buns with weiners and spoon bean mixture over all.

TOMATO WEINERS
Place weiners in a skillet and cover with canned tomatoes or tomato sauce. Sprinkle lightly with salt, a little sugar and a pinch of oregano. Simmer until weiners have split and the sauce has become thick.
Spoon over toasted bread or English muffins.
Top with a slice of cheese.

WEINER STEW
(Serves 4-5)
½ pound (approx.) diced bacon
2 onions, chopped
1 can (12 oz.) whole kernel corn
1 can (1 lb.) kidney beans
1 pound weiners, cut in 1" pieces
Salt and pepper
Sauté bacon and onion until limp and opaque. Drain fat.
Add rest of ingredients. Add salt and pepper to taste.
Cover and simmer 15-20 min.

WEINER—VEGETABLE CHOWDER
(Serves 3-4)

¼ cup chopped green pepper
3-4 weiners, sliced
1 can bean and bacon soup
1 can vegetable soup
¼ cup chopped onion
2 tbls. margarine

Melt margarine in a saucepan and sauté green pepper, onion, and weiner slices.

Add soups plus 1½ cans water. Blend well.

Simmer 10 min.

PADDLERS CHOWDER
(Serves 4-5)

6 weiners, thinly sliced
2 tbls. margarine
4 cups water
1 pkg. potato with leek soup (Wylers)
2 small cans milk
1 can whole kernel corn, undrained
⅔ cup shredded sharp cheese
1 tsp. prepared mustard

Brown weiner slices in margarine.

Add water and soup mix. Blend well with wire whip.

Simmer, partially covered 10 min. Stir occasionally.

Add remaining ingredients and heat only until cheese melts.

WEINERS AND RICE
(Serves 3-4)

In a skillet:
Sauté 6-8 weiners, sliced, in
2 tbls. margarine
Add 1 can (1 lb.) stewed tomatoes plus water to make 2 cups.
Bring to a boil.
Add 1⅓ cups minute rice.

Simmer, covered, 5 min.

Add 1 can (1 lb.) kidney beans
1 tsp. chili powder

Heat until bubbly.

CAMPERS WEINERS
(Serves 4-5)
1 lb. weiners, cut in half lengthwise.
2 tbls. margarine
3 tbls. water
1½ tbls. flour
¾ cup water (part drained green bean juice)
1 can tomato sauce
3 tbls. vinegar
1 tsp. sugar
1½ tsp. prepared mustard
1 can green beans, drained
   Sauté cut weiners in margarine in a skillet.
   Combine flour with 3 tbls. water.
   Add remaining ingredients and blend.
   Pour over weiners, cover, and simmer 25-30 ˙min.

WEINERS ORIENTAL
(Serves 3-4)
In a frying pan:
Cut up 6-8 strips of bacon
Cut up 1 lb. weiners in ½″ pieces.
   Brown together until bacon is crisp. Drain fat.
Add:
2 cans tomato sauce
1 can whole corn
1 can lima beans
   Simmer until well blended.
   Add ½ cup minute rice. Stir and let set, covered, 5 min.
   Spoon over canned Chinese noodles.
   Top with a dollop of processed cheese spread.

WEINER MIX-UP
(Serves 3-4)
Prepare rice and set aside. Keep warm.
Combine:
1 can cream of mushroom soup
1 can niblets corn, undrained
½ green pepper, cut up
1 stalk celery, cut up
½ tsp. Worcestershire sauce
1 lb. weiners, cut up
1 small jar pimiento pieces
   Simmer 15 min., covered.
   Spoon over mounds of rice.

SPANISH RICE AND FRANKS
(Serves 3-4)
6 weiners cut in 1" pieces
1 medium onion, sliced
½ green pepper, diced
2 cups minute rice
2 tbls. margarine
2 cups hot water
2 cans tomato sauce
1 tsp. salt. Dash of pepper
1 tsp. prepared mustard
  Sauté weiners, onion, green pepper and rice in margarine.
  Add rest of ingredients. Mix well. Bring to a boil.
  Simmer, uncovered, 5 min.

WEINERS N' POTATO SKILLET
(Serves 3-4)
1 pound weiners, cut into slices.
3 slices bacon, cut into pieces.
  Fry bacon and weiner slices together until bacon is crisp. Drain fat.
Add:
1 pkg. (5½ oz.) of au gratin potatoes
2¼ cups water
1 small can evaporated milk
1 can (1 lb.) peas, undrained
  Cover and cook 15-20 min. until potatoes are done.
  Stir occasionally.

MEXICAN SCRAMBLE
(Serves 2)
In a saucepan, sauté:
1 stalk celery, chopped
½ small onion, chopped
¼ tsp. dry garlic chips
¼ tsp. chili powder
2 tbls. margarine
Add 1 can (1 lb.) beans and franks
1 small can Mexican niblets corn
  Heat thoroughly, stirring once or twice.
  Serve with heated tortillas, or over corn chips, crushed.

PORK-APPLE-CABBAGE SKILLET
(Serves 4-5)

4 pork chops (or use freeze-dried and prepare per instructions)
2 red apples, cored and cut in eighths
1 small head cabbage
1 cup apple juice
2 tsp. instant bouillon (or 2 cubes)
1 tsp. caraway seed
Salt and pepper

Brown meat on both sides.
Cub cabbage in wedges, then across wedges in ½″ slices.
Remove meat, add apple, cabbage, apple juice and bouillon.
Place meat on top, sprinkle with caraway seed, salt and pepper.
Cover and simmer 20 min.
Dip crusty bread in the pan juices.

SAUSAGE RECIPES

If you have no sausage, substitute bacon or ham, canned or fresh.

FRUITY BEANS
(Serves 5-6)

1-2 pkgs. brown and serve sausages
1 can apricot halves
2 cans (1 lb. each) baked beans
⅓ cup brown sugar, packed
1 tsp. dry mustard

Brown sausages and drain fat.
Drain apricots (save the juice to add to your breakfast juice).
Combine all ingredients.
Simmer 15-20 min.

SAUSAGE AND BEANS
(Serves 2)
6-8 sausage links
½ chopped green pepper
1 can (1 lb.) barbeque beans
Shredded sharp cheese
In a saucepan:
Cook sausage until browned. Drain most of the fat.
Add green pepper and cook till tender.
Add beans and heat until bubbly, stirring occasionally.
Sprinkle cheese over each hot serving.

SAUSAGE AND DUMPLINGS
(Serves 3-4)
1 or 2 pkgs. brown and serve sausages
1 can (1 lb. 2 oz.) tomato juice
1 can whole kernel corn, drained (save juice)
½ tsp. salt
Measure corn juice and add water to make ⅓ cup liquid.
1 cup Bisquick
Brown sausages on all sides. Drain excess fat.
Add tomato juice and salt. Heat to boiling.
Add drained corn and reheat.
Mix corn juice liquid and Bisquick and drop by spoonfuls into liquid.
Cook uncovered 10 min., cover and cook 10 min. more.

EGG PLANT AND SAUSAGE STEW
(Serves 3-4)
2 pkgs. (8 ea.) brown and serve sausage (or use canned)
1 cup chopped onion
1 green pepper cut in chunks
1 medium sized egg plant, peeled and cubed into ½" chunks
1 cup chopped fresh tomato
½ tsp. salt, dash of pepper
¼ tsp. oregano
In a large frying pan, cut up sausages into 1" chunks and brown.
Remove and keep warm.
Sauté onion and green pepper in sausage fat until soft.
Add egg plant and stir well to coat with fat.
Add tomatoes, seasonings and browned sausages.
Stir often until enough juice appears to simmer.
Cook, covered, over low heat 30 min.
DO NOT ADD WATER.
Optional: Use 1 can (1 lb.) stewed tomatoes, partly drained and
chopped, instead of fresh tomatoes, green pepper and part of onion.

Chef's secret: To peel egg plant easily, place in boiling water and cook approximately 15 min., turning it often to expose the whole skin. Remove from heat, drain, and immerse in cold water, then the skin should slip off.

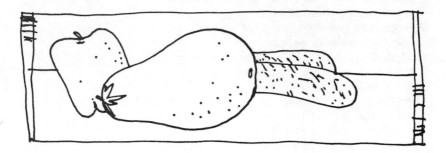

SAUSAGE AND SUCCOTASH
(Serves 4)

In a frying pan:
Cook brown and serve sausages (or bacon or ham)
Drain part of fat.
Add:
1 can (1 lb.) whole kernel corn, drained
1 can (1 lb.) lima beans, drained
1 tsp. salt
Dash of pepper
1 tsp. crushed dry parsley
 Heat until bubbly.

SAUSAGE PINEAPPLE SKILLET
(Serves 2)

1 pkg. (8 oz.) brown and serve sausages
¼ cup sliced onion
1 can (8¾ oz.) pineapple tidbits
1 tbls. brown sugar
¾ tsp. salt
Dash of pepper
¼ tsp. dry mustard
Pinch of ginger
1⅓ cups minute rice
 Brown sausages in a skillet. Drain all except 1 tbls. fat.
 Add onion and sauté, stirring often.
 Drain pineapple, measuring syrup.
 Add water to make 1⅓ cups liquid.
 Add rest of ingredients except rice. Bring to a boil.
 Add rice, cover and simmer 5 min.

ZUCCHINI AND SAUSAGE
(Serves 3-4)
2 pkgs. brown and serve sausage
2 lbs. small sized zucchini, sliced ½" thick.
1 small onion, sliced thin.
2 large firm tomatoes, chopped
½ tsp. salt, dash of pepper
Grated cheese.
  Brown sausages and remove from pan.
  Cook onion in sausage fat.
  Add zucchini and sauté slowly 5 min., stirring often.
  Add tomatoes and salt, place sausages on top.
  Cover and cook 5 min. longer.
  Sprinkle with grated cheese.

SWEET-SOUR SAUSAGE
(Serves 2-3)
Prepare minute rice and set aside while you combine the following:
1 pkg. brown and serve sausages, browned (drain fat)
1 can pineapple chunks, drained (save juice)
½ cup whole cranberry sauce
1 tsp. instant chicken bouillon
½ cup boiling water
2 tbls. brown sugar
2 tbls. vinegar
1 green pepper cut in chunks
2 tbls. corn starch
2 tbls. water
  Combine pineapple juice and cranberry sauce.
  Dissolve bouillon in hot water. Add brown sugar and stir.
  Add vinegar and pour onto sausages. Cover and simmer 10 min.
  Add pineapple and green pepper. Cover and cook 10 min.
  Push ingredients to sides of pan. Combine cornstarch and 2 tbls. water.
  Stir into sauce and cook until thinkened, stirring constantly.
  Spoon over rice.

SAUSAGE N' APPLE RINGS
(Serves 2)
1 pkg. brown and serve sausage
2 apples, cored and cut into ½" rings (do not peel)
  In a skillet, brown the sausages. After fat has started to accumulate, add apple rings. Cover pan and cook to soften apples.
  Turn sausages and apples to brown both sides.
  Add a little water if the pan is too dry.2

BULK SAUSAGE RECIPES
POTATOES N' SAUSAGE
(Serves 2-3)
½ lb. sausage (or use canned or freeze dried)
2 large potatoes, diced
1 large onion, chopped
Salt and pepper.

Crumble sausage into fry pan.

Add potatoes and onion and cook over low heat until potatoes are tender.

Add salt and pepper after draining extra fat.

SAUSAGE-YAM-APPLE CASSEROLE
(Serves 5-6)
1 can (24 oz.) yams in syrup, drained
1 lb. pork sausage, shaped into 5-6 patties, ½" thick
4 unpeeled large apples, cut in thick wedges
Salt
2 tbls. brown sugar

Brown sausage patties on both sides. Drain fat.

Slice yams and arrange on top of sausages.

Cover with apple wedges and sprinkle with salt and brown sugar.

Cover bottom of pan with syrup drained from yams.

Cover pan and simmer until apples are soft.

BREAKFAST-SUPPER
(Serves 4)
(Millie Jones — Northridge, Calif.)

Combine:
5 eggs
¼ cup milk
Salt and pepper to taste
Add:
⅓ cup grated parmesan cheese
⅓ cup cheddar cheese
1 tsp. caraway seeds

Fry half a pound of sausage until the pink color is gone. Drain part of fat.

Add three slices of white bread, cubed.

Continue to fry, stirring often until cubes are light brown.

Add egg mixture and cheese and stir, turning often with a spatula until eggs are cooked.

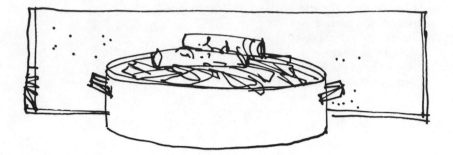

CANNED SAUSAGES
SAUSAGE PILAF
(Serves 3-4)

¼ cup margarine (½ stick)
1 large onion, chopped
1 cup uncooked rice
2½ cups hot water
2 tsp. instant chicken bouillon
2 cans Vienna sausages, sliced
½ tsp. sage
Salt and pepper.
    Melt margarine in a skillet.
    Add onion and sauté until clear.
    Add water and bouillon and bring to a boil.
    Add sausages, sage, salt and pepper.
    Cover and simmer on low heat 20 min. or until liquid is absorbed.

SAUSAGE STEW
(Serves 2-3)

2 cans sausages
1 medium onion, diced
1 green pepper, diced
1 can kidney beans
1 can (1 lb.) tomatoes
1 tsp. chili powder
1 cup water
    Brown sausages, onion and pepper together.
    Drain fat and add rest of ingredients.
    Simmer 15-20 min.
    Serve with thick chunks of French bread.

CABBAGE SURPRISE
(Serves 3-4)

2 cans sausages
1 can (1 lb.) apple slices, drained (save juice)
1 small head cabbage, chopped
Salt and pepper

Brown sausages in a skillet. Remove and keep warm by wrapping in a paper-towel-lined foil packet.

Add drained apples and sauté in sausage fat.

Add cabbage and apple juice, salt and pepper. Simmer covered until cabbage is tender but still a little crunchy.

Lay cooked sausage on top of cabbage and reheat before serving.

Add water sparingly only if needed.

NOODLES N' SAUSAGES
(Serves 3-4)

2 cans Vienna sausage, cut up
2 cans (8 oz.) tomato sauce
1 tbls. dry onion flakes
1 tsp. oregano
1 tsp. salt
3 cups uncooked noodles, broken
1 cup shredded mild cheese

Brown sausages in margarine

Add tomato sauce, onion, oregano, salt. Heat until simmering.

Stir in broken noodles, cover and simmer 20 min.

Sprinkle cheese over each serving.

Chef's secrets:
- *Freeze-dried diced ham or bacon bar can be substituted for sausages.*
- *Dried mushrooms could be soaked and added to the recipe.*

SAUSAGE RONI
(Serves 3-4)

2 cans Vienna sausage, cut up
½ onion, sliced fine
1 pkg. Chicken Rice-A-Roni
1 can peas, drained (save juice)
Water

Brown sausages, onion and Rice-A-Roni in margarine.

Add juice from peas and water to make required amount of liquid called for on box.

Add flavor packet and stir.

Cover and simmer 15-20 min.

Remove from heat and let stand a few minutes to loosen any stuck to the pan.

SOUP CAN SUPPER
(Serves 3-4)

1 can cream of vegetable soup
1 can cream of chicken soup
1 can condensed onion soup
2 cups milk (use dry milk and water)
1 can (8 oz.) cream style corn
1 can Vienna sausage, sliced.

Combine all, cover and heat slowly until soups come just to boiling.

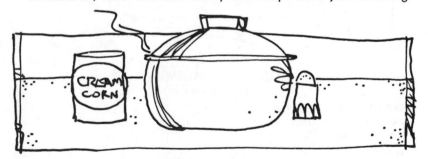

DINNER IS SERVED
Bacon and Sausages

Chef's secrets:

- Salt pork can be substituted for bacon in many recipes. Spear with a sharp-tined fork, then pour with boiling water to wash off the salt brine. Slice fine, then cut up into small pieces so it will cook quickly.
- Bacon bar also can be used as a substitute, but don't overdo.
- Cook extra bacon with breakfast slices. Wrap in a paper towel, then in a plastic bag. Add to your freeze-dried green beans at dinner for a delicious change.

SPANISH RICE

Dice a few strips of bacon and sauté with onion slices.
Add 1 can tomato soup, 1 can water, 1/2 tsp. sugar, salt and pepper.
Add 1 cup uncooked white rice and steam, covered, 25-30 min.

FRIED RICE
(Serves 2)

1/4 bacon bar (or 3 slices bacon, chopped)
2 eggs, whipped with a fork
1 can cooked rice
1/2 tsp. dry onion flakes
2 tbls. soy sauce
1/2 tsp. salt, dash of pepper
    Sauté bacon until crisp, drain fat.
    Scramble eggs with bacon over low heat.
    Add rice gradually, stirring into eggs with a fork.
    Add onion and seasonings. Stir often. Cook 5 min.

MEXICAN RICE
(Serves 2-3)

    In a frying pan combine: 1 1/3 cup water, 1 1/3 cup minute rice and 1/2 tsp.
salt. Bring to a boil, cover and remove from heat 5 min.
    Put hot rice in a bowl, set aside.
    Fry four or five strips of bacon until crisp. Drain on a paper towel.
    Sauté cooked rice in the hot bacon fat until browned. Add crumbled
bacon.
    Combine: 1 can (4 oz.) diced green chilis and 3 eggs. Beat well.
    Add to frying pan and cook until set.

SLUMGUM
(Serves 1-2)

4 slices bacon, diced
1 small onion, diced
1 can (1 lb.) tomatoes, plain or stewed
1/4 lb. sharp cheese, diced
    Sauté bacon and onion together.
    Add tomatoes. Heat until bubbly.
    Add diced cheese, and heat until melted.
    Serve spooned on sourdough French bread.

SOUPER SCRAMBLED EGGS
(Serves 4)

Cook 4 slices bacon, diced, until crisp. Drain some of the fat.
Combine and add:

8 beaten eggs
1 can vegetable soup
¼ tsp. salt, dash of pepper

Cook slowly, stirring often until eggs are set.
Variation: Use cream of chicken, celery or mushroom soup.

BACON POTATO MIX-UP
(Serves 3-4)

4 slices bacon, diced
1 tbls. sugar
1 tsp. salt
1½ tbls. flour
⅓ cup vinegar
⅓ cup water
4 cups diced, cooked potatoes
Parsley flakes.

Cook bacon in a skillet until crisp. Drain on a paper towel.
Drain fat, reserving 2 tbls.
Combine sugar, salt, flour, vinegar and water and add, cooking until thickened.
Add potatoes, bacon and parsley flakes and heat thoroughly.

HOT POTATO SCALLOP
(Serves 2-3)

4 slices bacon, diced
1 pkg. scalloped potato mix
1 tbls. dry onion flakes
3 cups boiling water
½ tsp. sugar
2 tbls. vinegar

In a large skillet, fry bacon until crisp. Drain on paper toweling.
Drain fat.
Combine potato slices, sauce mix and onion in skillet. Add hot water and sugar.
Stir cover and cook over low heat for 30 min. or until potatoes are done.
Add vinegar and bacon bits. Stir and reheat.

BACON N' BEANS
(Serves 5-6)
Fry 6 slices bacon until crisp, drain and crumble.
Sauté 1 green pepper, chopped, in drippings.
Stir in: 2 cans (1 lb. ea.) pork and beans
2 cans (1 lb. ea.) drained whole kernel corn
⅓ cup barbeque sauce
Heat and simmer 10 min.

BACON 'N GARBANZO BEANS
Fry several cut up bacon slices and drain fat.
Add:
1 can (1 lb.) stewed tomatoes
1 can tomato sauce
2 cans drained garbanzo beans
Heat thoroughly, and serve with French bread.

FRENCH ZUCCHINI
Cut up 2-3 strips bacon and sauté in frying pan.
Wash and trim ends of small zucchini.
Quarter lengthwise and lay in pan in rows on top of bacon.
Slice peeled fresh tomatoes on top.
Add ½ of Good Season's French Dressing Mix, mixed up.
Simmer 10 min. covered.

TEEPEE CORN
(Serves 2)
Fry 4 slices bacon and drain fat.
Add:
1 can creamed corn. When hot add:
4 eggs, lightly beaten.
Stir until as thick as desired.

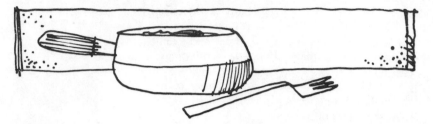

STERNMANS STEW
(Serves 4)

4 slices bacon, chopped
1 small onion, chopped
1 can cream of celery soup
1 can turkey-noodle soup
1 soup can water
1 soup can milk
1 can whole-kernel corn
1 tbls. parsley flakes
1 tsp. celery flakes
Dash of pepper

In a large saucepan sauté bacon and onion until golden, and bacon is crisp.

Stir in soups, milk and water. Add remaining ingredients and simmer 5-10 min., stirring occasionally.

CORN CHOWDER
(Serves 4)

Small cube (1½ square) salt pork, sliced and diced fine
1 small onion, sliced
2 cups diced raw potato
1 can (1 lb.) tomatoes or tomato soup
1 can cream style corn
½ tsp. salt, dash of pepper
2 cups water (approximately)
1 small can evaporated milk

Fry salt pork until browned. Add onion and sauté until golden and limp. Add vegetables, seasonings and water. Simmer until potatoes are tender. Stir in milk and reheat. DO NOT BOIL.

HURRY CORN CHOWDER

Sauté cut-up bacon and chopped onion until bacon is crisp.

Add peeled, diced raw potatoes, celery slices, whole-kernel corn, undrained. Add 2½ cups water and simmer until potatoes are tender.

Add 1 pkg. Wyler's Potato With Leek soup mix. Simmer 5 min.

Add 1 small can evaporated milk. Reheat, DO NOT BOIL.

RIVER BANK CHOW MEIN
(Serves 6-8)

4 slices bacon, cut into small pieces and browned
1 small head cabbage, cut into small pieces
2 large stalks celery, sliced diagonally
1 large carrot, shredded
1 medium onion, chopped
1 green pepper, chopped
1 tsp. salt, dash of pepper
½ cup water
1 large can evaporated milk

Fry bacon pieces until crisp. Do not drain fat. Add vegetables, salt and pepper, stir well in bacon drippings. Add water, cover and simmer 15 min. Add milk and reheat until steamy.

CHAYOTE (Chah-YO-tay)
A Mexican green squash

Fry 4-6 slices bacon until crisp. Drain on paper towel and set aside.

Wash and slice thin or dice chayote squash (do not peel). Include seed to be cooked.

Place in the pan with a SMALL amount of water, a sprinkle of salt and 1 tsp. dry onion flakes. Cover and simmer until tender, 10-12 min.

Drain water if necessary.

Add a dash of pepper and ¼ tsp. oregano, and crumbled bacon. Stir, mixing well.

Variation: Add 1 small can niblets corn.

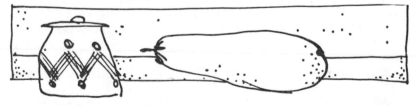

NOPOLITOS SCRAMBLED
(Serves 3-4)

5-6 slices bacon, cut up
1 small green pepper, diced
1 small onion, diced
1 medium sized firm tomato
1 jar nopolitos (in Mexican food section of market)
6 eggs, beaten

Fry bacon until crisp. Add pepper, onion and tomato and cook until browned. Add nopolitos and simmer until all is done.

Add beaten eggs and cook until well set.

CORN TACOS
(Serves 3-4)
Spread a thin film of margarine on one side of a tortilla. Fry quickly on both sides, margarine side first. (Or use pre-shaped and cooked shells). Set aside and keep warm by wrapping in paper towels and then in a turkish towel. Prepare as many tortillas as desired, or 3-4 for each person.

In that frying pan cook 5-6 slices bacon until crisp.

Drain the juice from 2 cans of whole-kernel corn (save juice).

Add the corn to the hot skillet and sauté 2-3 minutes.

Add 1 green pepper, finely chopped, 1 onion, chopped, 1 celery stalk, sliced.

Add garlic, chili powder and pepper to taste.

Add corn liquid and a small amount of evaporated milk.

Cover and simmer until liquid is almost gone. Spoon this mixture onto the cooked tortillas, roll up and enjoy.

HOMINY SCRAMBLE
(Serves 3-4)
Scald salt pork. Cut up into small pieces, fry until crisp.

Add enough fat to make approximately 2 tbls.

Lightly brown 1 can (2½ cups) hominy in the drippings.

Beat together 4 eggs, ½ tsp. salt, dash of pepper.

Add to hominy and cook until eggs are set, stirring often.

CABBAGE AND POLISH SAUSAGE
(Serves 2)
In a frying pan place 2 Polish sausages and 2-3 tbls. water.

Simmer, covered, turning sausages once or twice, until water is evaporated.

Brown sausages over low heat until they split. Place at the edge of the pan.

Add 1 small onion, sliced thin, and 1 small head of cabbage, shredded.

Stir into sausage fat, coating well. Add small amount of water, ½ tsp. caraway seed, ½ tsp. garlic powder, dash of pepper.

Stir well, cover, and cook 5-7 minutes more, or until cabbage is limp.

POLISH SAUSAGE 'N CORN
Simmer Polish sausages in ¼" of water in a covered frying pan 10 min. (Do not add more water).

Remove cover and allow any liquid to evaporate.

Turn sausages often to brown.

When they start to crack open, add a can of whole-kernel or Mexicorn and heat.

MEXICAN BEANS
(Serves 3-4)
6-8 slices dry salami, cut into eighths
1 can (1 lb.) kidney beans
1 can niblets corn
1 can tomato sauce
¼ tsp. oregano

Brown sausage pieces slowly in a small amount of margarine. Add remaining ingredients and heat thoroughly. Serve spooned over heated tortillas.

MIXED-UP BEANS
(Serves 4-5)
1 can (1 lb.) baked beans
1 can (1 lb.) cut green beans, drained
1 can (8 oz.) lima beans
1 can (8 oz.) garbanzo beans, drained
2 tsp. dry onion flakes
Bias cut slices of dry salami

Combine all ingredients and simmer over medium heat for 10-15 min., stirring occasionally.

HOT BOLOGNA SANDWICHES
(Serves 3)
6 slices bologna
1 tbls. margarine
1 can mushroom gravy
2 tbls. chili sauce
¼ tsp. Worcestershire sauce
3 hard rolls, split
Sliced cucumber, zucchini, onion

In a skillet, brown the bologna in margarine. Add gravy, chili and Worcestershire sauce. Heat, stirring occasionally. Place 1 slice bologna on each half roll.

Top with mushroom sauce and garnish with slices of cucumber, zucchini or onion.

HAM, SPAM,
AND LUNCHEON MEATS

The meats in these recipes are interchangeable. If a canned or cured ham is not available, substitute your favorite luncheon loaf. The recipe will be delicious, whichever you choose.

PEACHY LUNCH
(Serves 3-4)
(Lois Pitzer — Long Beach, Calif.)

1 can (12 oz.) luncheon meat, sliced
1 can (16 oz.) peach slices, drained

Brown meat slices on both sides in a skillet. Push to one side of pan. Place peach slices in center. Spoon about ¼ cup syrup over meat. Heat for 5 min.

CORN CHOWDER
(Serves 3-4)

½ can Spam, diced
2 medium sized onions, chopped
3 medium sized potatoes, sliced
3 cups water
1 tsp. salt, dash of pepper
1 can whole corn, undrained
1 can tomato soup
1 small can evaporated milk

Brown diced Spam in margarine in a deep pot. Add onions and sauté until clear. Add potatoes, water and salt and pepper. Cook until potatoes are tender. Add corn and tomato soup. Simmer 5 min. Just before serving, add canned milk. Stir and serve immediately.

FRIED TOMATO SLICES

Fry lunch meat, sliced, in margarine until browned.
Push to sides of skillet.
Cut *firm* tomatoes into ½'' thick slices.
Dip into a mixture of corn meal, salt and pepper. Coat both sides.
Fry tomato slices several minutes on each side, until coating is crisp.

HAM AND CABBAGE SKILLET
(Serves 2-3)

1 onion, sliced
⅓ cup margarine
1 can ham luncheon meat, cubed
1 small head cabbage, thinly sliced
¼ cup water
2 tbls. brown sugar
2 tbls. vinegar
Salt and pepper

Sauté onion in margarine until tender. Add luncheon meat and brown lightly. Add cabbage and water and cook, covered, for about 10 min. until tender. Stir occasionally. Combine sugar and vinegar, salt and pepper and add to skillet. Heat 5 min. more.

SCRAMBLED CORN
(Serves 3-4)
(Lois Pitzer — Long Beach, Calif.)

1 can (12 oz.) luncheon meat
Margarine
3 eggs slightly beaten
1 can (1 lb.) cream style corn
¼ tsp. salt, dash of pepper

Cube luncheon meat and brown in a little margarine. Combine remaining ingredients and add to meat. Cook over low heat, stirring, until eggs are set.

HAM A LA KING
(Serves 3-4)

2 pkgs. cream sauce mix, made up and set aside
1 lb. processed American cheese, cubed small
1 lb. canned ham, chopped (or Spam)
1 can whole kernel corn, niblets style
½ green pepper, cut up

Sauté ham, corn and green pepper in a small amount of margarine. Add ready mixed cream sauce and cheese cubes. Heat until cheese melts and cream sauce is cooked. Serve over buns or English muffins.

SKILLET B-B-Q

At home combine:
1 tbls. dry onion flakes
3 tbls. sugar
1 tsp. prepared mustard
½ cup catsup
2 tbls. vinegar
1 tsp. Worcestershire sauce
   At camp: Heat this mixture in a frying pan. Add sliced Spam and sliced canned yams. Simmer until hot and bubbly.

HAM DASH NO. 1
(Serves 2-3)

1 can chopped ham, cubed
⅛ tsp. thyme
2 tbls. margarine
1 can (10½ oz.) chicken gravy (or use mix, made up)
1 can (1 lb. 7 oz.) sweet potatoes, drained
1 can (8 oz.) small white onion, drained
1 tsp. dry parsley
   In a skillet, brown ham with thyme in margarine. Add gravy, potatoes, onions and parsley. Simmer, covered, 15-20 min.

HAM DASH NO. 2
(Serves 2-3)

1 can chopped ham, cubed
1 small onion, chopped
¼ tsp. thyme
2 tbls. margarine
1 can (10½ oz.) mushroom gravy (or use a mix, made up)
1 can green beans, drained
Water
1 cup minute rice
   In a skillet, brown the ham with onion and thyme in margarine. Add gravy and beans. Add water to bean juice to make 1 cup. Add and simmer, covered, 15 min. Stir occasionally. Add rice, stir, set off flame for 5 min., covered.

CELERY ROOT SAUTÉ
(CELERIAC)
(Serves 2-3)

Peel one celery root and cut into shoestring strips.

Cook in salted boiling water about 8 min. or until tender.

Drain and save the juice to add to tomato juice cocktail.

Add 2 tbls. margarine to pot. Coat strips.

Add chopped ham, sliced, and brown meat on both sides in the same pan.

Season to taste.

Chef's secret: At home: If the leaves of celery root are fresh, cut them off and dry in the oven for seasoning.

POTATO CAKES AND HAM

Prepare potato cakes using instant mashed potatoes. Season well.

In a large skillet fry ham slices on one side.

Turn and place a slice of cheese on each.

Fry potato cakes in center of pan while the cheese melts on the ham placed around the outside of the pan.

SCALLOPED POTATOES AND HAM
(Serves 3-4)

1 can Spam, cubed
1 pkg. scalloped potato mix
4 tbls. dry milk
1 envelope sour cream sauce mix
3 tbls. dry milk
1 tbls. dry onion flakes
2 tbls. dried parsley
1 tbls. dry green pepper flakes
Water
2 tbls. margarine

In a large pan put:

Cubed Spam

Potato mixed with 4 tbls. dry milk

Margarine

3 cups water

Heat to boiling, then simmer, stirring often, until potatoes are tender.

Combine:

Sour cream mix

3 tbls. dry milk

Onions, parsley, pepper

½ cup water

Stir into potatoes, heat.

POTATO — EGG SCRAMBLE
(Serves 3)
(Lois Pitzer — Long Beach, Calif.)
½ can luncheon meat, sliced
1 can potatoes, rinsed, dried and sliced
Salt and pepper
4 eggs, beaten

Brown the meat in a small amount of margarine. Add sliced potatoes and seasoning. Fry until light brown. Add eggs and stir-cook until eggs are set.

Variation: Add dry onion flakes. Serve with catsup.

HASH N' CHEESE SKILLET
(Serves 3)
1 can luncheon meat, cut in strips
1 pkg. (5½ oz.) dry hash brown potatoes with onion
1 can (1 lb.) cut green beans, undrained
1 can (6 oz.) evaporated milk
1½ cups water
1 jar (5 oz.) process cheese spread (your choice)
Pepper

In a skillet combine all ingredients. Cover and cook over medium heat, stirring occasionally. Simmer until potatoes are tender, about 10 mins.

CREAMED HAM
(Serves 2)
1 can Spam, cut into cubes
1 can (12½ oz.) peas and carrots, drained
1 envelope white sauce mix
Salt and pepper
1 can Chinese noodles

Brown Spam cubes in a small amount of margarine. Add drained vegetables. Use juice from vegetables to mix the white sauce. Add. Season and simmer 10 min. Serve over noodles.

SPAM CHOWDER
(Serves 4-5)

2 tbls. margarine
1 can Spam, cubed
1 tbls. dry onion flakes
3 tbls. flour
1 can (1 lb.) mixed vegetables
2-2½ cups milk (1 cup dry milk, 2-2½ cups water)
Dash of pepper
Dry celery and parsley flakes

Brown Spam cubes in margarine. Drain a little of the juice from the vegetables to mix with flour. Add the rest of the ingredients, stirring constantly. Bring to a boil, then simmer 10-15 min.

HAM-POTATO SKILLET
(Serves 2-3)

In a skillet:
Brown 1 can Spam, cubed, in small amount of margarine.
Add:
1 can cream of mushroom soup
1 small can evaporated milk
1 tbls. dry onion flakes
½ tsp. salt, dash of pepper
1 can potatoes, rinsed and sliced
1 can carrots, undrained

Simmer approximately 10 min. Use dry potatoes and carrots to lessen weight.

SAUCED HAM
(Serves 2)

In a skillet:
Brown ½ can Spam, cubed, in small amount of margarine.
Add:
1 can cream of mushroom soup
½ cup water (use juice from green beans)
⅓ cup dry milk
1 can (1 lb.) green beans, drained

Heat to boiling and serve over hamburger buns, split and warmed on the lid as the mixture cooks.

SKILLET BEANS
(Serves 2)
Place slices of luncheon meat in a skillet.
Drizzle with molasses. Heat until sizzling.
Add a can of baked beans
1 tsp. dry onion flakes
1 tsp. prepared mustard
Heat until bubbly.

BEAN HAWAIIAN
(Serves 5-6)
1 can Spam, cubed
1 tbls. margarine
1 can (9 oz.) sliced pineapple, drained
1 can (1 lb. 12 oz.) baked beans
1 can (1 lb.) kidney beans
1 can (small) garbanzo beans
2 tbls. brown sugar
¼ tsp. ground cloves
   Brown cubed Spam in the margarine, stirring often. Drain the pineapple (juice is the cook's bonus) and cut into small pieces right in the can. Add to meat along with the rest of the ingredients. Heat slowly, stirring occasionally.
   Chef's secret: Canned brown bread is a nice addition.

ORANGE HAM AND YAMS
(Serves 2-3)
Melt 1 tbls. margarine in a frying pan.
Sauté sliced Spam. Remove and keep warm.
Mix 1 tbls. cornstarch, 1 cup orange juice and 1 tbls. honey.
Pour into frying pan, using wire whip to keep it smooth.
Cook until thickened.
Add 1 can yams, drained, and Spam slices.
Heat through.
   Use canned ham instead of Spam.
   Use reconstituted orange crystals (Start, Tang) for orange juice.

YAMS HAWAIIAN
(Serves 2-3)
Melt one tbls. margarine and ¼ cup molasses in a skillet.
Add sliced luncheon meat and 4 pineapple slices.
Cook 8-10 min. turning pineapple as it browns.
Turn ham and place pineapple on top.
Add yams, drained, and brown while ham cooks on the other side.

PERKIN SPANISH RICE
(Serves 3-4)
(Mary Perkin—Tujunga, Calif.)

2 tbls. margarine
1 small onion, chopped
1 can Spam, cubed
2 pkg. Spanish Rice Seasoning mix
1⅓ cups minute rice
2-2½ cups water

In a skillet, brown onion and Spam in margarine. Add seasoning mix, rice and 1 cup water. Cook over medium heat, adding water as needed until rice is done.

PRONTO SPANISH RICE
(Serves 2-3)
Lightly brown in ¼ cup margarine:
1 can diced luncheon meat
1⅓ cups minute rice
1 small onion, sliced
½ green pepper, sliced
Add:
1½ cups hot water
2 cans (8 oz. each) tomato sauce
1 tsp. salt, dash of pepper

Mix well, bring to a boil. Simmer 5 min.

MINUTE SPAM N' RICE
(Serves 3-4)
In a skillet sauté:
2 tbls. margarine
1 can Spam, cut into strips
Add:
1 can condensed onion soup plus water to make 2 cups
Bring to a boil.
Add 1⅓ cups minute rice
Reduce heat and simmer, covered, 5 min.
ADD:
¼ cup chopped parsley
⅓ cup sweet pickle relish

Stir over low heat to blend.

SOUP N' RICE
(Serves 3-4)

1 can Spam, cubed
1 cup celery, chopped
1 small onion, chopped
1 can mushroom soup
1 can chicken noodle soup
½ cup *uncooked* rice
1 cup water

Brown Spam cubes in margarine. Sauté celery and onion. Add soups, rice and water. Bring to a boil and simmer, covered, 15-20 min.

RICE FLEMENCO
(Serves 3-4)

1 small onion, chopped
¼ cup each, diced green pepper and celery
¼ tsp. minced dry garlic
2 tbls. margarine
1 can (1 lb.) tomatoes, cut up
1 cup minute rice
1 can peas, drained (save juice)
1 cup water (add water to pea juice to make 1 cup)
½ tsp. salt, dash of pepper
1 tsp. oregano
1 can Spam cut in 6 slices (or use ham, cubed or sliced)

Sauté onions, celery, peppers and garlic in margarine. Add remaining ingredients except Spam.

Slice Spam and put on top of other indredients in center of skillet. Bring to a boil, cover and simmer over low heat 10 min. or until rice has absorbed the liquid.

SPEEDY FRIED RICE
(Serves 2)

¼ lb. ham or bacon cut into small pieces
2 eggs, lightly beaten
1 can cooked rice (look in Oriental food section of market)
1 tbls. chopped onion or 1 tsp. dry onion flakes
2 tbls. soy sauce
½ tsp. salt, dash of pepper

Fry meat until browned and remove from skillet. Cook eggs over low heat. Add rice gradually, stirring with a fork. Add onion and seasonings, stirring often. Cook about 5 min. Add meat and cook 2-3 min. more.

Serve with applesauce.

SPAM N' RICE SKILLET
(Serves 3-4)

2 tbls. margarine
1 can luncheon meat, cut in strips
1 can condensed onion soup plus water to make 2 cups liquid
1⅓ cups minute rice
1 tsp. dry parsley flakes

Heat margarine in a skillet. Add meat and sauté. Gradually add soup and water, then stir in rice. Add parsley. Cover and simmer 5 min.

ORIENTAL FRIED RICE
(Serves 6-7)

¼ cup margarine (½ stick)
1 small onion chopped
2 cups diced luncheon meat
2⅔ cups minute rice
4 eggs, lightly beaten
2 cups chicken broth
2 cans (3 oz. each) mushrooms, undrained
2 cans (1 lb. each) peas, drained
2 tsp. soy sauce

Sauté onion, meat and rice in margarine about 5 min.

Stir in eggs. Add broth, mushrooms with liquid, peas and soy and bring to a boil.

Remove from heat, cover and let stand 5 min.

Before serving, stir to fluff.

CHOP SUEY
(Serves 4-5)

3 tbls. margarine
1 can Spam, cut in strips
3 cups bias-cut celery
1 large onion, sliced
1 envelope Lipton Beef Flavor Mushroom Mix
1¼ cups water
¼ cup soy sauce
1 can (1 lb.) bean sprouts, drained
1 can (5 oz.) water chestnuts, drained and sliced
1 can (5 oz.) bamboo shoots, drained

Sauté Spam, celery, onion until crisp-tender.

Add Mushroom Mix, water, soy sauce. Simmer 5 minutes, stirring constantly.

Add rest of ingredients and simmer, stirring constantly until heated through.

Serve over canned noodles.

MACARONI WITH MEAT
(Serves 1-2)

½ can luncheon meat, cubed
1 tsp. dry minced onion
1 tbls. margarine
1 can (1 lb.) macaroni and cheese
Pinch of marjoram

In a saucepan, brown meat and onion in margarine.

Add macaroni and marjoram and heat, stirring occasionally.

Chef's secret: Golden Grain Macaroni and Cheese is tasty if freeze-dried ham bits or cubed luncheon meat and a drained can of peas and carrots are added to it. Use the liquid drained from the peas and carrots for a part of the liquid to cook the macaroni.

LUNCH MEAT N' NOODLES
(Serves 4-5)

Cook 1 pkg. (6-8 oz.) wide noodles in salted water and drain.

To the noodles add:
1 can cream of chicken soup
½ cup milk (¼ cup dry milk, ½ cup water)
1 can luncheon meat, cut into strips
½ green pepper, chopped
1 tsp. minced dry onion
1 can peas, drained (use liquid to add to dry milk)
1 tsp. salt

Simmer, stirring occasionally for 12-15 min.

DRIED BEEF,
CORNED BEEF AND HASH

CREAMED BEEF
(Serves 2-3)

1 pkg. (4 oz.) sliced dried beef
1 tsp. dry onion flakes
2 tbls. margarine
1 can cream of celery soup
1 cup milk (or 1 small can evaporated milk and water to make 1 cup)

Rinse the dried beef in hot water, drain on paper towels. In a saucepan, brown the beef and onion flakes in margarine. Stir in soup and milk. Heat thoroughly, stirring often. Serve over buns, toast, cooked rice or shredded wheat.

DRIED BEEF-MACARONI MIX-UP
(Serves 2-3)
(Lois Pitzer—Long Beach, Calif.)

1 pkg. macaroni and cheddar
1½ cups hot water
1 can cream of celery or mushroom soup
1 jar (4 oz.) dried beef torn into small pieces

Cook macaroni as directed on package. Drain. Add water, soup, dried beef and cheese sauce mix from macaroni package. Heat to boiling; simmer until thick. (2-3 min.)

DRIED BEEF 'N BEANS
(Serves 2-3)

1 tbls. dry onion flakes
3 tbls. margarine
1 pkg. (3 oz.) dried beef, chopped
2 tbls. flour
1 can (1 lb.) lima beans, drained
1 small can evaporated milk.

Sauté onion and beef in margarine. Blend in remaining ingredients. Cook over low flame, stirring until thickened.

CREAMED CHIPPED BEEF
(Serves 3-4)

¼ cup (½ cube) margarine
1 small green pepper, chopped
1 small onion, chopped
¼ lb. dried beef, rinsed and shredded
¼ cup flour
2 cups milk (use dry milk or evaporated milk and water)

In a skillet: Cook green pepper and onion in margarine until tender. Add beef. Cook and stir a few minutes longer. Remove from heat. Blend flour into meat mixture. Slowly add milk, stirring constantly.

Replace over flame, stirring until mixture boils and thickens.

Chef's secret: Serve with Dutch oven Spoon Bread.

CREAMED CORNED BEEF AND CABBAGE
(Serves 3-4)

1 small cabbage, shredded
½ tsp. salt
½ cup water
1 cup milk (or ⅓ cup dry milk and 1 cup water)
1 tbls. flour or instant potato
1 can (12 oz.) corned beef, broken into small pieces

Simmer cabbage in salted water until done. Drain. Pour milk over cabbage. When hot, stir in flour and corned beef. Reheat.

EGGS 'N HASH
(Serves 3)

1 tbls. dry onion flakes
2 cans (1 lb. each) corned beef hash
2 tsp. bacon drippings or margarine
3 eggs

Heat bacon drippings in a skillet. Mix onion flakes into the hash. Spread hash evenly over bottom of pan. Cover and cook over low heat 10 min. With the back of a large spoon make 3 dents in the hash. Break an egg into each nest. Cover and cook until eggs are done.

CHEESY LIMAS 'N HASH
(Serves 3-4)

2 tbls. margarine
1 small onion, minced (or use dry flakes)
1 can (16 oz.) corned beef hash
1 can (12 oz.) lima beans, drained
½ lb. American cheese, cubed
Salt and pepper

Melt margarine in a skillet and sauté onion. Spread hash evenly in skillet and brown, about 5 min. Spoon limas on top of hash. Sprinkle cheese cubes over top. Reduce heat, cover and cook until cheese is melted, 5-10 min.

HASH 'N CARROT PIE
(Serves 2-3)

Sauté:
1 small carrot, shredded
1 small onion, chopped
2 tbls. margarine

Combine 1 can (15 oz.) corned beef hash with 1 egg.

Add carrot and onion and pack down in skillet with a spatula. Brown, then turn over. Sprinkle with sharp cheese, shredded. When cheese melts, cut in wedges to serve.

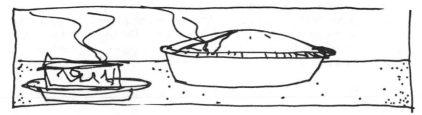

CORNED BEEF SAUCE
(Serves 4-5)

1 can tomato sauce
2 tsp. Worcestershire sauce
2 tbls. vinegar
1 cup water
1 tsp. dry onion flakes

Combine and simmer 5 min.
Add 2 cans (12 oz. each) corned beef, broken up.
Simmer 15 min.
Serve over rice, noodles, spaghetti.
Chef's secret: Dip sliced, chilled corned beef hash in flour seasoned with a dash of ground cloves. Brown in hot bacon fat or margarine and serve with a dollop of mayonnaise.

CORNED BEEF 'N DUMPLINGS
(Serves 3-4)
2 cans split pea soup
1 soup can water
1 can (8 oz.) mixed vegetables
1 can (12 oz.) corned beef, cubed
Combine and bring to a boil.
Prepare dumplings with:
1 cup biscuit mix
⅓ cup water
¼ tsp. marjoram
Mix with a fork and drop by spoonfuls over simmering stew.
Cook uncovered 10 min., covered, 10 min. more.
Serve dumplings and stir soup mixture before serving.

TOMATO CORNED BEEF
(Serves 2)
(Melba Blackstone—Los Angeles, Calif.)
Add 2 cups water to 2 one-cup pkgs. tomato Cup-A-Soup mix. Bring to a boil. Add ¾ cup minute rice. Simmer a few minutes. Add a small can of corned beef, broken up. Add salt, basil and garlic powder to taste.

FAMILY STEW
Let each person carry a different ingredient:
Suggestions: A can of corned beef, a green pepper, an onion, a small cabbage, a pkg. of freeze-dried vegetable, a couple of beef bouillon cubes, or a pkg. of Wyler's Potato With Leek Soup. Prepare the vegetables while the pot of water is heating. Cook until all the vegetables are tender.

CORNED BEEF AND CABBAGE
Boil cabbage wedges and dry onion flakes (or fresh sliced onion) until almost done. Drain. Add a can of corned beef, broken up. Season and serve.

KIDNEY BEANS AHOY
(Serves 3-4)
1 can (1 lb.) kidney beans
1 can (1 lb.) tomatoes
1 can (12 oz.) corned beef, cut into cubes
1 large onion, chopped
3 tbls. margarine
Cook onion in margarine until transparent.
Add beans, tomatoes and corned beef.
Simmer until thickened.
Serve on hamburger or wiener buns.

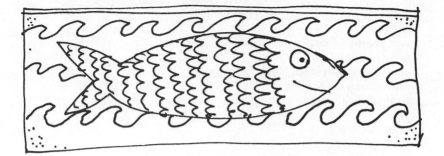

TUNA

TUNA AND NOODLES
(Serves 2-3)
Cook 1½ cups (8 oz. pkg.) broken noodles with half an onion, sliced, in unsalted water until noodles are done. Drain.

Add:
1 can cream of mushroom soup
1 small can evaporated milk
¼ cup water
1 can tuna, drained
Reheat until bubbly and thoroughly hot.
Add 1 cup shredded processed cheese. Stir until melted.

Chef's secret: Add drained tuna to Chicken Rice-A-Roni. Include a canned vegetable, drained (use the juice as part of the liquid in the recipe), to extend the amount.

MACARONI AND TUNA FISH
(Serves 3-4)
½ lb. macroni (elbow)
1 can (10 oz.) concentrated cheddar cheese soup
½ soup can milk (use dry milk and water; measure milk generously)
1 can (7 oz.) tuna fish, drained
Cook macaroni and drain well.
Stir in soup, milk and tuna fish. Cover, heat until bubbly.

CURLY TUNA CASSEROLE
(Serves 2-3)
1 pkg. (8 oz.) curlies (pasta section of food market)
1 can condensed mushroom soup
1 can tuna, drained
In a 4 qt. kettle, boil curlies in salted water until tender, 8-10 min.
Add soup and tuna and heat thoroughly.
Variation: add chopped pimiento, dry parsley, or dry celery flakes.

TUNA COMBO
(Serves 2-3)

Combine:
1 can cream of celery or mushroom soup
1 can tuna, drained
2 chopped hard-cooked eggs
1 tbls. chopped pimiento
Heat, stirring constantly.
Sprinkle with chopped fresh parsley.
Serve on wiener buns.

TUNA ON TOAST
(Serves 2-3)

Combine:
1 can cream of mushroom soup
½ cup water with ¼ cup dry milk
1 can tuna, drained
1 can drained peas (use juice with water to add to dry milk)
2 sliced hard-cooked eggs
Heat thoroughly and serve on toast or English muffins.
Butter split muffins and place butter side down in a hot skillet until browned.

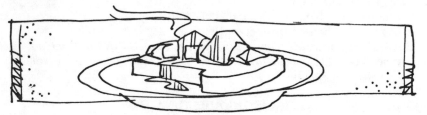

SKILLET TUNA SCALLOP
(Serves 4-5)

¼ cup (½ cube) margarine
4 cups water
3 cups milk (use dry milk and water)
2 tbls. dry onion flakes
1 tsp. basil
2 pkgs. (5⅜ oz. each) scalloped potatoes
2 cans tuna, drained
1 can (1 lb.) peas, drained (use in the water measurement)
Heat margarine, water, milk, onion and basil until simmering.
Add potatoes and flavor packet (if there is one).
Cover and simmer 20 min.
Break up tuna and add along with the peas. Cover and heat 5-10 min.
Variation: use canned salmon or shrimp in place of tuna.

CREAMED TUNA

2 cups reliquified dry milk
3 tbls. margarine or bacon drippings
3 tbls. instant potato
2 cans (7½ oz. each) tuna, drained
Heat milk and stir in margarine or bacon drippings, and instant potato.
Cook until slightly thick.
Break tuna into small chunks and stir into creamed mixture. Reheat.
Serve over potato cakes, rice or noodles.
Variation: add freeze dried vegetables such as peas or corn.

TUNA AND POTATOES
(Serve 2-3)

3 slices bacon, diced
1 small onion, sliced
1 can (1 lb.) potatoes, drained, rinsed, and diced
1 can tuna, drained
Sauté bacon and onion until golden. Add potato dices and tuna.
Heat thoroughly. Sprinkle with parmesan cheese.

TUNA JUBILEE
(Serves 2-3)

1 can (4 oz.) shoestring potatoes
1 can cream mushroom soup
1 can tuna, drained
1 can (6 oz.) evaporated milk
1 can (3 oz.) mushroom pieces, drained
1 small jar chopped pimiento
(Reserve some potatoes to sprinkle on top of each serving.)
Combine all indredients and heat thoroughly. Simmer 10 min., stirring
occasionally.

POTATO CHIP TUNA
(Serves 2-3)

2 cans (7 oz. each) tuna, drained
1 can cream of celery soup
⅓ soup can milk
1 tsp. dry minced onion
Heat, stirring often, until bubbly.
Spoon over crushed potato chips.
Variation: Add drained vegetable or sliced pimiento.

TUNA N' RICE
(Serves 3-4)
In a skillet, combine:
2 cans tuna, drained
1 can chicken broth plus water to make 2 cups
Bring to a boil and add 1⅓ cups minute rice.
Reduce heat, cover and simmer 5 min.
Add 1 chopped hard cooked egg and 1 small jar of pimiento, chopped.
Stir over heat to blend.

VEGETABLE 'N TUNA SKILLET
(Serves 3-4)
1 small onion, chopped
2 stalks celery, cut in thin slices
2 tbls. margarine
1½ cups minute rice
1½ cups water (part canned vegetable juice)
2 cans tuna, drained
1 can mixed vegetables, drained (add juice to water, above)
1 can cream of celery soup
½ tsp. salt
Sauté onion and celery in margarine until tender. Add remaining ingredients. Stir just to moisten. Bring to a boil, cover, simmer 5 min.

TUNA 'N GREEN BEANS
(Serves 3-4)
1 can cream of mushroom soup
½ cup milk
1 can tuna, drained
1 can green beans, drained
Dash of pepper
Conbine soup and milk in saucepan. Heat, stirring constantly.
Add rest of ingredients. Heat thoroughly.
Serve over Chinese noodles or crushed potato chips.
Chef's secrets:
- *Crush potato chips by cutting a small slit in one end of the bag to allow air to escape. Mash by hand. NO MESS.*
- *Combine the liquid drained from canned vegetables with V-8 or instant bouillon for a nourishing before-dinner "cocktail".*

TUNA JUMBLE
(Serves 3-4)

4 strips bacon, diced
½ cup chopped onion
¼ cup chopped green pepper
1 cup water (hot if possible)
3 chicken bouillon cubes (or 3 tsp. instant)
1 cup minute rice
1 can (1 lb.) tomatoes
1 tsp. dry parsley
1 tsp. dry celery leaves
2 cans tuna, drained
Salt and pepper

Sauté bacon with onion and green pepper.
Pour hot water over bouillon cubes to dissolve.
Add rest of ingredients. Mix well.
Cover and simmer 5-7 min.

SEASCAPE SOUP
(Serves 3-4)

1 medium onion, chopped
1 tbls. margarine
1 can cream of celery soup
1 can clam chowder
1½ cans water
1 can tuna, drained

In a saucepan, sauté onion in margarine.
Add remaining ingredients and simmer 8-10 min.
Serve with oyster crackers.

Chef's secrets:
- *Add bacon bar sparingly to clam or corn chowder.*
- *Sauté rinsed salt pork, cut into small pieces, in margarine with onion.*

FISHING PIER CHOWDER
(Serves 2)
(Mildred Howell—Granada Hills, Calif.)

¼ cup sliced celery
1 tbls. dry onion flakes
1 tbls. margarine
1 pkg. Wyler's Potato Soup With Leek
2½ cups water (part juice from green beans)
½ cup milk
1 can (7 oz.) minced clams
1 can (8 oz.) cut green beans, drained
Sauté celery and onion in margarine.
Stir in water, then soup mix.
Add milk, clams, green beans.
Heat, stirring occasionally; simmer 5 min.

CHINESE TUNA
(Serves 2-3)

2 tbls. margarine
2 stalks diced celery
1 small onion, diced
1 can tuna, drained
1 can mushroom soup
⅓ can water or milk
1 can Chinese noodles
Sauté diced celery and onion in margarine. Combine other ingredients except noodles. Heat and simmer 10 min. Serve over Chinese noodles.

TUNA CHOW MEIN
(Serves 2-3)

2 tbls. margarine
1 small onion, chopped
2 stalks celery, chopped
1 can tuna, drained
1 can mushroom soup
¼ cup water
½ cup slivered almonds or cashews
1 can chow mein noodles
Sauté onion and celery in margarine.
Add tuna, break up and stir.
Add soup and water and heat thoroughly.
Add nuts and serve over chow mein noodles.

SCRAMBLED EGGS WITH SALMON
(Serves 4)
1 can (8 oz.) salmon, drained
4 tbls. margarine
6-8 eggs, beaten with a fork
Salt and pepper
   Heat drained salmon in margarine. Add beaten eggs, salt and pepper.
   Stir and lift to let egg flow to bottom of pan. Cook until set.

CHINESE VEGETABLES AND SHRIMP
(Serves 3-4)
Sauté together: 1 tbls. margarine, 1 medium onion, chopped until
golden.
Combine: 2 tbls. catsup and 2 tsp. cornstarch. Stir into sauté onion.
Add:
1 can (1 lb.) chop suey vegetables, undrained.
1 tsp. sugar
¼ tsp. chili powder
1 can (4½ oz.) shrimp, drained and rinsed
   Stir until blended and cook until slightly thickened.
   Serve over cooked noodles or chow mein noodles.

PASTA AND RICE

Stick-to-the-ribs combinations
for hearty outdoor appetites.

TOMATO-CHEESE MACARONI

1 cup raw macaroni
Salted water
    Boil macaroni until tender, approximately 8-10 min. Drain.
To the pot of cooked macaroni add:
1 can tomato soup
½ cup milk (dry milk and water or diluted evaporated milk)
2 cups grated sharp cheese
2 tsp. dry parsley
    Combine thoroughly and heat, using a low flame, until cheese melts and
all is bubbly.
Chef's secrets:
• *Add a blob of margarine or a few drops of salad oil to the macaroni
  cooking water to keep tubes from sticking together.*
• *Add oregano to tomato or cheese recipes.*

MUSHROOM MACARONI
(Serves 3-4)

2 cups uncooked macaroni
3 tbls. margarine
2-3 tbls. flour
1 pkg. Lipton Beef Mushroom Mix Soup
2 cups milk (2 cups water, 1 cup dry milk)
2 cups shredded sharp cheese
    Cook macaroni in boiling salted water 8-10 min. Drain.
    Add margarine and stir until melted.
    Carefully open soup pkg. and add the flour. Combine well in the pkg.
    Add to macaroni and stir well.
    Add milk and cheese. Simmer over low heat until cheese melts and bub-
bles and the liquid evaporated to a creamy consistency.

SHORT-CUT MACARONI

Cook the macaroni in salted water and drain well.
Stir in a cheese spread of your choice.
Combine until macaroni is coated well and there are no lumps of cheese.

KIDNEY BEANS 'N RICE
(Serves 3-4)
1 large onion, chopped
2 tbls. margarine
1 cup raw rice
1 tsp. salt, dash of pepper
2 cans (1 lb. each) kidney beans, drained. Save juice.
Approximately 3½ cups tomato juice
½ cup grated Parmesan cheese
   Sauté onion in margarine until limp. Add rice, salt and pepper.
   Add enough tomato juice to the bean juice to make 4 cups liquid.
   Add juice to the rest of the ingredients. Bring to a boil.
   Lower heat and cover. Simmer about 30 min. until rice is tender.
   Add beans and heat.
   Serve sprinkled with cheese.
   Add more tomato juice if it becomes too dry.

VEGETABLE PILAF
(Serves 2-3)
2 tbls. margarine
1 medium onion, chopped
2½ cups water
1 envelope vegetable soup mix
1 cup minute rice
½ tsp. dry parsley
   Sauté onion in margarine in a skillet. Add water, soup mix and parsley.
   Bring to a boil, then simmer 25 min. Add rice, remove from heat, cover
and let stand 5 min.
   *Chef's secret: Pre-flavored rice is double the cost of plain rice. Add your
own instant bouillon or cube and your oven dried parsley or celery leaves
for flavor.*

SPANISH RICE PRONTO
(Serves 2-3)
1 can (1 lb.) stewed tomatoes
1 envelope onion soup mix
1 tbls. margarine
1 cup minute rice
½ cup grated cheese
   Combine tomatoes and onion soup and margarine.
   Heat to boiling. Add rice, cover and remove from heat for 5 min. Top
each serving with grated cheese.
   *Chef's secret: When cooking instant rice above 3,000 feet, boil it 1-2
minutes before you remove it from the flame to steam. Quick cooking
types need to cook 11-12 min. instead of 9 min. You probably will need to
add a little extra water.*

Add variety to your camp rice:

Dissolve 1-2 beef or chicken bouillon cubes in the water before you add the rice.

Add onion soup mix to the water if you like the concentrated flavor.

Use tomato juice, diluted tomato sauce or tomato paste as the liquid, and season with dried parsley, celery or green pepper flakes.

Use the liquid drained from canned vegetables plus water to meet the required liquid amount.

Sauté ½ cup chopped celery in margarine until tender. Add water, salt and rice.

Add ¾ cup grated cheddar or process American cheese to cooked rice and mix lightly with a fork.

Christmas Rice: Add chopped pimiento, chopped stuffed ripe olives, minced parsley, and finely chopped chives to your cooked rice.

MEXICAN FRIED RICE
(Serves 2-3)

1⅓ cups minute rice
2 tbls. margarine
1⅓ cups water
1 pkg. Spanish Rice Seasoning Mix

Sauté rice in margarine until golden. Add water and seasoning mix. Stir to blend. Bring to a boil, then cover, and simmer 10 min. Allow to stand off the heat for 5 min. more.

SOUPER RICE
(Serves 2-3)
(Lois Pitzer — Long Beach, Calif.)

1 can vegetable beef soup
½ soup can minute rice
½ can water

Empty the soup into a saucepan. Fill the empty soup can half full of minute rice. Add enough water to fill the can. Combine rice and soup and bring to a full boil. Cover, reduce heat and simmer 5 min.

You may add canned, fresh or frozen vegetables. Cook fresh or frozen ones before adding. You also can add meat.

SOUP-MIX IDEAS

A packet of soup mix tucks away in a small corner,
but it could make an important survival meal.

QUICK CHOWDER

To 1 pkg. chicken noodle soup mix, add 3½ cups water. Cook as directed
on package.

Add ½ cup dry milk and 1 can (8 oz.) minced clams and juice, or
1 can (8 oz.) niblets corn, or both.

CHIPPED BEEF SOUP
(Serves 2)

5 oz. dried chipped beef, pulled apart
1 tbls. margarine
1 pkg. Wyler's Potato With Leek Soup
3 cups water
¼ cup dry milk
Simmer 5 min.

Chef's secrets:

- *Drop freeze-dried meat balls and freeze-dried vegetables into beef or vegetable soup mix.*
- *Combine split pea soup mix and 2 tsp. onion soup mix. Add water as suggested on pea soup package. Add diced lunch meat, Vienna sausage, sliced wieners or small amount of bacon bar.*

TOMATO-CHEESE SOUP
(Serves 2-3)
(Mildred Beatty — Monrovia, Calif.)

2 tbls. margarine
2 cups sharp cheddar cheese, shredded
1 can tomato soup
Salt and pepper
¼ tsp. sage
1 egg, well beaten

Melt cheese in margarine. Add tomato soup and seasonings. Add egg,
stirring constantly.

Serve on toast, rice or shredded wheat biscuits.

*Chef's secret: Make a before-dinner soup in the coffee pot so dinner can
be cooking while you sip, and the sauce pan won't be tied up.*

ONION PILAF
(Serves 4-5)
2 tbls. margarine
1 cups quick cooking cracked wheat
1 pkg. onion soup mix
3 cups water

Melt margarine and stir in cracked wheat. Brown for 2-3 min.

Add onion soup mix and water. Cover, bring to a boil, then simmer for about 15 min.

Serve with grilled steaks or hamburger patties.

Chef's secrets:
- *Add instant mashed potatoes to thin soups to thicken them.*
- *Dry soup mixes make a good base for one-pot combinations. Try chicken noodle soup with freeze-dried diced chicken and freeze-dried peas. You could make a pot pie by adding biscuit mix dumplings.*

Following are soup mix combinations which you might like to try:
- Chicken soup with cream of leek soup.
- Onion sprinkled with parmesan cheese.
- Split pea soup with marjoram added.
- Cream of potato soup — Add dry milk, or evaporated milk and a can of clams, oysters, salmon or tuna.
- Beef and vegetable soup mix — Add freeze dried meatballs.
- Onion or mushroom soup — Use as the liquid for cooking rice.
- Mushroom or Cream of Leek soup — Use half of the recommended liquid. Use as a sauce over poached salmon or sauted trout or catfish.
- Chicken soups — Add freeze-dried whole kernel corn and crumbled bacon bar.

Chef's secret: Add flavor to stews and soups with croutons. Butter and cube bread slices. Toss in a hot skillet until dry and crispy. To flavor, add whichever herb you will need to pep up the dish they will be used in.

SOUPED-UP DUMPLINGS

To any pot of soup, especially a watery one, add a half recipe of *biscuit mix dumplings* to which you have added dry celery flakes, dry parsley, dry onion or other herb for flavor. Cook dumplings as directed on package.

Corn Muffin Mix, using less liquid then called for, makes excellent dumplings. Keep the dough quite stiff.

Press a small cube of sharp cheddar cheese into the center of biscuit mix biscuits. Cover cheese completely. Drop into hot soup and cover the pot. Simmer 20 min.

TAKE-ALONG SOUPS

Cook soup, stew or chowder at home and freeze in a well-washed milk carton. When ready to leave, wrap in a paper towel to absorb condensation, put it in a plastic bag, and finally in an insulated bag. It will keep until time to reheat for dinner. Add one of the above dumplings to make a hearty meal.

VEGETABLES

Vegetables make a grilled meat meal complete.
Use fresh vegetables whenever possible.
The ones suggested in these recipes will keep
several days with care.

Any vegetable juice drained from cans
can be used in several ways, so don't waste it.

SWEET AND SOUR BEANS
(Serves 4)

In a large frying pan, sauté 6 slices diced bacon with 1 onion, chopped.
Add
1 can (1 lb.) tomatoes, cut up
3 tbls. vinegar
¼ cup packed brown sugar
1 tbls. Worchestershire sauce
Bring tomato mixture to boiling, then simmer uncovered to reduce liquid.
Add 2 cans (1 lb. each) red kidney beans. Simmer uncovered until beans are heated, adding 1 tsp. dry minced parsley.

BEAN CASSEROLE
(Serves 2-3)

4 slices bacon, diced
2 cans (1 lb.) pork and beans
1 can (1 lb.) kidney beans, drained
1 pkg. onion soup mix
½ cup each catsup and water
1 tsp. prepared mustard
2 tsp. molasses
Sauté bacon and drain fat. Add rest of ingredients and simmer, covered, 15-20 min.

BEANS, BEANS, BEANS

Combine all kinds of beans (pork and beans, chili beans, kidney beans, garbanzo beans). Add onion, celery, salt and basil. Add 1 can (4 oz.) diced green chilis. Simmer 20-30 min. Top each serving with sharp cheddar or Jack cheese, grated or shredded.

Serve with corn bread.

Variation: omit diced green chilis and add 1 pkg. spaghetti or taco sauce mix.

QUICK CHILI
(Serves 3-4)
(Lois Pitzer — Long Beach, Calif.)

1 can bean and bacon soup
1 can tomato soup
1 can (10½ oz.) chili with beans
1¼ cup water

Combine and simmer 10-15 min.

REFRIED BEANS I
(Serves 2-3)

1 can kidney beans, drained and mashed. Save juice.
3 tbls. bacon drippings or olive oil
1 small onion, chopped fine
1 clove garlic, mashed
½ green pepper, chopped fine
1 tsp. chili powder (or less)

Heat the fat in a skillet. Add onion, garlic, green pepper. Sauté over low heat until tender.

Stir chili powder into mashed beans and add to skillet. Cook slowly, stirring continuously, adding bean liquid as needed.

REFRIED BEANS II
(Serves 2-3)

1 can (1 lb. 4 oz.) refried beans
1 pkg. taco seasoning mix plus ¼ cup water
¾ cup shredded cheddar cheese
¼ cup chopped onion

Combine beans, seasoning mix and water in a saucepan. Bring to a boil, then reduce heat and simmer 5 min.

Garnish with shredded cheese and chopped onion.

Serve with or spooned over hot tortillas.

BEANS 'N MUFFINS
(Serves 2)

1 can (1 lb.) kidney beans
1 small jar diced pimientos
Shredded sharp cheese
English muffins, split and toasted

Toast muffins by buttering and placing cut side down in a hot skillet until browned. Remove and keep warm in a towel.

Heat kidney beans over low heat. Add pimientos and cheese and stir until cheese is melted. Pour over toasted muffins.

FRITOS 'N BEANS
(Serves 2)

1 can chili beans
1 tbls. dry onion flakes
¼ cup sliced black olives
1 can tomato sauce
½ tsp. salt

Heat thoroughly and spoon over crushed Fritos. Top with shredded sharp cheese.

HUSH PUPPIES CON CARNE
(Serves 4-5)

1 cup cornmeal
2 tsp. baking powder
½ tsp. salt
1 tbls. dry onion flakes
1 egg
¼ cup water
Melted fat

AT HOME: Combine the cornmeal, baking powder, salt, onion, and place in a sturdy plastic bag.

AT CAMP: Add egg and water to the cornmeal mix. Beat hard for several minutes and form into patties. Brown in hot fat, turning to cook both sides. Keep hush puppies warm in a towel while you heat 2 cans (1 lb.) each Chili with Beans in the same pan.

Chef's secret: Be a gourmet show-off. Stuff canned pimiento halves with a slice of sharp cheddar cheese. Heat in a "slow" skillet until the cheese wilts.

FRUITED BEAN BAKE
(Serves 2)

1 jar (18 oz.) Boston baked beans
½ cup chopped dried fruit (apples, pineapple, raisins, etc.)
½ cup beer

Combine ingredients and simmer 15-20 min

2-VEGETABLE POT
Slice fresh carrots into an inch of salted water in a regular coffee pot. (Revere, 1½ qt. size is excellent). Cook 5 min.

Snap off the tough ends of asparagus, wash.

Stand asparagus stalks upright in the same water. Continue to cook the carrots while you steam the asparagus 10-12 min.

Pour the cooking water out of the spout to drain. Save and add to a mix along with dry milk for next morning's omelet.

Chef's secret: Add a spoonful of mint jelly to hot, buttered carrots.

VEGETARIAN EGGS
(Serves 3-4)
3 medium-sized tomatoes, peeled and chopped
½ cup water and ½ tsp. bouillon (instant chicken)
3 small onions, peeled and chopped
1 medium-sized green pepper, seeded and chopped
2 tsp. cider vinegar
1 tsp. salt
4 eggs
Salt and pepper
Spear the tomatoes with a fork, hold each one over the flame, turning to heat the skin until it splits. Remove skin and chop tomatoes coarsely.

Heat chicken bouillon and water in a skillet. Add onions, green pepper, tomatoes, vinegar and salt. Cover and cook vegetables 7 min., stirring once. With the back of a spoon make 3-4 depressions in the mixture and break an egg into each one. Sprinkle with salt and pepper, cover and cook over low heat until eggs are set.

SOUP 'N VEGETABLE CHOWDER
(Serves 2-3)
1 can cream of chicken soup
1 can chicken noodle soup
1 can water
1 can niblets corn
1 can lima beans
¼ tsp. sage
Salt and pepper
1 small can evaporated milk
Combine all ingredients except milk. Simmer 10-15 min.

Stir in evaporated milk just before serving. DO NOT BOIL.

Chef's secret: DON'T throw away the juice in a can of vegetables. It can be used in sauces, gravies and soups or as part of the liquid when cooking rice, macaroni, spaghetti or dumplings. Seasoned, it makes a tasty beverage.

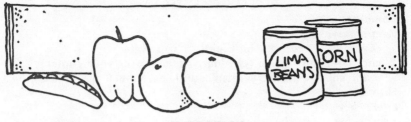

SUCCOTASH
(Serves 3-4)
1 can (1 lb.) lima beans
1 can (1 lb.) whole kernel corn, drained
2 tbls. margarine
1 tsp. salt, dash of pepper
¼ cup canned milk
Cook over low heat until bubbly and hot. Add milk just before serving.

VEGETABLE GOULASH
Combine chopped vegetables (carrots, cabbage, potatoes, peas, onions, etc.) with:
1 can mushroom pieces, drained
1 can stewed tomatoes
1 green pepper cut in small chunks
½ tsp. garlic chips
Simmer in 3 tbls. fat with a dash of pepper, ½ tsp. salt and a sprinkle of marjoram. Simmer about 20 min.

VEGETABLE COMBO
(Serves 4-6)
2 tbls. margarine or oil
4 small zucchini or summer squash, sliced
1 small onion, chopped
1 green pepper, diced
½ cup water
1 large fresh tomato, diced
1-2 cans niblets corn
(Water)
Salt and pepper
Heat margarine in a large pot. Stir in squash, onion, pepper and water. Cover and simmer, stirring once or twice. Cook about 5 min. Add tomatoes and corn, salt and pepper. Cook 5 min. more or until vegetables are tender. Add water if needed.

Chef's secret: Raw carrots keep well. Take along a small, flat grater so you can add shredded carrot to your one-pot meal. It will cook quickly when shredded.

VEGETABLE CHEESE SAUCE
Combine:
½ cup mayonnaise
½ cup milk (¼ cup dry milk and ½ cup water)
½ cup shredded cheese (cheddar, American or your choice)
Add to cooked, drained vegetables and heat about 5 min. over low heat. Stir carefully.
Chef's secrets:
- *Instead of using salted water when cooking fresh vegetables, try using an oil and vinegar salad dressing for the cooking liquid. Sliced zucchini, thin sliced celery root, shredded cabbage or thin sliced potatoes simmered in Italian dressing about 10 min. all are especially good. Use the rest of the dressing for the salad.*
- *To keep vegetables fresh, wash well, wrap in a damp turkish towel, put in a plastic bag and then wrap in a well-furred towel kept damp by occasionally dipping in water and wringing out . . . cooling by evaporation.*

TOMATO-CHEESE SAUCE
(Serves 3-4)
In a saucepan melt: 2 tbls. margarine. Stir in 1 tbls. flour and mix well with a wire whip. Add 1 can tomato soup
1 tsp. salt
1 tsp. Worcestershire sauce
¼ tsp. marjoram
½ tsp. sugar
2 cups shredded sharp cheese
1 egg, beaten
Stir constantly with the wire whip until thickened. Serve spooned over English muffins, croutons or crushed crackers.

TOMATO-BEAN SCRAMBLE
(Serves 2)
In 4 tbls. margarine, brown 2 heaping tbls. flour in a skillet. Add 1 can tomato sauce and 1 can red kidney beans. Heat thoroughly. Top with shredded sharp cheese.

BOSTON MACARONI
(Serves 3-4)
Cook 2 cups elbow macaroni in salted water until tender. Drain. Add 1 can tomato sauce and several slices of dry salami, chopped. Heat thoroughly and add 1 cup diced American cheese. Stir until cheese melts.

SCRAMBLED SOUP
(Serves 2)
In a saucepan, combine:
1 can tomato soup
1 scant can of milk
Beat 2 eggs lightly with a fork. Pour into soup, stirring constantly just until eggs are set.

Ladle over toast or crackers in a bowl.

Chef's secret: Add a little sugar to pots containing tomatoes or tomato sauce to cut sharpness and improve flavor.

HOBO SOUP
(Serves 4)
1 can (50 oz.) tomato juice
1 pkg. each beef and vegetable soup mixes
Simmer 15-20 min.

Variation: Add shredded fresh carrot, chopped celery, chopped green pepper, small can of mushroom pieces, drained, or beef jerky broken into pieces.

Top with biscuit mix dumplings.

GRILLED TOMATOES NO. 1
(Serves 2 or 4)
2 medium sized tomatoes, sliced in half
1 tsp. dry Italian Salad Dressing Mix
Grated parmesan cheese
Place tomatoes cut side up in a greased skillet. Sprinkle salad dressing mix over cut side of tomato. Top with cheese.

Cook, covered, until tomatoes are heated through.

GRILLED TOMATOES NO. 2
Cut tomatoes in half. Pepper and salt the cut halves, then coat the cut surface with bread crumbs. Heat 2 tbls. margarine until sizzly hot. Add tomatoes and cover. Cook about 10 min.

CORN OYSTERS
(Serves 2)
Combine:
⅓ cup creamed corn
⅓ cup bread crumbs
1 egg, beaten
¼ tsp. salt, dash of pepper
½ tsp. sugar
Drop by spoonfuls on a hot greased frying pan. Flatten with the back of the spoon. Brown both sides.

Serve with a packaged gravy mix for dinner, or syrup for breakfast.

TOMATO-CORN CHOWDER
(Serves 2-3)
Combine and heat:
1 can tomato soup
1 can niblets corn
1 cup milk (¼ cup dry milk and 1 cup water)
2 tbls. margarine
Salt and pepper
Do not boil, but serve very hot, with chunks of French bread.
Chef's secret: Try adding chili powder to canned corn.

CORNY BEAN CHOWDER
(Serves 2-3)
Sauté:
1 large onion, thinly sliced in
2 tbls. margarine
Add:
1 can tomato soup
¾ cup water
1 can (1 lb.) kidney beans, undrained
1 can (1 lb.) whole kernel corn, undrained
¼ tsp. oregano
Salt and pepper
Simmer 15 min. Add: 1 small can evaporated milk. Heat, do not boil.

SAUTEED CORN 'N PEPPERS
(Serves 2)

Sauté 1 green pepper, chopped fine, in 2 tbls. margarine until soft. Add 1 can niblets corn and ¾ tsp. salt and a dash of pepper. Cook about 5 min. more.

CORN FRITTERS
(Serves 2-3)

1 can whole kernel corn
1 cup milk
1 egg
1 tsp. salt
1 tbls. sugar
1½ tsp. baking powder
1 cup flour

Combine thoroughly and fry by spoonfuls on a hot greased griddle, turning once.

BACKPACK CORN FRITTERS
(Serves 2-3)

This is the same recipe as the one above, but uses all dry ingredients for transporting.

At home measure and combine:
½ cup dry milk
1 tbls. whole egg powder
1 tsp. salt
1 tbls. sugar
1½ tsp. baking powder
1 cup flour (try using whole wheat or rye)

Seal dry ingredients in a sturdy plastic bag.

At Camp: Soak ½ cup freeze dried corn in 1 cup water for 5 min. Add corn and water to dry ingredients and mix well. Add more water if necessary.

Fry by spoonfuls on a hot greased griddle.

CORN RAREBIT
(Serves 3-4)
1 can (12 oz.) whole kernel corn
2 cans tomato soup
½ pound American cheese, shredded
I tsp. sugar
Salt and pepper
Shredded Wheat biscuits

Combine corn and soup. Heat over low flame. Add shredded cheese and stir until melted. Add seasonings, serve over Shredded Wheat biscuits or toast.

CORN 'N PEPPER FRITTERS
(Serves 4)
2 cans (1 lb. ea.) whole kernel corn
2 tbls. sugar
½ tsp. salt
½ cup evaporated milk
2 eggs, beaten
¼ cup chopped green pepper
1½ cups sifted flour
1½ tsp. baking powder

Combine corn, sugar and salt. Add milk, eggs and green pepper. Combine flour with baking powder and add to corn mixture. Beat well. Drop by spoonfuls onto a greased skillet. Cook slowly until puffed. Brown on both sides. Serve with warmed tomato sauce.

EGGPLANT STEW
(Serves 3-4)
1 eggplant, peeled and diced
1 can mushroom pieces, drained (or use fresh)
1 cup tomatoes, chopped
2 green peppers, chopped
1 clove garlic, minced

Combine and sauté in 3-4 tbls. margarine or bacon drippings until hot and well coated. Season with salt, pepper and a sprinkle of marjoram. Cover and simmer 20 min.

SPANISH OMELET
(Serves 2)
1 tbls. margarine
4 eggs, slightly beaten
2 tbls. diced green chilis
½ tsp. salt

Heat margarine in a small frying pan. When browned, pour in egg mixture. Lift edges to let uncooked egg flow under to cook. Serve with refried beans and corn tortillas.

EGGS ITALIANO
(Serves 3-4)
Sauté:
3 tbls. margarine
⅛ tsp. garlic chips
2 medium sized green peppers, chopped
1 medium onion, chopped
When pepper is tender, add:
6 eggs, beaten with
¼ cup milk
½ tsp. salt, dash pepper
Pinch of oregano

Cook slowly, stirring often. Sprinkle parmesan cheese on each serving.

SCRAMBLED EGGS ORIENTAL
(Serves 3-4)
Sauté together: 3 tbls. margarine
½ small onion, chopped
½ can bean sprouts, drained and chopped
½ can water chestnuts, chopped
Combine and beat together:
6 eggs
2 tsp. soy sauce
½ tsp. salt, dash of pepper

Pour egg mixture over vegetable mixture. Stir until eggs are set.

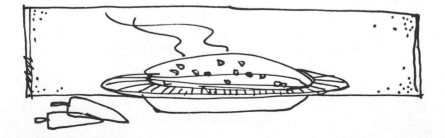

QUICK CABBAGE

Remove the outer leaves from a small head of cabbage. Cut into quarters, then cut across the leaves in small slices to create shreds. Place shreds in boiling salted water, as little as needed. Cook 10 min. and drain immediately. Add salt and pepper and margarine enough to coat the cabbage. Serve with meat from the grill.

CABBAGE ORIENTAL
(Serves 3-4)

1 small head cabbage, shredded
3 tbls. margarine
½ medium onion, sliced
1 can bamboo shoots, drained
2 tbls. soy sauce
2 tbls. vinegar
1 tbls. sugar

Sauté cabbage and onions in margarine until limp. Add remaining ingredients, stirring well. Cover and cook over medium heat about 15 min. until cabbage is done.

IRISH SOUP
(Serves 3-4)

2 medium potatoes, peeled and diced
1 onion, chopped
2 carrots, sliced thin
1 medium cabbage, shredded

Add vegetables to 3 cups boiling water. Add: ½ tsp. thyme, 1½ tsp. salt, dash of pepper. Bring to a boil, then simmer, covered, 25-30 min.

POTATO SURPRISE
(Serves 3-4)

2 cans (1 lb. each) whole potatoes
¼ cup margarine (½ stick)
1 large onion, chopped
2 cloves garlic, minced
1 tbls. dry parsley flakes
1 tsp. salt
½ tsp. basil

Drain potatoes and rinse well in cold water. Pat dry with paper towels. Cut potatoes in ¼" slices. Sauté onion, garlic and parsley flakes in margarine until golden. Add seasonings and the sliced potatoes. Heat 3-5 min. more.

POTATO CAKES

Cook Instant Potato according to package directions, except double the amount of dry milk needed to mix. Drop mixture by spoonfuls into bacon drippings in a hot frying pan. Brown on both sides.

Variation: Season potato mix with packaged sauce mix like spaghetti, taco, etc.

Chef's secret: Add 3 tbls. vinegar to hash brown potato mix just before serving.

SWEET POTATO SKILLET
(Serves 3-4)

1 can (1 lb.) sweet potatoes, drained
2 tbls. margarine
1 tsp. lemon juice
¼ cup sugar

Brown sweet potatoes in margarine in a frying pan. Combine lemon juice and sugar. Drizzle over potatoes. Serve with ham or luncheon meat.

SIMMERED CELERY

Wash and diagonally slice celery stalks into 1″ pieces. Add 1 or 2 bouillon cubes to water to almost cover celery slices. Simmer until tender, covered. Save cooking water to add to V-8 cocktail.

GREEN BEANS IN LEMON SAUCE
(Serves 3-4)

¼ cup margarine (½ stick)
1 small onion, chopped
1 tsp. dry parsley flakes
½ tsp. marjoram
3 tbls. lemon juice
Salt and pepper
2 can (1 lb. each) green beans, drained

Sauté onion in margarine until golden. Add parsley, marjoram, lemon juice, salt and pepper. Stir well. Add drained green beans and heat, stirring gently.

Chef's secret: Add a little bacon bar to green beans for additional flavor.

GREEN BEAN CRUMBLE
(Serves 3-4)

2 cans (1 lb. each) green beans, drained
1 tbls. soy sauce
1 can bamboo shoots, drained
½ tsp. salt, dash pepper
½ cup crushed chow mein noodles
6 tbls. shortening

Combine beans and soy sauce in a bowl. Add bamboo shoots, salt, pepper and crushed noodles. Melt shortening (or use margarine) in a pan. Add bean mixture, stirring until well coated with noodle crumbs. Heat thoroughly.

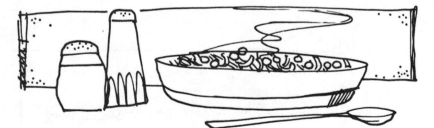

CELERY AND PEAS
(Serves 2-3)

½ cup celery, sliced diagonally
1 tbls. dry onion flakes
2 tbls. margarine
½ tsp. salt, dash of pepper
1 can peas, drained

Sauté celery and onion flakes in margarine 5 min. Add seasoning and peas and heat.

PEAS AND CHESTNUTS
(Serves 2-3)
2 tbls. margarine, melted
1 tbls. soy sauce
1 tsp. Worcestershire sauce
1 can water chestnuts, drained and chopped
1 can peas, drained (or use freeze dried, soaked)

Melt margarine in a saucepan and add soy and Worcestershire sauce. Add chopped water chestnuts. Stir to coat well. Add peas, stir and simmer 5-10 min.

SUMMER SQUASH
(Serves 2-3)
2 tbls. margarine
1 pound summer or zucchini squash, thinly sliced
1 medium onion, sliced
½ tsp. salt, dash of pepper

Heat margarine in a frying pan. Add all the ingredients and stir to coat with margarine. Cover and simmer 10 minutes or until tender.

Chef's secret: Cook fresh vegetables only until barely tender. Overcooking destroys vitamins.

COOKED CUCUMBER
Peel cucumber or not, as desired.

Slice thin and cook in a small amount of salted water 5-8 min.

Drain, mash with a fork and season with butter, salt and pepper.

Instead of plain salted water try using a bouillon cube or instant bouillon added to the water. Omit salt.

ZUCCHINI IN TOMATO SAUCE
(Serves 4-5)
5 tomatoes
¼ cup margarine (½ stick)
½ tsp. salt, dash of pepper
½ tsp. basil
1 pound zucchini, washed and sliced fine
1 tsp. dry parsley flakes

Peel and cut up tomatoes, in margarine, stirring constantly until thick. Add seasonings and sliced zucchini. Simmer 12-15 min. Sprinkle with parsley flakes, and stir lightly.

ZUCCHINI 'N MUSHROOMS
(Serves 2-3)

1 lb. zucchini, washed and thin sliced
1 tbls. dry onion flakes
1 can (8 oz.) mushroom pieces, drained (save juice)
1 fresh tomato, peeled and cut into chunks
Garlic powder, pepper
Dry celery flakes

In a skillet, place zucchini, onion flakes and the liquid drained from the mushrooms.

Cover and simmer 5 min.

Add mushrooms and tomato and sprinkle with garlic powder, pepper and celery flakes.

Simmer 5 min. more.

MEXICAN SQUASH FRY
(Serves 3-4)

1½ lb. summer squash, trimmed and sliced thin
2 medium-firm tomatoes
1 medium onion, sliced into rings
1 can (4 oz.) diced green chilis
4-6 tbls. margarine
Salt and pepper

Melt margarine in a large skillet. Sauté squash about 5 min. Add remaining vegetables. Mix gently. Add salt and pepper. Sauté until well heated, stirring carefully. Do not overcook.

DINNER BREADS

It is easy to take bread and rolls enough
to last for a few days,
but when your wilderness trip lasts more than a week,
you can use these camp bread recipes to see you through.

Many campers like to make their own flour mix. It can be used for all flour requirements. The following combination is wholesome and nourishing:

CAMP FLOUR MIX

2½ lbs. white flour
2½ lbs. whole wheat flour
1¼ lbs. yellow corn meal
1¼ lbs. soy flour
¾ lb. wheat germ

Mix thoroughly and keep in a closed container in your refrigerator.

When preparing for a trip, measure and pre-mix all dry ingredients into a plastic bag for each recipe. Use the flour mix in place of all-purpose flour.

GRIDDLE SCONES
(Makes 14-18)

2 cups Camp Flour Mix (or all-purpose flour)
1 tbls. each baking powder and sugar
½ tsp. salt
¼ cup margarine
⅓ cup milk
2 eggs

Combine flour with baking powder, sugar and salt. Cut the margarine into the dry ingredients with a pastry blender or 2 table knives.

Beat the eggs and milk together and add to the dry ingredients, blending thoroughly. Turn out onto a lightly floured surface and knead about 5 times. Using a bottle for a rolling pin, roll out the dough to ½" thickness and cut into rounds using a can with both ends cut out, about 2" diameter.

Place the scones on the UNGREASED surface of a griddle or frying pan over medium heat. Bake about 10 min., turn and bake the other side about 10 min. Bake slowly so they are light brown on the surface, but baked clear through. Serve hot with margarine.

FRY BREAD

Mix together and stir until shortening is melted:
2 cups warm water
1 tsp. salt
3 tbls. soft shortening (or margarine)
Stir together and add:
2½ cups Camp Flour Mix (or all-purpose flour)
1 tbls. baking powder

Add approximately 2½ cups more flour to make a soft dough.

Roll out ½" thick on a floured surface. Cut into pieces 3" long and 2" wide. Cut a slit in the center of each.

Fry in deep fat, turning once, to a golden brown. Drain on paper towels and sprinkle with salt, seasonings or powdered sugar if to be used for a dessert.

Chef's secret: To keep breads or pots warm, place them on a rock that has been heated in the campfire.

WAYS TO PREPARE TORTILLAS

Before starting, heat a flat rock in the campfire. Rake it from the coals and use it to keep the tortillas warm. Stack tortillas, as heated, in a covered pot or wrap in foil to keep hot on the rock until ready to serve.

DEEP FRIED TORTILLAS: Heat about ¼" salad oil in a small frying pan over medium heat. Fry tortillas, one at a time, turning often, until sizzly around the edges. Drain on paper towels. Add more oil as needed.

SOFT TORTILLAS: Use an ungreased heavy skillet or griddle and have it medium hot. Place tortillas, one at a time, in the skillet. Turn in about 30 seconds and heat other side.

FRIED TORTILLAS: Thinly spread margarine on one side of a tortilla. Place tortilla in the hot frying pan, spread side down. Heat for several seconds and turn with tongs. When it starts to puff, it is done. It will take only a few seconds on each side.

Chef's secret: Tortillas are the most versatile bread of all. They can be rolled, torn, cut or used as a scoop or a plate. They keep well, and can be reheated.

TORTILLAS
(Makes 12)

If you would rather make your own tortillas, here is an easy recipe:

1 cup flour
½ cup corn meal
¼ tsp. salt
1 egg
1½ cups cold water

Combine all ingredients in a bowl and beat until smooth.

Spoon 3 tablespoons of batter onto a medium hot UNGREASED griddle or skillet. Turn when the edges look dry, but not brown.

Fill with heated canned chili beans, freeze-dried cooked vegetables or meats, and top with sharp cheese and crisp vegetables such as green pepper strips, tomato slices, lettuce leaves, or shredded raw carrots. Top with sliced olives or pickle relish. Slices of mild Jack cheese add flavor.

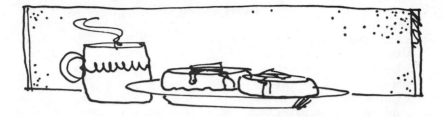

TOASTED ENGLISH MUFFINS

Split, butter and heat buttered side down on the edges of the griddle or frying pan. Scramble the eggs in the center over the flame.

Chef's secret: Heat breads at the same time your meal is cooking by placing them in a foil pie pan, covering tightly with foil and placing the pan on the pot in place of a lid. (Be sure you have the right size pan.)

BANNOCK
(4 servings)

4 cups flour
6 tbls. sugar
1 tsp. salt
4 tsp. baking soda

Mix the dry ingredients. Cut in 1/3 cup solidified bacon fat with a fork, adding small amounts of water or milk until the dough gathers into a ball. Flatten into a pancake not more than one inch thick, and dust top and bottom with flour. Heat a greased cast iron frying pan. Brown the Bannock and turn. Continue to bake for about 15 min. or until done.

SPEEDY BANNOCK

1 cup biscuit mix
Water to knead into a stiff dough

Knead several times on a flat surface and flatten into a 1/2" round. Press into a well-greased frying pan and brown on both sides. Place beside the fire at a tilt to catch the heat and bake slowly for half an hour.

Add raisins or fresh berries, if desired.

PAN BREAD

Mix biscuit mix and water to a soft dough.

Fry flattened spoonfuls in margarine on both sides and serve with jelly or honey.

Variations:

Add

1/4 cup raisins
1 tsp. instant bouillon
1 tsp. dry onion chips
1 tsp. dry parsley or celery flakes

HUSH PUPPIES

Combine:
2 cups corn meal
1 tsp. salt
2 tsp. baking powder
½ cup dry milk
1 cup water
1 tbls. dry onion flakes

Shape into patties and fry in bacon fat in a medium hot skillet. Brown on both sides.

Variations: Add left over cooked corn or other vegetable to the batter before cooking. Or add crumbled crisp fried bacon or a tsp. of bacon bar.

CORN MEAL BISCUITS

1¼ cups hot water
2 cups corn meal
1 tsp. salt

Mix all ingredients thoroughly. Batter should be stiff. Spoon into *well-greased* skillet and flatten with a spatula to ½" thick. Brown about 10 min. on each side.

CHAPTER EIGHT

What's for Dessert

The following desserts are quick and easy if you have done your "home work." Measure and pre-package as many of the dry ingredients as you can. Don't forget to include directions.

FRUIT FRITTERS

2 cups biscuit mix
¾ cup dry milk
1⅔ cup water
1 egg, beaten
1 can (1 lb.) cut up fruit, drained

Mix biscuit mix and dry milk. Add water and beaten egg. Combine.

Add drained fruit and drop by spoonfuls into a medium hot, greased skillet. Brown both sides.

Serve with the syrup saved from the fruit:

Heat the syrup and add 1 tbls. margarine and ½ tsp. cinnamon. The syrup also can be used to replace part of the water in the recipe.

SKILLET PUDDING
(Serves 5-6)

¼ cup margarine
2 slices white bread cut into cubes, or 1½ cup croutons
¼ cup sugar
1 can cherry pie filling
2 tbls. chopped nuts (optional)

Melt margarine in a frying pan. Brown the bread cubes in the fat. Sprinkle sugar and stir until well blended. Add pie filling, stirring to combine. Heat through.

FRUIT FLUFF

In a skillet place canned peach or pear halves.

Put a large marshmallow in each center.

Combine the fruit syrup with ⅔ cup brown sugar, 2 tbls. lemon juice. Pour over fruit.

Cover and simmer until the marshmallows are soft and the fruit is heated.

GRAPEFRUIT SUPREME

Combine drained canned grapefruit sections and drained canned grapes.
Top with shredded coconut and a drizzle of honey.

SKEWERED FRUIT

Leave the peeling on firm bananas and cut in 1" slices.

Dip the cut ends in a brown sugar and cinnamon mix.

Alternate on square shafted skewers with unpeeled quartered orange
slices.

Hold over coals until hot and the banana peel turns brown.

Dip in more brown sugar-cinnamon mix to eat.

BACON BANANAS

Peel bananas and cut in half lengthwise, and then in half across the fruit.
Fry with bacon strips in a heavy pan until the bacon is as you like it. Turn
the bananas occasionally to brown both sides.

CRUMBY BANANAS
(Serves 3-4)

Peel 3-4 large firm bananas Cut each in half, then slice each half lengthwise.

Dip in evaporated milk, and roll in a mixture of ¼ cup fine graham
cracker crumbs and 1 tsp. cinnamon.

Heat 3 tbls. margarine in a frying pan over medium heat. Add banana
slices (do not crowd) and fry until lightly browned and crispy. Turn carefully with wide tongs.

HONOLULU PUDDING

Combine:
1 pkg. vanilla pudding
1½ cups fruit juice drained from:
1 can (9 oz.) pineapple tidbits
2 cans (11 oz. ea.) mandarin oranges
1 can (1 lb.) fruit cocktail

Cook pudding and fruit juices until clear. Allow to cool, stirring occasionally. Add fruit and stir thoroughly.

Serve warm or chilled. For individual servings, spoon into plastic foam or
insulated cups.

CAMPER'S CREPE SUZETTES

Prepare pancakes from a mix, but make a thinner batter by adding a little more liquid than called for. Wrap in foil to keep warm.

In the same skillet melt 1 tbls. margarine.

Add 1 can (1 lb. 5 oz.) cherry pie filling to which you have added 1 tbls. lemon juice. Heat until bubbly.

Dip each pancake in the hot pie filling, coating both sides. Lift out carefully to a plate. Spoon a few cherries onto the pancake and roll it up. Sprinkle with sugar.

SKILLET DOUGHNUTS

Combine:
2 cups biscuit mix
⅔ cup milk

Drop by spoonfuls, one at a time, in hot *deep* bacon grease.

When turned and browned on both sides, drain and roll in cinnamon sugar.

SKILLET COOKIES
(Martha Kaiser — Valencia, Calif.)

1 cup shortening
1 cup sugar
3 eggs
4 cups flour
4 tsp. baking powder
1 tsp. salt
1½ tsp. cinnamon

Cream shortening, sugar and eggs. Combine the dry ingredients and add.

Stir in raisins and drop by teaspoonfuls on a hot greased skillet or griddle. When the top puffs, turn and brown the other side.

NO-BAKE CRISPIES

In a double boiler melt together:
3 tbls. margarine
½ lb. marshmallows

Remove from heat and add 1 can (4 cups) Chinese noodles. Press into greased 9" x 13" pan. Sprinkle with chocolate chips and press into mixture. Allow to cool and harden.

NO-BAKE COOKIES

½ cup margarine
⅓ cup dry milk
½ cup water
2 cups sugar (half brown and half white)
6 tbls. cocoa
3 cups quick cooking oats
1 cup coconut, or nuts, or raisins

Put margarine, milk, water, sugar and cocoa in a saucepan and bring to a full boil. Remove from heat and fold in the oats while the mixture is still hot. Add coconut, nuts or raisins. Drop by spoonfuls onto waxed paper or foil to cool.

SWEET BREAD

Cut stale white bread slices in half.
Dip in sweetened condensed milk.
Roll in cinnamon sugar or flaked coconut.
Fry slowly on a greased griddle or frying pan until browned on both sides.

RICE CAKES

½ cup minute rice
½ cup water
½ tsp. salt
¼ cup soft margarine
½ tsp. cinnamon
½ tsp. almond extract
2 eggs, unbeaten
1½ cups biscuit mix
1 cup milk (or use dry milk and water)

Bring rice, water and salt to a boil. Cover and remove from heat. Let set 5 min.
Add margarine, cinnamon, almond and eggs. Combine well.
Add dry biscuit mix, then gradually add milk, stirring until blended.
Fry this mixture as you would pancakes.
Top with heated pie filling.

QUICK DESSERTS

Top pound cake with fresh or canned fruit for a shortcake.
Slice pound cake. Butter slices and toast in a frying pan.

Spread with jam or marmalade.

Top graham crackers with cream cheese and jelly, marmalade or pie filling.

CANDIED BACON: Cut bacon strips in 2" pieces and place in a frying pan. When fat begins to accumulate, sprinkle bacon pieces with brown sugar and turn heat very low allowing the bacon to simmer in the fat. When the sugar is carmalized, lift out with a slotted spoon or tongs, and place on foil or waxed paper to cool. (The hot sugar sticks to paper towels.)

FRUIT FONDUE
In a double boiler, combine and heat:
2 tbls. margarine
¼ cup milk
1 pkg. creamy type frosting mix

Cut up bananas, apples and oranges into chunks. Also try large marshmallows and cubes of pound cake.

Use square shafted skewers on sharpened sticks to spear the "dippers". Leave the frosting mix over hot water to serve.

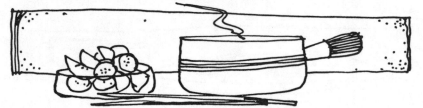

APPLESAUCE DESSERTS
7-UP FRUIT COMBO
1 pkg. (3 oz.) raspberry gelatin
1 cup applesauce
1 can (9 oz.) crushed pineapple
1 tbls. lemon or orange juice
1 bottle (7 oz.) 7-UP

Dissolve gelatin in *heated* applesauce. Add rest of ingredients and stir until smooth. Serve warm or cooled.

APPLEMALLOW
Add ½-1 tsp. cinnamon to a can of applesauce. Stir it in the can. Pour the applesauce over miniature marshmallows and combine. Serve heated or cold.

APPLERICE
Add ¼ cup minute rice to a can of applesauce in a saucepan. Add a few dates or raisins heat to a boil, cover and let set 5 min. Serve with milk or mixed coffee lightener.

SAUCED DESSERTS

In a saucepan combine:

Canned applesauce and 3-4 tbls. flavored gelatin. Heat and stir to dissolve gelatin.

Canned applesauce and 1 cup miniature marshmallows. Heat and stir to dissolve marshmallows.

Canned applesauce and ½ cup fresh cranberries. Cook together until berries pop, about 5 min. (Add a little water if it is too dry.)

Canned applesauce and 2 tsp. red hots. Heat and stir to dissolve the red hots.

MINT APPLESAUCE:

Add 2 drops of mint flavoring to a can of applesauce.

CRAN-APPLE SAUCE:

Combine

1 can cranberry sauce

1 can applesauce

MOLASSES APPLESAUCE:

To a can of applesauce add cinnamon to taste and 1 tbls. molasses. Stir in the can.

APPLE DUMPLINGS

In a skillet combine a can of apple pie filling with ½ cup water.

Bring to a boil. Cut refrigerator biscuits into fourths and place on top of the apples. Sprinkle with cinnamon sugar.

Cover tightly and simmer 20 min.

PUDDINGS

The following pudding recipe is written in two versions to show how a recipe can be changed to fit camping requirements.

HAWAIIAN PUDDING

(Marie Hughes — Monrovia, Calif.)

2 cups dry milk

6 cups water

½ of an 8 oz. pkg. coconut

⅔ cup sugar

1½ tsp. vanilla

1 cup cornstarch, lightly packed

1 tsp. cinnamon

Put 5 cups water and 2 cups dry milk in a 3 qt. saucepan. Add coconut, sugar and vanilla. Bring just to boiling point.

Mix 1 cup cornstarch in 1 cup water and add, stirring constantly. Stir until thickened.

Pour into 9" square pan to cool. Sprinkle with cinnamon. Cut in squares and eat in your hand, or on a paper towel.

HAWAIIAN PUDDING

Camping Method:

At home: Combine and mix well with a wire whip:

2 cups dry milk
⅔ cup sugar
1 cup cornstarch, lightly packed
1 tsp. cinnamon

Put into sturdy plastic bag and seal well. Also pack: ½ of an 8 oz. pkg. of coconut to which you have added 1½ tsp. vanilla.

At camp: In a 3 qt. kettle heat 6 cups water to steaming, but not boiling. Add coconut-vanilla packet first, then dry milk packet, stirring constantly until thickened and bubbly.

Pour into 9" square pan to cool. Sprinkle with cinnamon. When cold, cut in squares and eat in hand or on paper towel. (Make this in the morning. It takes a long time to cool.)

Chef's secret: If you have a 9" x 9" aluminum Dutch oven you can use it to cool your pudding. (See Chapter 9)

VANILLA-RICE PUDDING

2½ cups water
½ cup minute rice
¼ cup raisins
1 cup dry milk
1 pkg. (3 oz.) vanilla pudding mix
Dash of cinnamon

Combine water, rice and raisins. Bring to a boil, cover, and let set 5 min. Combine dry milk, pudding mix and cinnamon and add to rice.

Cook, stirring constantly, until thick. Serve warm or cold. Top with a blob of jelly.

Top vanilla instant pudding with any of the following:

Salted nuts

Jams or jellys

Crushed peanut brittle

Crushed peppermint candy

Crushed English toffee

Instant coffee

Ice cream toppings

Add almond extract to vanilla pudding. (¼ tsp.)

Add banana flakes to vanilla pudding.

VANILLA-FRUIT PUDDING
1 can pineapple tidbits, drained
1 can mandarin oranges, drained
1 can seedless grapes, drained
½ cup tiny marshmallows
1 heaping tablespoon flaked coconut.

Drain fruits and use the liquid to make *cooked* vanilla pudding. Add marshmallows and coconut along with the drained fruits. Chill.

Chef's secret: This pudding will chill faster if it is spooned into foam coffee cups.

ORANGE PUDDING
Combine:
1 pkg. instant vanilla pudding
1 cup dry milk
Add:
2 cups water
1 can (11 oz.) mandarin oranges, drained

Make pudding using the dry milk and water. Stir in mandarin oranges and keep in a cool place until served.

CHOCONUT PUDDING
¼ cup peanut butter
2 cups milk

Combine peanut butter and ¼ cup milk until smooth. Slowly add remaining milk. Beat until well blended.

Add: 1 pkg. (4½ oz.) instant chocolate pudding and blend well. Cover and chill.

CHOCO-CHEESE PUDDING
Mix freeze-dried cottage cheese per directions. Add instant chocolate drink mix, some sugar and a dash of salt for a tapioca-like dessert. (Or use fresh cottage cheese.)

Chef's secrets:
- *For a richer flavor, add semisweet chocolate bits or ¼-½ tsp. instant coffee to instant chocolate pudding.*
- *Alternate large marshmallows and chocolate drop cookies on a skewer. Heat over coals until gooey, turning often.*

CHAPTER NINE

The Fragrant Campfire

Dutch Oven Cooking

A cake, with its tempting aroma, is baking while a dozen canoeists sit around the campfire on a lonely river sand bar miles from electricity or gas. Someone calls, "Time!" and the lid is lifted carefully from the Dutch oven. The center tests done and the cake edges have pulled away from the sides. All is well. The coals are dumped from the lid and scraped away from the oven for a 10-minute cooling period. Paper towels substitute for plates as the cake is squared and served.

If that sounds like something you would like to try, your choice of Dutch oven depends upon your activities. If you car-camp, then the traditional heavy cast iron oven may be your choice. If you canoe, you might like a cast aluminum one. Each has its advantages and disadvantages.

Cast iron requires a certain amount of care. It should NEVER be soaked in a detergent. This will remove the "seasoning." Brust is a major enemy but prompt thorough cleaning and drying will control it. Cast iron is rugged and durable — but also heavy. Be sure the legs are well spaced to keep it steady.

My choice includes two rectangular cast aluminum Dutch ovens. One is 6½" x 9", the other 9" x 9". They came from Outdoor Cookware Co., 134 So. Virginia, Hobart, Indiana 46342 (Send for a brochure.) They are lighter weight, they heat and cool fast and do not warp or rust. A plastic scouring pad is all I ever need to clean them. They need no seasoning, so detergents can't hurt them.

Eddie Bauer, P.O. Box 3700, Seattle, Wash. 98124 carries round cast aluminum Dutch ovens in 10" and 12" diameters if you prefer the traditional shape.

Cast iron utensils can be found in many outdoor shops and catalogues. Be sure the Dutch oven you select has a flat lid with a rim to hold coals.

If you are grilling a steak for dinner, rake out some of those coals ahead of time and bake a package of potatoes, au gratin or scalloped. To get a fast start, you can grease the oven, put on the lid and pre-heat while you mix up the casserole. The cooking time will be approximately the same as with your oven at home.

I have found that my rectangular Dutch ovens get more even heat if the coals do not quite touch the outside edges. I do not put any coals underneath, but the lid is covered, of course.

Many of the one-pot meals described in Chapter 8 can be cooked in a Dutch oven. The lid can be used for frying when inverted, so you can try out some breakfast recipes, too.

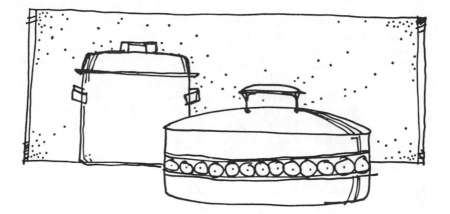

CASSEROLES
TUNA CASSEROLE
(Serves 2-3)

Combine:
1 can mushroom soup
1 can tuna, drained
1 cup crushed saltine crackers
½ cup milk
1 can peas, drained
½ tsp. salt, dash of pepper
    Pour into greased Dutch oven. Bake about 25 min.

HAM AND YAMS
(Serves 3-4)

2 or 3 lb. canned ham
1 can (1 lb. 4½ oz.) sliced pineapple, drained
2 cans (1 lb. each) canned yams
    Cover bottom of Dutch oven with pineapple slices. Slice ham about ½"
thick and place on top of pineapple.
    Slice yams and place on top of ham. Add about ¼ cup pineapple juice,
cover and bake 30 - 40 minutes. Use larger oven (9x9).

APPLES AND YAMS
(Serves 2-3)

1 can yams, sliced ½" thick
2 tart cooking apples, peeled, cored, thin-sliced
    Generously butter a Dutch oven. Arrange yams and apples in layers.
Sprinkle each layer with brown sugar and cinnamon. Bake about 30 min.

FRUIT AND BEAN BAKE
(Serves 2-3)
1 jar (18 oz.) Boston baked beans
¾ cup chopped mixed dried fruit
½ cup beer
Combine and bake 15 - 20 min.

DUTCH OVEN POTATOES
At home: Boil medium sized potatoes in their jackets about 10 min.
At camp: Heat ¼ cup bacon fat in your Dutch oven. When oil is hot coat each potato with the hot fat and stack in the oven. Sprinkle with garlic and onion salt and pepper.
Bake about 20 min.

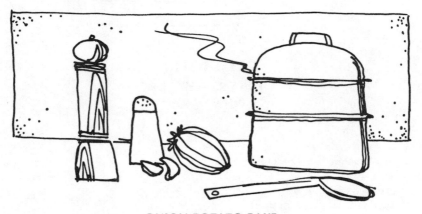

ONION-POTATO BAKE
Scrub medium sized potatoes and slice lengthwise ¾" - 1" thick. Do not peel.
Peel and slice onion ½" thick.
Overlap slices of potato and onion in a Dutch oven.
Add 1 can beef or chicken bouillon and bake until potatoes are done.
Variation: Instead of bouillon add ½ cup oil and vinegar French dressing.

EASY MEAT LOAF
(Serves 2-3)
Combine
1 lb. ground beef
2 tbls. chopped green pepper
1 egg
1 envelope Sloppy Joe seasoning mix
Mix well, form into loaf.
Bake 30 min. or until done.
Variation: Instead of Sloppy Joe mix, use spaghetti mix, taco mix, etc.

DUTCH OVEN DINNER
(Use larger oven)
Prepare meat loaf at home and freeze *hard* to use for first dinner.
2 lbs. hamburger
1 envelope onion soup mix
2 eggs
¼ cup catsup
1½ cups soft bread crumbs or 1 cup crushed soda crackers
(save these cracker crumbs)
¾ cup warm water   .
Mix thoroughly and shape into loaf that will fit your Dutch oven. Wrap in foil, then a plastic bag and freeze until needed.
At Camp: Place mostly thawed meat loaf in a heated Dutch oven. Surround meat with scrubbed, halved potatoes and carrots. Bake approximately one hour.

CHILI-RELLENO CASSEROLE
(Large oven)
(Sue Montepert — Newport Beach, Calif.)
Prepare at home:
2 cans (7 oz. each) whole green chilis, washed, seeded and drained
½ lb. Jack cheese, shredded
½ lb. cheddar cheese, shredded
Place cleaned chilis in a plastic container with tight lid. Keep the two cheeses separate in plastic bags.
Take along:
2 eggs
3 tbls. flour
1 large can evaporated milk
1 large fresh tomato
At camp: Grease a 9" x 9" rectangular or 10" round Dutch oven.
Line the bottom and sides with cleaned chilis. Leave the ends hanging out over the edges.
Put Jack cheese in first. Top with cheddar cheese.
Combine egg, flour and evaporated milk and pour over cheese.
Cover with the green chili ends.
Bake about 35-40 min.
Remove cover and top chilis with peeled, sliced fresh tomato.
Replace cover and bake 10-15 min. longer.
While you have a cake baking in the Dutch oven try:

DINNER IN A CAN

For each person: Grease a one pound coffee can.

Place meat in the bottom (hamburger pattie, canned beef and gravy, canned chicken or Spam)

Top with drained canned vegetables. Add a slice of fresh tomato. Dot with margarine, salt and pepper.

Cover tightly with heavy foil. Place on grill or near coals and heat until bubbly.

BREADS

ONION-CHEESE BREAD

Combine:

1½ cups biscuit mix
2 tbls. dry onion flakes
⅓ cup dry milk
1 egg, slightly beaten with . . .
½ cup water
1 tbls. shortening, melted in the heated Dutch oven
½ cup sharp cheese, shredded

Spread the dough in a greased Dutch oven. Top with:

1 tbls. poppy seeds
2 tbls. melted margarine
½ cup cheese, shredded.

Bake 20 - 25 min.

HAWAIIAN CORN BREAD

Dip sliced luncheon meat in beaten egg. Coat with crushed cracker crumbs and flaked coconut.

Place each meat slice on a slice of pineapple in a greased Dutch oven.

Top with a package of corn bread mix, mixed up.

Bake for the time suggested on the package.

CORN BREAD
(Serves 2)

At home, sift together:

¼ cup corn meal
¼ cup flour
¼ tsp. soda
⅛ tsp. salt
1 tbls. sugar
¼ cup dry milk

At camp: Melt 1 tbls. margarine in a heated Dutch oven. Add:

¼ cup water
1 tsp. lemon juice or vinegar

Combine with the dry ingredients and stir until smooth. Pour into the warmed Dutch oven (greased with margarine).

Bake 10-15 min. or until the bread pulls away from the edges of the pan and tests done in the center.

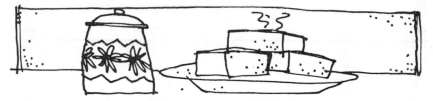

MEXICAN CORN BREAD
(Small oven)

½ of a 4 oz. can of diced green chilis
½ cup shredded cheddar of Jack cheese
1 pkg. (8½ oz.) corn bread or muffin mix
¼ cup dry milk
½ cup water
1 egg

Prepare corn bread mix with milk and eggs and water. Pour half of the mixture into a greased Dutch oven.

Sprinkle chilis and cheese over the batter.

Cover with the remaining batter. Bake about 25 min.

SPOON BREAD

Pour 1 cup BOILING water over ½ cup corn meal.
Beat in:

½ cup milk
½ tsp. salt
1½ tsp. baking powder
1 tsp soft margarine
2 eggs, well beaten

Pour into buttered Dutch oven. Bake 20-25 min. until set.

DUTCH BREAD
(Large rectangle oven)

Melt 3 tbls. margarine in a 9" x 9" oven or the 10" oven. Use the melted margarine to grease the sides of the oven.

Combine:

2 cups biscuit mix
⅓ cup dry milk
¾ cup water
1 egg

Sprinkle the bottom of the Dutch oven with onion and garlic salt and grated Parmesan cheese.

Spread ingredients over bottom of the oven. Cover and bake about 15 min. or until browned on top.

Variations: Instead of garlic and onion salt, sprinkle caraway seed, dry onion flakes, instant bouillon, nuts or raisins.

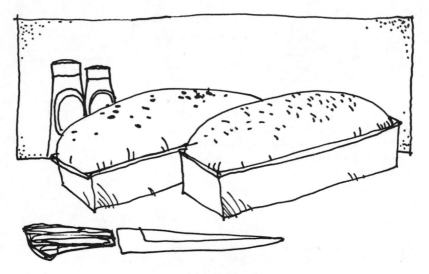

CAKES
CHERRY CAKE
(6½" x 9" oven)

1 can cherry pie filling
1 pkg. loaf size yellow cake mix (Jiffy)
⅓ cup margarine, melted

Spread pie filling in a buttered Dutch oven. Sprinkle the cake mix evenly over the top. Drizzle with the melted margarine.

Bake 35 - 45 min.

SNACK CAKE

At home, sift together:

1½ cups flour
1 tsp salt
3 tbls. cocoa
1 tsp. baking powder
1 cup granulated sugar

At camp: Put the dry ingredients in a greased Dutch oven.

Make 3 holes. Add 1 tsp. vinegar, 1 tsp. vanilla and 5 tablespoons salad oil.

Pour 1 cup water over the whole thing. Mix well.

Bake 25 - 30 min. or until it tests done.

DUMP CAKE
(Large Dutch oven)
(Ruth Carson — Turlock, Calif.)

Grease a 9" x 9" Dutch oven bottom and sides.

Spread ingredients, as is and as listed, in the Dutch oven.

1 can (1 lb. 5 oz.) pie filling
1 can (8 oz.) crushed pineapple
1 box yellow or white cake mix
½ cup chopped nuts
½ cup coconut
½ lb. (2 sticks) margarine, cut into small pieces

Place lid and bake approximately 40 min.

Chef's secret: Use the left-overs for your breakfast coffee cake.

JAM CAKE

Bake a loaf cake mix (Jiffy, yellow or white)

Spread the hot cake with apricot or peach jam, or orange marmalade. Serve warm.

Chef's secret: Betty Crocker Snackin' Cake works well in a 6½" x 9" Dutch oven. Add one tbls. salad oil to the batter to keep from sticking. Allow 10 min. to cool before serving.

"FRUIT" CAKE
(6½" x 9" oven)

Using a small cake mix (Jiffy or Cinch), spread half the batter in a greased Dutch oven. Top with drained, canned fruit slices or applesauce on the dough. Cover with the rest of the batter. Top with Grape Nuts.

Bake 35 - 40 min.

Variation: Use the juice drained from the canned fruit for the liquid to mix the cake batter.

DUTCH BANANA CAKE
(6½" x 9" oven)
Mix up 1 pkg of Jiffy or Cinch yellow or white cake mix, BUT take out 2 tbls. of liquid called for.

Mash 2 ripe bananas to add to the cake mix batter.

Bake about 25 min. in a greased oven.

Chef's secrets:
- *Top a hot Dutch oven cake with mint patties, marshmallow spread or chocolate candy bars broken into squares.*
- *Add a dash or two of nutmeg or cinnamon to spice or applesauce cake mixes.*

TOMATO SOUP SPICE CAKE
(9" x 9" oven)
1 pkg. (2 layer) spice cake mix
1 can tomato soup
½ cup water
2 eggs

Prepare cake mix as directed on the package using soup and water for the liquid.

Bake in a greased and floured Dutch oven 30 - 35 min. or until done.

CROUTON UPSIDE DOWN CAKE
Put margarine and brown sugar in the bottom of a heated Dutch oven. Stir together while margarine melts, then spread evenly.

Arrange drained canned fruit on top. (Peaches or pineapple)

Top with a thick layer of plain croutons. Sprinkle with cinnamon and sugar. Pour some of the fruit juice over the top of the croutons.

Cover and bake until bubbly and croutons are browned.

DUTCH CAROB CAKE
(9" x 9" oven)
At home combine in a plastic bag:

1½ cups unsifted flour
1 cup sugar
¼ cup Carob powder for baking (in health food stores)
1 tsp. soda
½ tsp. salt

At camp: Put dry ingredients in a bowl.

Add

⅓ cup margarine melted in a pre-heated Dutch oven
1 tbls. vinegar
1 tsp. vanilla
1 cup cold water

Stir to blend. Spread batter in the greased Dutch oven.

Cover and bake 20 - 30 min. or until it tests done with a toothpick or twig.

BAKED FRUIT

BREAD CRUMB TOPPING
Can be made at camp or at home to take along.
Spread evenly in a frying pan:
½ cup soft margarine (1 stick)
¼ cup packed brown sugar
1½ cup fine bread crumbs
Cinnamon to taste
Heat and stir until lightly browned. Cool and store in tight container. Use as crust for pie fillings or as a topping.

DESSERT TOPPING
(2½ cups)
(Make at home) Combine all ingredients:
½ cup melted margarine
¼ cup packed brown sugar
1 cup sifted flour
½ cup chopped nuts, or coconut, or Grape Nuts cereal
Heat oven to 400 degrees. Spread topping in a flat pan.
Bake 15 min., stirring once. Cool and store in a covered container in the refrigerator. Can also use as topping on breakfast cereal.

APPLE CRISP
1 can Comstock apple slices
1 tbls. lemon juice
⅓ cup sifted flour
1 cup quick oats
½ cup packed brown sugar
½ tsp. salt
1 tsp. cinnamon
⅓ cup melted margarine
Melt margarine in the pre-heated Dutch oven.
Combine dry ingredients; add melted margarine. Mix until crumbly.
Put apples in the greased Dutch oven. Sprinkle with lemon juice.
Top with crumb mixture. Bake for approx. 30 min.

STUFFED APPLES

Core apples and place in a greased Dutch oven. Fill the cavities with raisins, chocolate bits and sugar, plain or with cinnamon added.

Cover with the Dutch oven lid, and bake 30 - 45 min. or until fork tender.

Add a little water if the apples are not juicy.

CRUSTLESS PIE
(6½" x 9" oven)

At home, mix following ingredients and put in a *sturdy* plastic bag:

¾ **cup sugar**
½ **cup flour**
2 tsp. baking powder
Dash of salt
1 tsp. cinnamon
½ **cup chopped nuts**
Also take:
2 large cooking apples
1 egg
1 tbls. salad oil

At camp: Peel, core and slice apples, then cut slices into smaller pieces. This makes the dessert easier to serve. Add apples to the dry mix bag and coat slices well. Add egg and oil and mix again.

Spread into greased Dutch oven (mixture will be quite dry).

Bake 35 - 45 min. till apples are fork tender.

Cool 10 - 15 min. for easier serving.

Top each serving with a chunk of sharp cheddar cheese.

CRAN-APPLE CRUNCH

In a pre-heated Dutch oven, melt ½ stick margarine and grease the sides of the Dutch oven.

In a bowl combine:

½ **cup quick oats**
⅓ **cup packed brown sugar**
3 tbls. flour
¼ **tsp. salt**

Add melted margarine and mix well. (Or use one of the toppings on pg. ??.)

In the Dutch oven place:

1 can of whole cranberry sauce
1-2 peeled and chopped apples

Mix together.

Sprinkle with a topping. Bake 40 - 45 min.

Add chopped nuts to the topping if desired.

Chef's secret: For a fast, easy dessert, generously butter white slices of bread and lay them butter side down to line a Dutch oven. Add canned pie filling. Cover with buttered bread slices, butter side up. Bake until bread is browned.

FRUIT COBBLER
(9" x 9" oven)

2 cans (1 lb. each) pie filling
2 cups biscuit mix
2 tbls. sugar
1 tsp. cinnamon
⅓ **cup dry milk**
¾ **cup water**

Grease the Dutch oven. Add pie filling and place over hot coals until the pie filling is bubbly.

Mix dry ingredients and add water. Spoon over fruit.

Add cover and bake until dough is done, about 20 min.

PIE FILLING DELIGHT

Heat the Dutch oven and melt ½ cup margarine, spreading it around the sides of the oven generously.

Combine:

1 can (3½ oz.) flaked coconut (1⅓ cups)
1 cup sifted all purpose flour
¾ **cup packed brown sugar**
⅔ **cup fine cracker crumbs (14 saltines put through blender).**

Stir in margarine, mixing well. Press half the mixture in the bottom of the oven.

Spread with a can of pie filling. Top with remaining crumb mixture and press down gently.

Bake 25 - 30 min.

GRANOLA APPLE DELIGHT

¼ cup margarine melted in the pre-heated Dutch oven, added to . . .
1½ cups granola. Mix well and set aside.
1 can (1 lb. 9 oz.) apple pie filling
½ cup raisins
Cinnamon
Lemon juice to taste.

In the greased Dutch oven combine: pie filling and raisins.
Sprinkle with cinnamon and lemon juice. Cover with granola crumbs.
Bake 15 - 20 min.

CROUTON COBBLER

Melt ¼ cup margarine in a pre-heated Dutch oven, spreading around the sides to grease well.

Add 2 cups plain croutons and stir into the melted margarine to coat.
Reserve 1 cup of coated croutons for topping.

Add ½ tsp. almond flavoring to a can of cherry pie filling (or your choice) and stir gently.

Pour pie filling over the coated croutons. Top with the reserved croutons, pressing them in to make a "crust."

Sprinkle with cinnamon sugar.

Bake 25 - 30 min.

Variation: Crumb mixture: Combine at home:
½ cup brown sugar
½ cup flour
½ cup oatmeal
½ cup nuts, chopped
½ cup coconut
½ cup margarine

Variation: Combine 4-6 cups fresh, cleaned berries with 1 tbls. lemon juice and ⅔ cup packed brown sugar, instead of canned pie filling.

CHERRY CASSEROLE

Melt ¼ cup margarine in pre-heated Dutch oven
Add 2 cups plain croutons and mix well.
Combine:
1 jar (1 lb. 4 oz.) cherry preserves with . . .
½ cup water
Smooth preserves over croutons in the Dutch oven and cover with a generous sprinkle of cinnamon sugar.
Bake 25 - 30 min.
Use any fruit preserve.

SHREDDED WHEAT PUDDING

Melt 2 tbls. margarine in a pre-heated Dutch oven and coat the sides. Crumble 2 shredded wheat biscuits into the melted margarine.

In a bowl combine:

2 eggs
2 cups milk
¾ cup molasses
1 tsp. cinnamon
¼ tsp. salt

Pour over Shredded Wheat. Bake 30 - 40 min.

Serve with butterscotch ice cream topping.

GINGERBREAD PUDDING

3 cups applesauce
1 pkg. (13 oz.) gingerbread mix

Ingredients for the mix per instructions.   Pour applesauce into a greased Dutch oven. Cover and heat until bubbly.

Prepare gingerbread batter and pour over hot applesauce.

Cover and bake approximately 30 min. or until gingerbread topping is done.

GINGERBREAD
(9" x 9" oven)

At home combine:

2½ cups flour
2 tsp. soda
2 tsp. ginger
2 tsp. cinnamon
¼ tsp. ground cloves
¼ tsp. nutmeg
½ tsp. baking powder

Seal in a sturdy plastic bag with instructions.

At camp: Melt ¾ cup margarine in heated Dutch oven. Spread up the sides.

Combine:

melted margarine
2 eggs, beaten
¾ cup brown sugar, packed
¾ cup molasses

Add the pre-mixed dry ingredients and stir well. Add 1 cup *boiling* water.

Bake in larger rectangle oven 30 - 40 min. or until it tests done.

CHAPTER TEN

Bake Aheads

An accomplished one-burner cook takes time to plan, prepare and pre-package. These are recipes to be prepared at home for wholesome, nutritious "take-along" food.

RAISIN NUT BREAD
(1 loaf)

1 cup raisins
1½ cups boiling water
¼ cup sugar
1 tbls. margarine
1 egg, beaten
1⅓ cups flour
1 tsp. soda
¼ tsp. salt
½ tsp. vanilla
½ cup nuts, chopped
    Pour boiling water over raisins and then allow to cool.
    Cream together sugar, shortening, egg.
    Combine dry ingredients and add.
    Add raisins, vanilla and nuts. Mix well.
    Pour into greased loaf pan. Bake 350 degrees for 1 hr. or until done.

RAISIN BRAN BREAD
(1 loaf)

1 cup raisins
1 cup boiling water
1 cup graham flour
1 cup All Bran cereal
1 cup oatmeal
1 tsp. salt
¾ cup sugar
1 tsp. soda
1 cup sour milk
    Pour boiling water over raisins. Cool to lukewarm.
    Combine dry ingredients, add sour milk, then add raisins.
    Pour into greased loaf pan. Bake 350 degrees, 1 hour or until done.

PEANUT BUTTER BREAD
(1 loaf)

2¼ cups sifted flour
1 tsp. salt
½ cup sugar
3 tsp. baking powder
1 cup milk
2 eggs
1 cup crunchy peanut butter
    Sift dry ingredients together. Combine milk, eggs and peanut butter and
beat thoroughly until smooth. Add to dry ingredients and blend well.
    Pour into greased loaf pan. Bake 350 degrees, 1 hour, or until done.

EASY NUT BREAD
(1 loaf)

Combine in a large bowl:

¼ cup shortening, melted and cooled
1 egg
1½ cups milk

Sift together and add:

3 cups sifted flour
4 tsp. baking powder
1 tsp. salt
¾ cup sugar

Mix thoroughly, then fold in 1 cup broken nuts.
Pour into greased loaf pan, set for 20 min.
Bake 350 degrees, 1 hr. 10 min. or until done.
Chef's secret: Flavor improves and it cuts easier if left 12-24 hrs.

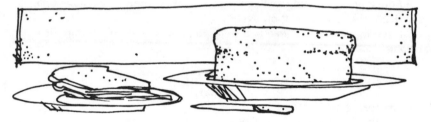

PRUNE BREAD
(1 loaf)

¾ cup honey
1 cup sugar
1½ cups flour
1 cup whole wheat flour
1 tsp. soda
1 tsp. cinnamon
1 cup walnuts, broken
½ cup chopped dried prunes
1 cup boiling water

Combine honey and dry ingredients.
Add 1 cup boiling water and mix well.
Grease *and flour* a loaf pan. Add prune mixture.
Bake 1½ hours at 350 degrees or until done.
Cool before removing from pan.
Chef's secret: An interesting bread substitute can be made by boiling wide lasagne noodles until tender (add a tsp. of salad oil to the boiling water, plus salt). Drain and pat dry with paper towels. Cut into 2" pieces and fry in deep fat until crisp. Drain on paper towels and sprinkle with salt or Parmesan cheese, grated.

PRUNE SPICE BREAD
(1 loaf)

2⅓ cups sifted flour
1 tsp. allspice
½ tsp. ground cloves
1 tsp. cinnamon
1 tsp. baking powder
½ tsp. soda
¼ cup soft margarine
1 cup sugar
3 eggs
½ cup dairy sour cream
1 tsp vanilla
1 cup chopped cooked prunes

Sift dry ingredients together. Cream margarine and sugar. Add eggs and mix well.

Add sour cream and vanilla to eggs, mix well, then add dry ingredients and prunes. Combine thoroughly.

Place in greased loaf pan and bake 350 degrees for 50-60 min. or until done.

FIG BREAD
(1 loaf)

1 cup dried figs
3½ cups sifted flour
¾ cup sugar
1 tsp. salt
4 tsp. baking powder
3 tbls. shortening
1 tsp. grated orange rind
1 egg, beaten
1 cup milk

Clip stems from figs and cut up into small pieces.

Sift flour, sugar, salt and baking powder together. Cut shortening into flour mixture until thoroughly blended.

Combine orange rind, egg and milk. Add to dry ingredients and beat. Fold in cut-up figs.

Pour batter into greased and floured loaf pan. Bake 375 degrees, 1½ hrs. or until done.

SOY DATE BREAD
(1 loaf)

Cream together:
2 tbls. shortening
1 cup brown sugar
Add:
1 cup dates, stemmed and chopped
½ cup nuts, broken
Combine:
1 tsp. salt
1 cup flour
1 cup soy flour
¾ cup dry milk
1 pkg. dry yeast
Add to the rest of the ingredients and mix well.
   Add: 1½ cups warm water and beat thoroughly to combine.
   Pour into greased loaf pan. Let rise ½ hour in a warm, draftless place.
   Bake 1 hr. at 300 degrees or until done.
   This is a heavy bread so be sure the center tests with a clean toothpick.

ORANGE DATE BREAD
(1 loaf)

Combine and cool:
1 cup boiling water
1 pkg. (8 oz.) pitted dates, chopped
¼ cup margarine
Add:
1½ tbls. grated orange peel
1 cup orange juice
2 eggs, beaten
Combine in a large bowl:
2 cups unsifted flour
2 cups quick cooking oats
⅔ cup sugar
2 tsp. soda
2 tsp. baking powder
1 tsp. salt
1 cup chopped walnuts
   Add the date mixture to the dry ingredients and stir just to moisten.
   Pour into greased and floured loaf pan. Bake 350 degrees about 1 hr. 20 min.
   Cool in pan 10 min., then turn out on wire rack to cool.

APPLE BREAD
(1 loaf)
(Diane Kowerduck — Northridge, Calif.)

1 cup sugar
½ cup margarine
2 eggs
2 tbls. sour milk
1 tsp. soda
1 cup graham flour
1 cup flour
1 tsp. salt
1 tsp. vanilla
2 cups chopped apple
½ cup raisins
½ cup broken walnuts

Cream the sugar and margarine. Add eggs and milk.
Combine the dry ingredients and add.
Mix in vanilla, apples, raisins and nuts.
Pour into greased loaf pan and top with: 2 tbls. each sugar, flour, margarine, and 2 tsp. cinnamon that has been cut fine with a pastry blender. Bake 350 degrees, 1 hr.

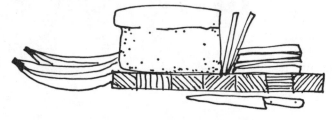

BANANA WHEAT BREAD
(1 loaf)

Combine thoroughly:
½ cup melted margarine
1 cup sugar
2 eggs, slightly beaten
3 medium bananas, peeled and mashed
Sift together:
1 cup sifted flour
½ tsp. salt
1 tsp. soda
1 cup whole wheat flour
Add to the banana mixture alternately with:
⅓ cup hot water

Stir in chopped nuts, about half a cup.
Pour into greased loaf pan and bake 325 degrees for 1 hr. and 20-30 min.

PINEAPPLE BREAD
(1 loaf)

Combine:
2 cups sifted flour
½ cup sugar
1 tsp. baking powder
½ tsp. salt
Add:
1 cup raisins
½ cup chopped nuts
Combine and add:
1 egg, beaten
1 tsp. vanilla
2 tbls. melted margarine
Add:
1 cup crushed pineapple, well drained
1 tsp. soda
Stir until well blended. Pour into greased loaf pan.
Bake 350 degrees, 1 hour or until done.

CARROT BREAD
(1 loaf)

Combine:
1 cup sugar
½ cup salad oil
Combine and add:
1½ cups flour
2 tsp. baking powder
½ tsp. soda
¼ tsp. salt
1 tsp. cinnamon
Add:
1 cup grated carrots
2 eggs, one at a time. Beat well between each addition
½ cup chopped nuts
Pour into greased loaf pan and bake 55-60 min. or until done.
Chef's secret: Cover the batter with foil for the first 15-20 min. to reduce cracking.

CHILI CHEESE CORN BREAD
(Serves 3-4)

Cream together:
½ cup margarine
½ cup sugar
Add:
2 eggs
½ of a 4 oz. can diced green chilis
½ of a 1 lb. can creamed corn
¼ cup shredded Jack cheese
¼ cup shredded cheddar cheese
Combine and add:
½ cup flour
½ cup corn meal
2 tsp. baking powder
¼ tsp. salt

Mix all ingredients thoroughly.
Pour into a greased and floured 8″ x 8″ x 2″ pan.
Bake at 350 degrees for ½ hour. Turn oven down to 300 degrees.
Bake until browned and a toothpick comes out of the center clean.
Cool and store in foil.
At camp: Reheat on a grill or a hot rock for a delicious bread to go with soup.

BRAN BREAD
(1 loaf)

1 cup whole bran cereal
1 cup buttermilk
½ cup raisins
¼ cup molasses
¼ cup packed brown sugar
1 tbls. salad oil
1 cup flour
1 tsp. baking soda
¼ tsp. salt

Soak the bran in buttermilk.
Combine raisins, molasses, brown sugar, oil and bran mixture.
Sift dry ingredients together and add. Stir thoroughly.
Pour into greased and floured loaf pan. Bake 350 degrees, 50-55 min.
Serve with baked beans.

PUFF BREAD
(Makes 2 doz.)

Sift together:
2 cups flour, sifted
¾ tsp. salt
1½ tsp. baking powder
1½ tbls. sugar
Cut in:
1 tbls. shortening until the mixture is fine grained.
Add:
⅔ cup milk (approximately) to make a dough just firm enough to roll.

Cover bowl and let stand for 45 min.

Roll ¼" thick on a lightly floured board. Cut in 3" squares.

Heat about 1" of oil in an electric frying pan to 300 degrees.

Add a few pieces at a time. Turn at once so they puff evenly, then brown both sides. Drain on paper towels.

Chef's secret: Take along to serve with Dutch oven Chili Relleno Casserole (Chapter nine).

CRANBERRY NUT BREAD
(1 loaf) (Freezes well)

2 cups flour
1 cup sugar
1½ tsp. baking powder
½ tsp. soda
1 tsp. salt
¼ cup shortening
¾ cup orange juice
1 tbls. grated orange rind
1 egg, beaten
½ cup nuts, chopped
1 cup whole fresh cranberries

Combine dry ingredients, then cut in shortening to look like cornmeal.

Combine orange juice, rind, egg, and add to dry ingredients. Mix just enough to dampen. Add nuts and cranberries.

Bake in greased loaf pan, 350 degrees for 1 hr. or until done.

CRACKERS
WHEAT CRACKERS
2 cups whole wheat flour
2½ tsp. salt
5 tbls. salad oil
¾ cup water
Combine flour and salt. Add oil and mix thoroughly.
Add water and mix well.
Roll dough very thin on a floured board. Cut and place on cookie sheets.
Bake 425 degrees — 8-10 min.
Variation: Sprinkle with sesame or poppy seeds. Roll lightly before cutting.

HARDTACK
Combine and mix thoroughly:
5 cups rye flour
1 tsp. salt
1 tsp. sugar
1 tbls. caraway seed
Add just enough water to make a stiff dough.
Roll out to ¼" thickness and cut into squares.
Bake on a greased flat cookie sheet until bone-dry, approximately 20 min. in a 325 degree oven. Cool and store in an airtight container.
Variation: Try seasoned salt instead of regular salt. Try brown sugar instead of white sugar. Try regular flour instead of rye.

RYE WAFERS
(3½ doz.)
Combine all ingredients in a bowl and mix until smooth:
¼ cup margarine — melted and cooled
1 cup unsifted rye flour
¾ cup unsifted white flour
1 tsp. baking powder
1 tsp. sugar
2 tsp. caraway seed
½ cup milk
Chill 1 hour. Divide in half and roll out on a lightly floured board.
Form very thin rectangles, cut in 2" squares with a sharp knife.
Place on cookie sheets and bake 375 degrees for 8-10 min. or until lightly browned.
Store in airtight container in a cool place.

PILOT BISCUITS

Combine:
4 cups flour
2 tbls. sugar
1 tsp. salt
Cut in:
¼ cup margarine with a pastry blender
Add:
1 cup milk to make a stiff dough
   Roll about ¼" thick on a floured board. Cut with a large round cookie cutter. Prick surface with a fork many times, and brush with milk.
   Place on ungreased cookie sheets. Bake 425 degrees — 15-18 min. until light tan.
   Variation: Add 1 cup rye, whole wheat or soaked cracked wheat flour to 3 cups white flour instead of using 4 cups white flour.

GRAHAM CRACKERS
(3 doz.)

Cream together:
½ cup margarine
⅔ cup packed brown sugar
Combine:
2¾ cups graham flour
½ tsp. salt
½ tsp. baking powder
¼ tsp. cinnamon
   Combine all ingredients and add ½ cup water a little at a time. Mix well.
   Stand about half an hour to make the dough easier to handle.
   Roll out on a floured board to ⅛" thickness.
   Cut in 2" squares and put on a greased cookie sheet.
   Bake 350 degrees for 20 min. or until lightly browned.
   Variation: Brush tops with melted margarine before baking and sprinkle with cinnamon sugar.

DESSERT BARS
COCONUT CRUNCHIES
(3 doz.)

Combine:
½ cup margarine
½ cup sugar
½ cup packed brown sugar
1 egg, beaten
½ tsp. vanilla
Combine and add:
1 cup flour, unsifted
½ tsp. baking powder
½ tsp. soda
¼ tsp. salt
1 cup quick cooking oats
1 cup Grape Nuts
½ cup shredded coconut.

The dough is stiff. Combine well. Drop by tsp. onto greased cookie sheets. Bake in a 375 degree oven 10-12 min. or until browned.

PECOCHO BARS

For the *base*, combine:
2½ cups flour
1¼ cup brown sugar, packed
¼ tsp. salt
½ cup margarine
⅓ cup peanut butter

Combine to the consistency of coarse crumbs with a pastry blender. Add:
1 egg, beaten
1 tsp. vanilla

Press into ungreased jelly roll pan. Bake 350 degrees for 25 min. Cool. For the *topping*: Melt together in a double boiler:
1 cup chocolate chips
½ cup peanut butter

Stir in: ½ cup coconut.
Spread on the cooled base and let the topping harden.
Cut into squares.

FRUIT BARS

Melt:
½ cup shortening and let it cool
Add:
½ cup molasses
2 eggs, and beat well
Sift together:
¾ cup sifted flour
½ tsp. baking soda
½ tsp. salt
½ tsp. each of nutmeg, cinnamon, ground cloves
Add to mixture.
Stir in:
1 cup chopped nuts
1 cup chopped raisins
Pour into greased 9″ x 9″ baking pan. Bake 375 degrees — 25-30 min.
Cool 5 min. and cut into squares.

DATE WHEAT BARS
(40 bars)

Combine:
1½ cups packed brown sugar
3 eggs, beaten well
Add:
¼ tsp. salt
½ tsp. vanilla
1 cup whole wheat flour
1 cup chopped nuts
½ cup chopped dates
Mix thoroughly and pour into 2 greased 7″ x 11″ pans.
Bake 325 degrees about 25 min.

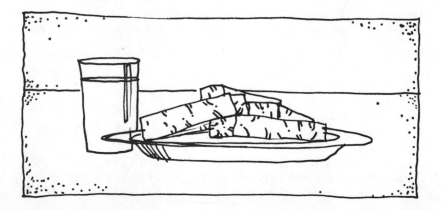

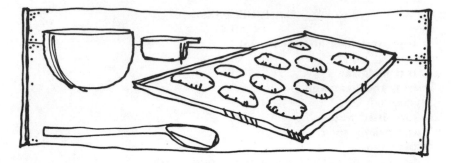

COOKIES
MACAROONS
(4 doz.)
Combine:

2 (8 oz.) pkgs. shredded coconut
1 can (15 oz.) sweetened condensed milk
1 tsp. vanilla
Drop by teaspoonfuls onto well-greased cookie sheet.
Bake 350 degrees, 10-12 min.
Variations: Add chocolate or butterscotch bits to the batter.

NOODLE COOKIES
Melt together in a double boiler:
2 pkg. (6 oz. each) butterscotch morsels
1 cup peanut butter
Stir to combine smoothly. Add:
1 can (5½ oz.) Chinese noodles
1 pkg. (6-8 oz.) salted Spanish peanuts
Stir to coat the noodles and peanuts, then drop by spoonfuls onto a length of waxed paper and allow to cool and dry.
Variations: Use a can of shoe string potatoes or crushed potato chips.

PEANUT BUTTER COOKIES
(Can be baked in a reflector oven)
Combine:

1½ cups chunky peanut butter
1 cup sugar
2 unbeaten egg whites
Drop by teaspoonfuls onto an ungreased cookie sheet.
Bake 350 degrees, 10 min. (Leave on the pan a few minutes to cool or they will break apart.)

PEANUT COOKIES
(3 doz.)

Combine and cream together:
½ cup margarine
¼ cup chunky peanut butter
½ cup packed brown sugar
1 egg
Beat together until fluffy, then add:
½ cup honey
Combine and add:
1 cup whole wheat flour
1 cup quick cooking oats
½ cup wheat germ
½ cup salted peanuts
   Drop by spoonfuls onto greased cookie sheets. Bake 375 degrees, 10-12 min.

PEANUT CRUNCHIES

Cream together:
1 cup shortening
1 cup sugar
1 cup packed borwn sugar
Add:
3 eggs
Combine and add:
2 cups flour
1 tsp. soda
1 tsp. cream of tartar
Add:
1 tsp. vanilla
1 cup corn flakes
1 cup oatmeal
1 cup salted peanuts
   Drop by spoonfuls on a greased cookie sheet and flatten.
   Bake at 350 degrees, 10-12 min.

ORANGE OATMEAL COOKIES
(4 doz.)
In a large bowl, combine:
1 cup soft margarine
2 eggs
⅓ cup orange juice
1 tsp. vanilla
Sift together and add:
2 cups sifted flour
1 tsp. each soda and salt
½ cup granulated sugar
Add:
1 tbls. grated orange rind
2 cups quick-cooking oats
½ cup firm packed brown sugar
Mix thoroughly, then add:
1 cup raisins
¾ cup chopped nuts
Drop by teaspoonfuls on greased cookie sheets.
Bake 375 degrees, 10-12 min.

CARROT COOKIES
(4 doz.)
Cook 2 cups shredded carrots in a small amount of boiling salted water until tender. Drain and mash.
Cream together:
¾ cup soft margarine
1 cup brown sugar, packed
Add:
1 egg
1 tsp. vanilla
cooked carrots
Beat until fluffy.
Combine and add:
2 cups flour
2 tsp. baking powder
½ tsp. salt
Mix thoroughly and drop by spoonfuls onto ungreased cookie sheets.
Bake 375 degrees, 10-12 min.

FIG COOKIES
(2½ doz.)

1½ cups sifted flour
1½ tsp. baking powder
½ tsp. each salt and cinnamon
1 egg, beaten
¼ cup milk
⅓ cup margarine
¾ cup brown sugar
½ cup each chopped figs and chopped nuts

Sift dry ingredients. Add beaten eggs to milk.

Cream butter and sugar and add dry ingredients alternately with milk.

Add figs and nuts. Shape into 2 rolls. Wrap in foil or waxed paper and chill until firm.

Slice thin and bake 375 degrees about 20 min.

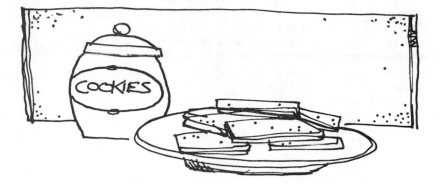

CORNMEAL COOKIES
(3 doz.)

Combine:
1 cup (½ lb.) margarine
½ cup packed brown sugar
½ cup sifted powdered sugar
Add:
1 tsp. vanilla
⅔ cup yellow cornmeal
1⅓ cups unsifted flour
¼ tsp. salt.

Shape 1 tbls. dough into a ball, then roll in cornmeal to coat evenly. Place balls 2″ apart on greased cookie sheet. Flatten to ¼″ thickness. Bake 350 degrees, 10-12 min. Cool 5 min. before removing from pans to a wire rack.

GRANOLA COOKIES
(2 doz.)
Combine all ingredients thoroughly:
1 cup regular granola
¾ cup flour
½ cup soft margarine
⅓ cup sugar
¼ cup packed brown sugar
½ tsp. each baking soda, salt, vanilla
1 egg
Drop by spoonfuls onto greased cookie sheets.
Bake 375, 12 min.
Variations: Add 1 cup raisins, 1 pkg. (6 oz.) chocolate drops, 1 cup cut-up dates.

CORN FLAKE COOKIES
(2 doz.)
In a double boiler blend:
1 can (15 oz.) sweetened condensed milk
¼ cup brown sugar
Cook over boiling water until mixture thickens, about 10 min.
Remove from heat and add:
3 cups corn flakes
Drop by spoonfuls onto greased cookie sheet. Bake 350 degrees, 10-12 min. Remove from pan at once.

POTATO CHIP COOKIES
Combine and beat well:
1 cup margarine
¾ cup white sugar
¾ cup packed brown sugar
2 eggs
1 tsp. vanilla
Add:
2 cups crushed potato chips
1 pkg. (6 oz.) butterscotch chips
Sift together and add:
2½ cups flour
1 tsp. baking soda
Drop by spoonfuls on greased cookie sheet.
Bake 375 degrees, 10-12 min.
Chef's secret: Cut a small slit in one end of the potato chip bag to allow air to escape, then crush by hand while chips are still in the bag.

MOLASSES COOKIES
(3½ doz.)

In a large bowl combine:
⅔ cup soft shortening or margarine
½ cup sugar
1 egg
½ cup molasses
Sift together and add:
2½ cups sifted flour
1 tsp. each soda, salt, cinnamon, ginger
Mix thoroughly and add:
½ cup buttermilk
 Drop by spoonfuls onto greased cookie sheets.
 Bake 350 degrees, 10-12 min.
 Add 1 cup raisins if desired.

RYE COOKIES

Combine:
½ cup rye flour
½ cup quick-cooking oats
½ tsp. salt
½ tsp. baking powder
¾ cup chopped walnuts
In a mixing bowl combine:
⅓ cup cooking oil
1 cup packed brown sugar
1 tsp. vanilla
2 eggs
 Beat liquid mixture with an egg beater until sugar is well mixed in.
 Add dry ingredients, and pour into greased 9″ square baking pan.
 Bake at 350 degrees, 30-35 min.
 Cool and cut into squares. Dust with powdered sugar if desired.

SUNFLOWER COOKIES
(4 doz.)

Cream together:
½ cup margarine
½ cup packed brown sugar
½ cup white sugar
Add and beat thoroughly:
1 egg
½ tsp. vanilla
Add:
¾ cup flour
½ tsp. salt
½ tsp. baking soda
1½ cups quick cooking oats
Mix thoroughly and add:
½ cup shelled sunflower seeds (from health food store)
    Chill dough for several hours. Flatten spoonfuls onto a greased sheet.
Bake 350 degrees, 10-12 min.

STAMINA COOKIES
(3 doz.)

Cream together:
4 tbls. margarine
¾ cup packed brown sugar
Blend in:
2 eggs
2 tbls. water
½ tsp. vanilla
Combine and add:
1½ cups whole wheat flour
¼ cup dry milk
½ tsp. baking soda
½ tsp. salt
Add:
1 pkg. (6 oz.) chocolate chips
½ cup shelled sunflower seeds
¼ cup chopped peanuts
    Drop by spoonfuls on a greased cookie sheet.
    Bake 375 degrees, 8-10 min.
    Add ½ cup raisins, if desired

COFFEE CAKES

ORANGE HONEY COFFEE CAKE

Combine thoroughly:

1⅓ cups honey
¾ cup soft margarine
2 eggs
½ cup milk
2 tbls. lemon juice
Sift together and stir in:
3½ cups unsifted flour
¾ tsp. soda
¼ tsp. salt
1 tsp. cinnamon OR ground cloves
Add:
1 cup broken walnuts
⅔ cup diced candied orange peel (See Chapter 11)

Pour into greased and floured 9" x 13" baking pan. Spread batter evenly with spatula and "drop" pan sharply several times to settle batter.

Bake 400 degrees, ½ hour or until it tests done in the center.

Cool in pan 10 min. before cooling on rack.

ORANGE COFFEE CAKE

Combine:

½ cup light corn syrup
1 tsp. grated orange rind
½ cup orange juice
¼ cup melted margarine
Sift together and add:
2 cups sifted flour
½ tsp. salt
1 tbls. baking powder
Add:
2 eggs, well beaten
1 tsp. vanilla

Pour into a greased and floured 8" square baking pan.

Add topping.

Combine: 2 tbls. grated orange rind, ½ cup sugar, 1 tsp. cinnamon, 1 tbls. melted margarine. Bake at 400 degrees, 30 min. or until cake pulls away from the pan.

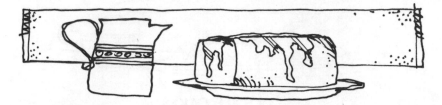

SAUCES TO SERVE ON POUND CAKE

PEANUT FUDGE SAUCE
Combine thoroughly and store in a tight container:
1 cup chocolate syrup
½ cup chunky style peanut butter

ORANGE SAUCE
Combine and bring to a rolling boil; stirring constantly:
1 cup sugar
¼ cup water
Boil 1 minute. Remove from heat and add;
1 can (6 oz.) frozen orange juice concentrate
  Cool and store in a tight container. Any frozen juice concentrate can be used for this recipe.

HOMEMADE CANDY BAR
  Combine salted peanuts, raisins, and a package of chocolate or butterscotch chips. Melt in a double boiler over hot water, stirring often. Drop by spoonfuls onto waxed paper to cool and harden.

CACTUS PEAR CANDY
(Nevi Otten — Torrance, Calif.)
  Cactus Pear Juice: Fruit must be *very* ripe. Do NOT cook. Wash fruit and stir with a wooden spoon in a large container of water to eliminate most of the spines. Put through two waters. Force fruit through a food mill or a doubled cheesecloth to eliminate seeds and pulp.

Soften 3 tbls. unflavored gelatine in ½ cup cold water.
Combine:
2 cups sugar
¾ cup cactus pear juice
juice from one lemon
  Bring to a boil, blend with the softened gelatin and simmer 20 min.
  Pour into a shallow (½"-1") pan that has been rinsed in ice water. Do NOT dry the pan.
  Let mixture stand at least 24 hours or until set. Cut in cubes and roll in powdered sugar.

DRY BREAD

SOUP STICKS

Spread sliced bread with margarine. Sprinkle with grated Parmesan cheese and a little salt. Cut into ½" strips. Place on a cookie sheet and bake at 350 degrees till browned.

CROUTONS

Thinly spread day old bread with margarine. Cut into ½" cubes.
Place in a flat pan and bake at 350 degrees until lightly browned and dry. Shake the pan occasionally or stir with a spatula.
Seasonings may be added to the margarine before spreading:
  Garlic or onion salt
  Dry crumbled celery leaves
  Dry crumbled parsley leaves
  Grated cheeses
  Marjoram or oregano
Chef's secret: At camp, if bread is getting too dry for sandwiches, spread generously with margarine, cut into small cubes and toss into a hot frying pan. Stir until browned. Use as topping for soups and stews, or with such desserts as applesauce or canned fruits to soak up some of the liquid.

CHAPTER ELEVEN

Make Aheads
Energy-Survival Foods

Food, and plenty of it, is the most important item to pack for an outing. If it is good, the mood of the campers will be up. Unimaginative, unpalatable food can make the whole trip an unhappy experience.

Energy-survival foods take time to prepare, but they are delicious and especially important on a wilderness trip.

DRIED FRUIT
FRUIT LOGS
Dried fruits . . . any or all: Apples, prunes, figs, apricots, peaches, pears, raisins, dates.
Nuts . . . your choice, kind and amount.
Dry cereal . . . Wheat Chex, Krumbles, Shredded Wheat (choose one).
Shredded coconut
Wheat germ
Brown sugar

Put all ingredients through the fine blade of a food grinder *three* times.

Shape and roll in crumbs made by putting oatmeal or sugar cookies in a blender with sugar and cinnamon. Or use crushed graham crackers.

Make each roll about as big as your thumb and three inches long.

Wrap individually in foil and store in a tightly sealed plastic bag.

Variation: Roll in a crushed Granola-type cereal.

DRY FRUIT MIX-UP
Put through a food grinder *three* times:

One pound each of the following: Pitted dates, pitted prunes, seedless raisins, shelled nuts. Shape into individual rolls, wrap in foil and store in freezer or refrigerator until used.

TRAIL BARS
Put through fine blade of food grinder:
½ lb. pitted dates
1 cup peeled, cored and sliced apples (or use dry ones)
1 cup seedless raisins
Combine and add to fruit:
2 cups crushed vanilla cookies
1½ cups chopped nuts
1 cup powdered sugar
1 cup granulated sugar
Add:
¾ cup honey
½ tsp. vanilla
Water if necessary

Knead and work with hands to mix well. Press into foil lined pan. Allow to "dry" for a few hours, then cut into bars after lifting from the pan by the edges of the foil. Roll in brown sugar and wrap individually in foil or plastic wrap. Store in refrigerator until ready to use.

QUICK ENERGY LOGS

¼ cup dry roasted cashews
1 cup walnuts
½ cup figs
½ cup pitted dates
½ cup raisins
¼ cup chopped dry apples
½ tsp. lemon juice
½ cup flaked coconut

Put nuts and fruits through the food grinder two times. Add lemon juice and mix.

Roll into small logs. Roll in coconut and let stand several hours to "dry".

Wrap individually in foil and store in refrigerator until ready to use.

DRIED FRUIT BARS

Apricots OR prunes, cut up to make one cup. Pour 3 tbls. melted margarine over chopped fruit.

Combine:
¾ cup flour
½ tsp. salt
1 tsp. baking powder
Add:
2 eggs, well beaten
1 cup brown sugar

Cream together well, then add the chopped fruit.

Line an 8" x 8" pan with foil and grease and flour it. Pour mixture into pan and spread evenly.

Bake at 325 degrees for 30-35 min.

Lift by edges of foil and cool on a rack before cutting into squares. Sprinkle with powdered sugar.

ENERGY BARS

OUTER SPACE STICKS
(Makes 2 doz.)
(Betty Warner — Santa Barbara, Calif.)

½ cup peanut butter, chunky or smooth
½ cup powdered milk
⅓ cup corn syrup or honey
1 envelope unflavored gelatin
1 tbls. wheat germ
Pinch of salt

Combine in order listed. Roll into individual logs and wrap in foil. No need to refrigerate.

GRANOLA GORP

1 pkg. (12 oz.) chocolate bits
1 pkg. (12 oz.) butterscotch bits
¼ cup of each of the following:
Honey
Chopped dates
Raisins
Dried apple
Shredded coconut
Cashews
Walnuts
Wheat germ
Quick cooking oatmeal
Granola cereal

Melt chips and honey in the top of a double boiler. Pour over rest of ingredients in a large bowl. Mix well.

Grease a large shallow pan, add mixture and spread evenly. Cool.

Break into chunks and put in plastic bags, securing the top.

KANDY BARS

2 tbls. margarine
2 cups miniature marshmallows
2 tbls. peanut butter
½ cup butterscotch bits
4 cups corn flakes

In a sauce pan, melt margarine and marshmallows, stirring often. Remove from heat. Add peanut butter, butterscotch bits, corn flakes. Mix until coated well. Press into a 8″ x 8″ foil-lined pan.

Chill in refrigerator. Lift from pan and cut into bars.

Variation: Use chocolate bits, raisins, dry cut-up fruit and coconut.

BEEF JERKY

Three to five pounds of lean beef will yield less than 1 pound of jerky.

Always use lean meat. Trim fat and gristle. Flank steak is a popular cut to use, but any lean beef is suitable.

Partially freeze 3-4 lbs. of meat (it is easier to slice). Cut into thin strips (¼″) about six inches long.

Soak overnight in the refrigerator in one of the following marinades.

Place the strips in a large flat pan in rows. If more than one layer, make the second layer go the other way for easier handling later.

Pour the marinade over, moving the strips to allow it to touch all the meat. Cover with a plastic film, laying it on the meat. Be sure all the meat is covered by the marinade.

After about 12 hours, drain and pat dry on paper towels. Lay the strips over oven racks or barbeque grill, not touching, to dry. Store in a tightly covered jar or sealed plastic bags.

TO SUN DRY: Shallow-line a large box, or the barbeque, with foil, shiny side up. This will concentrate the heat and catch any dropped meat. Cover with cheesecloth, fastened securely with clothespins. Take the jerky in at night so the meat does not absorb moisture from the air.

TO OVEN DRY: Temperature from the pilot light is sufficient in a gas stove. Set an electric oven at the lowest temperature and prop the door open. Remember, YOU ARE NOT COOKING THE MEAT, ONLY DRYING IT!

MARINADES

Combine:
1 tbls. salt
1 tsp. onion powder
1 tsp. garlic powder
½ tsp. pepper
⅓ cup Worcestershire sauce
¼ cup soy sauce

Combine:
½ onion, diced fine
¼ tsp. thyme
2 bay leaves
2 tbls. salt
2 cloves crushed garlic
½ tsp. pepper
2 whole cloves
½ cup vinegar
1 cup red wine
¼ cup Worcestershire sauce
¼ cup soy sauce

Combine:
⅔ tsp. garlic powder
⅔ tsp. pepper
2 tsp. onion powder
½ cup Worcestershire sauce
½ cup soy sauce

BEEF JERKY WITHOUT MARINADE

Prepare the meat as before by trimming away all fat and slicing thin.
Combine: ¼ cup salt to a gallon of water and heat to a simmer.
Dip meat strips in the hot brine until the meat is no longer red.
Drain well. Mix salt and coarse ground pepper and coat the meat well on
both sides.
Dry in sun or oven.

Chef's secrets:
• *Sprinkle meat well with a mixture of salt and seasoning (basil, oregano etc.). Pound seasonings into strips. Dry.*
• *If you want to use dry meat in a one-pot meal, simple dry the strips with no seasonings. The meat stays chewy after cooking.*

JERKY
(Nevi Otten — Torrance, Calif.)

Marinade:
2 bay leaves
¼ cup soy sauce
⅛ cup Worcestershire sauce
½ tsp. pepper
1 cup wine
½ tsp. onion salt
½ tsp. garlic salt
4 whole cloves
¼ cup vinegar
1½ tbls. salt
1 tsp. seasoned salt
1 tsp. Accent
2 tbls. minced onion
2 tbls. brown sugar

Combine all ingredients and add enough water to make 5 cups total.
Heat marinade just long enough to dissolve ingredients. When cool,
pour over layers of flank steak cut ¼" thick. Marinate overnight or about 12
hours.
Roll strips of steak with a rolling pin between paper towels. Lay on oven
racks for about two days until dried.

UP-TO-DATE PEMMICAN

Cut all the fat from lean beef and cut into thin strips. Dry in the sun or
oven until the meat breaks or crumbles.
Grind dry meat to a powder in an electric blender. For 8 oz. . . .
Add: 8 oz. dried fruit; 8 oz. nuts, chopped
Heat 2 tsp. honey with 4 tbls. peanut butter and stir into mixture. Put mix
in a tightly sealed plastic bag or a tight container. It will keep indefinitely in
a cool dry place.

PARCHED CORN
(Dick and Norma Thomas — Encino, Calif.)
Spread a bag of frozen whole kernel corn on a shallow pan. Bake at 250 degrees until dry, but not dark . . . about three hours. Stir occasionally. Cool and store in airtight container to use in soups, stews, etc.

To use for a trail snack, sprinkle the frozen corn with salt before drying.

SUN DRIED FRESH CORN
Drop cobs of husked corn into a large pot of boiling salted water.

When water returns to a boil, cook about 5 minutes, or until the milk in the kernels is set.

Lift from water and cool. Slice kernels from cob.

Spread cut corn in a shallow pan. Cover with a single thickness of cheesecloth. Place in hot sun 6-8 hours until dry to the touch.

Do not leave overnight. If it is not dry, return to the sun the next day. Or, place in low temperature oven to finish drying.

Store at room temperature in clean, covered container.

Chef's secret: To use parched corn, rinse the kernels clean in hot water and soak in a hot liquid such as water or broth for 5-6 hours. To serve as a vegetable, cover pan (without draining), bring to a boil and simmer about 45 min.

DRIED CORN CHOWDER
In a large saucepan, sauté: 4 slices of bacon, cut up, with 1 medium onion, finely chopped. Remove from pan and save.

Combine ¾ cup dried, rinsed corn and 1 can (14 oz.) chicken or beef broth (or use bouillon). Bring to a boil, cover and set aside for two hours to soak. Reheat and simmer 45 min. Add bacon and onion.

1 large can evaporated milk and 2 cups water, salt and pepper. Heat thoroughly, but do not boil.

FRUIT LEATHERS
You will need a level surface — a card table is ideal — and a roll of clear plastic film. Stretch plastic strips across the table surface overlapping edges and fasten with cellophane tape or masking tape. Place the table in full HOT sun. After the puree (below) is poured onto the sheets to dry, cover with a single layer of cheesecloth elevated by stretching over large jugs (cider or vinegar containers work well) at each corner, and fasten around the table legs with clothespins. Get some help when covering. The cheesecloth is light and enjoys a "dip" in the puree.

Fruit must be fully ripe. Wash and trim blemishes. Add sugar and heat as directed below. Remove and whirl in a blender or force through a food mill or wire strainer. Cool to lukewarm. Pour puree onto the plastic film and spread to ¼ inch thick with a spatula.

APRICOTS: Peel, remove pits, quarter, measure. Add one cup of sugar to 5 pints. Mash while heating to just below boiling point.

BERRIES: Strawberries; use ½ cup sugar for 5 pints. Bring just to full boil. Raspberries; use 1 cup sugar for five pints. Boil and stir until liquid is syrupy. Blackberries; use 1½ cups sugar for 5 pints. Boil until syrupy.

PEACHES: Peel and slice. Use one cup sugar for 5 pints. Mash while heating to just about boiling. If liquid is thin, boil until syrupy.

NECTARINES: DO NOT PEEL. Slice. Use 1 cup sugar for 5 pints.

PLUMS: Choose those with firm flesh. Slice. Use 1½ cups sugar for 5 pints. Mash while heating. If liquid is thin, boil until syrupy.

Drying may take as long as 24 hours, depending on the heat of the sun. Do not leave out overnight to avoid collecting moisture. It is dry when the whole sheet of fruit can be pulled away from the plastic.

To store: Roll up the sheets of fruit still on the plastic film. Place in a plastic bag and seal tightly. It will keep at room temperature about a month, four months in a refrigerator, a year if frozen.

In humid situations you may finish drying your fruit leather in a 150 degree oven with the door ajar. A gas stove pilot light should provide sufficient heat.

DRIED FRUITS

APPLE SLICES: Peel, core and thin-slice apples. Place on paper towels on cookie sheets and place in a WARM oven (150 degrees) until dry. Leave the door ajar. DO NOT BAKE. Store in paper bags in a warm dry place. When soaked in water, the slices will return to their original size and tenderness. Use them to make applesauce, baked goods or "as is" for a trail snack.

When cooking dried fruit, add a few drops of molasses to the water. Or, try frying fresh or rehydrated apple slices or canned drained slices in margarine and molasses for something different.

CRANBERRIES: Place washed and sorted fresh berries on a paper towel-lined shallow pan in the oven. The pilot light is enough on a gas oven; use the lowest setting with the door ajar on an electric oven. Dry until the berries can be pulverized in a blender. Store in air tight container.

To use: soak in water, boil for a few minutes, add sugar to taste. Use as a sauce, add dry to cake mixes, instant puddings, pancake mix, other desserts, cooked fruit or drink powders.

CANDIED CRANBERRIES: Wash 2 cups of fresh berries and spread an even layer on a shallow baking pan. Sprinkle with 1 cup sugar. Cover tightly with a lid or foil and bake at 350 degrees for one hour. Stir occasionally by shaking the pan vigorously, but leave the cover tight.

CANDIED CITRUS PEEL: ORANGE . . . Peel 4 large navel oranges and cut the rind into pieces 1/4" wide. Cover with cold water and heat to boiling. Boil for five minutes. Drain. Cover with cold water and heat to boiling again for 5 min. and drain. In the third water add 1 cup of sugar to each cup of cooked rind. Boil until the liquid becomes a thick syrup. Drain and roll in granulated sugar. Place on waxed paper to dry.

GRAPEFRUIT . . . Peel 1 large grapefruit and boil in four changes of water. In the fifth water, add 1 cup sugar and proceed as for orange rind.

PE-CO CANDY
(No Cooking)

Combine 1 cup peanut butter with 2 cups dry milk.

Add about 1/2 cup honey, a little at a time, until mixture sticks together well. Shape into small balls, roll in powdered sugar or fine cookie crumbs. Coconut flakes, chopped nuts or wheat germ also can be used.

Place on waxed paper to dry and get firm.

CHAPTER TWELVE

Foiled Cookery

Fire starters are important. However, the commercial liquid kind is not needed if you remember the following:
- The seed fluff from cattails or fire weed make good tinder.
- Cedar pencil shavings catch fire readily.
- Charcoal placed in cardboard egg cartons and tied tight, can be dipped in melted paraffin to make "sure fire" starters. For a small fire, cut the carton in half.
- Fuzz sticks, pitch knots and dry dead twigs from beneath evergreen trees all have proven their worth.
- Dry corn cobs, dipped in melted paraffin, also are useful.
- A half gallon milk carton full of charcoal briquettes is enough to cook one meal. Simply light the carton.

NEVER line a fire pit or circle an open fire with rocks taken from a wet area such as a stream or lake. Porous rocks absorb enough water to produce steam and explode violently when they get hot.

To foil cook, dig a shallow trench and line it with small smooth *dry* stones. Cover the stones with glowing coals and let set for 15 min. Add the foil wrapped food and cover with more coals. Remember to foil wrap with the shiny side inside so heat will not be reflected away.

Smoking flames do not cook efficiently. Wait until glowing coals can be shoveled out of the fire. Cooking will be much cleaner and quicker.

It is possible for a plastic bag to seal into a "balloon" when thrown on the fire. It will explode violently spraying melted plastic. This can result in a severe burn.

HOBO DINNER

For each serving, place 2 tbls. catsup on the center of each piece of doubled heavy foil. Cover with 1 ground beef patty, top with a slice of onion, salt and pepper. Add a handful of cubed raw potatoes and carrots. Twist top to seal. Cook over coals about 30 min.

Variations:

Cubed lamb, canned lima beans, canned small onions, and sliced fresh or canned mushrooms.

Slices of ham, pineapple, canned whole sweet potatoes, canned green beans.

Fresh caught and cleaned trout, bacon, sliced onion, cubed potatoes.

WIENERS IN FOIL

Place wieners in double heavy foil and spread with one or more of the following: mustard fine chopped onion, cheese strips, pickle relish. Wrap tightly and cook over coals for 10 min. turning once.

SAUCED DOGS
(Serves 3-4)

At home, grind together:
½ lb. hot dogs
¼ cup mild cheddar cheese
Add:
1 hard boiled egg, chopped
2 tbls. chili sauce
1 tbls. pickle relish
½ tsp. mustard
½ tsp. garlic salt
At camp: Spread this mixture on bu.is. Wrap in double heavy foil. Place on coals to heat for about 10 min.

WIENIE BEANS

For each serving, place in a double heavy foil square:
2 wieners, split
Spread with barbeque sauce
Spoon Boston baked beans over wieners and sauce.

Wrap tightly to heat on the coals. Toast split and buttered wiener buns in a hot frying pan. Top with contents of the foil packet.

Variations: Spread wieners with 1 tsp. pickle relish and top with 2 table-spoons of chili beans. Spread toasted buns with prepared mustard. Top hot contents of packet with shredded cheese.

BEANS 'N DOGS
(Serves 4)

8 wiener buns
8 wieners
1 can (15 oz.) chili and beans
1 cup crushed corn chips
Prepared mustard
Spread buns with prepared mustard. Slit wieners lengthwise almost through and place one on each bun. Combine chili beans and corn chips and spoon over each wiener. Close bun and wrap in doubled heavy foil. Place in campfire coals 10-15 min.

PEPPERONI BUNS
(Serves 4)
4 hamburger buns, split
1 jar (5 oz.) process cheese spread
1 pkg. (4 oz.) sliced pepperoni
Spread buns with cheese. Arrange pepperoni on bun bottoms and cover with the tops. Wrap in double heavy foil and place on the coals to heat about 10 min.

BEAN BOATS
(Serves 6)
6 hamburger buns
¼ lb. thin sliced dry salami
1 tbls. dry onion flakes
1 can (1 lb.) barbeque beans
6 slices processed cheese
Split buns and arrange slices of salami on top of bottom half. Combine onion and beans and spread over salami. Top with cheese and bun top. Wrap in double heavy foil. Heat in coals 15-20 min.

HOT CHICKEN SANDWICHES
(Serves 3-4)
1 can boned chicken
1 cup chopped celery
¼ cup sliced ripe olives
¼ cup shredded Jack cheese
¼ cup mayonnaise
1 tsp. dry onion flakes
Combine ingredients and spread on hamburger buns. Wrap in double heavy foil and heat over coals 15-20 min.

HAM'N GREEN BEAN BAKE
(Serves 3-4)
Combine:
1⅓ cups minute rice
1 cup diced ham or Spam
1 can (8 oz.) drained green beans
⅓ cup mayonnaise
2 tsp. dry onion flakes
Stir in 1⅓ cups hot chicken bouillon or chicken soup. Sprinkle with grated Parmesan cheese. Shape a triple thickness of heavy foil into a bowl. Add mixture and seal. Leave over hot coals for ½ hour.

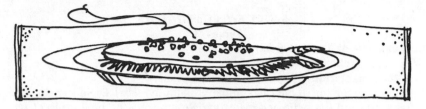

TROUT 'N APPLE
(Serves 4-5)
8 small to medium trout, cleaned
3 cooking apples, peeled, cored, and chopped fine
Cinnamon to taste

Place the cleaned fish on double heavy foil. Top with the chopped apples and a dash or two of cinnamon. Wrap the foil to seal securely, place on coals and add a cover of coals. Leave for 30-45 min. depending on size of fish.

FOIL BAKED FISH

Lay out a strip of heavy doubled foil and butter generously. Lay out a filleted fish on the foil. Sprinkle with salt and pepper. Cover with onion rings, lemon slices, tomato slices. Seal tightly with foil and place on a grill over the coals. When steam balloons the foil, prick it once. A large filleted fish is ready to eat in 20-30 min.

Chef's secret: If you use a variety of fish that tends to be dry, add a can of tomato sauce.

BAKED PERCH

Dig a shallow trench and line with small flat rocks. Heat with coals from the campfire while you prepare the fish.

For each fish: Use salad oil or margarine to grease a double thickness of foil. Salt and pepper the outside and cavity of the fish. Lay thin slices of lemon (if available) in the body cavity. Wrap tightly, sealing well. Place the fish on top of the coals, add more coals to cover. Fish will be ready in about 45 min.

VEGETABLES ON THE COALS: Foil wrapped potatoes will take about 45 min. to an hour depending on size.

Sweet potatoes, yams, large onions wrapped in foil take between 45 min. to an hour.

Foil wrapped corn on the cob takes 25-45 min. depending on maturity.

FOILED CARROTS
(Serves 2)

Scrape 2 carrots clean, trim ends. Place in double heavy foil. Add: 2 tbls. water, salt and pepper, dry celery and parsley flakes, pat of margarine. Seal tightly in the foil and place on the coals for 20-25 min.

SWEET SWEET POTATOES
(Serves 3-4)
1 can (18 oz.) sweet potatoes
¼ cup maple flavored syrup
1 tbls. margarine
Remove the top of the can completely. Strip off label. Drain some of the juice and add the syrup and margarine. Return some of the juice to cover the sweet potatoes. Cover the can top with foil. Place on a grill or near the coals and heat until bubbly, about 20 min.

BAKED SLICED POTATOES
Scrub and cut potatoes into thick slices. Use one potato per person. Do not peel the potatoes. Place each one on heavy double foil. Add 1 tbls. margarine. Sprinkle with garlic and onion salt and pepper. Seal foil tightly and cook on grill, turning often. Leave for 1 hr.

SCALLOPED TOMATOES 'N CHEESE
(Serves 3-4)
Arrange in layers in a double heavy foil "bowl":
1 can (1 lb. 12 oz.) tomatoes
Salt, pepper, 1 tsp. sugar
1½ cups soft bread crumbs
¼ cup melted margarine
1 cup grated American cheese
Seal and bake in the coals for 15-20 min.

FOILED ONIONS
(1 onion for 2 persons)
Peel one large onion and cut in half. Place a pat of margarine on the cut side and sprinkle with salt and pepper. Top with a half strip of bacon on each half onion. Wrap each in double heavy foil squares and seal tightly. Bake in coals 35 min. to 45 min.

FOILED CORN
(Serves 4)

4 ears of corn
Soft margarine
Onion salt and pepper

Remove husks, all but the last layer, and remove silk. With remaining husks pulled back, spread corn with margarine and sprinkle with onion salt and pepper. Replace the husks and wrap tightly with heavy foil, sealing well. Place on hot coals for 15 min. Turn and leave for 15-20 min. more.

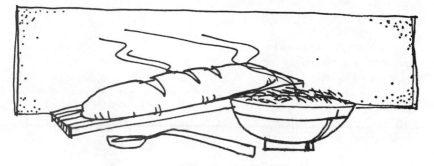

RICE ON THE COALS
(Serves 4)

Place two sheets of foil (14" square) on top of each other in a cooking pot. Press to form a pouch. Add:

1½ cups minute rice
1½ cups water
½ tsp. salt, dash of pepper
4 tsp. instant bouillon
1 tbls. margarine

Seal tightly, remove from pot and place on coals for about 15 min.

Variations: Add dry onion flakes, or 1 tsp. prepared mustard, or 1 tsp. Worcestershire sauce.

HERBED FRENCH BREAD
(Serves 6-8)

At home combine:

¼ lb. margarine
¼ tsp. basil
¼ tsp. marjoram
¼ tsp. dry parsley flakes
¼ tsp. Worcestershire sauce

Slice loaf of French bread on the diagonal and place in a plastic bag. At camp: Spread bread slices with herbed margarine. Wrap in heavy foil and heat on the coals.

CHEESE LOAF
(Serves 6-8)

1 loaf French bread (or use individual loaves)
⅓ cup margarine combined with 1 jar (5 oz.) sharp spreading cheese.

Cut the loaf in half lengthwise, spread cheese mixture between slices and put back together. Cut in diagonal slices, wrap in heavy foil and heat over coals.

MUFFIN BREAD
(Lois Pitzer — Long Beach, Calif.)

You will need:
2 - 9" foil pie pans
1 pkg. muffin mix
Margarine, jam or honey
Spring-type clothespins

Lightly grease foil pans. Prepare muffin mix according to directions and pour into one pan. Cover with the second pan, inverted. Secure rims together with the clothespins. Place on a grill over *low* coals, and bake 15 min. on each side, rotating pan occasionally for even baking. Cut into wedges and serve with margarine and jam or honey.

DESSERTS

BAKED BANANAS
(Barbara Reznick — Palos Verdes, Calif.)

Do not peel the bananas, but cut off the end tips to keep them from breaking the foil. Slit through the skin on the inside curve and fill with:
Raisins and cinnamon sugar
Chocolate or butterscotch chips
M and M's
Brown sugar
Chocolate candy bar squares and wheat germ
Cut up marshmallows

Place on foil and wrap tightly. Heat over coals 10-15 min.

FOILED DESSERTS
On a square of heavy duty double foil place:
1 slice of buttered white bread, buttered side down.
Canned fruit (apple slices, pineapple, peaches, etc.)
Jam or jelly
Sprinkle of cinnamon or nutmeg.
Seal tightly and heat over coals for 15 min.

APPLE RINGS
For each serving place 3-4 thick apple slices in heavy double foil. Sprinkle with brown sugar and grated orange peel. Dot with margarine and seal. Cook over low coals 10-15 min.

BAKED APPLES
For each serving place a cored apple on heavy doubled foil.
In the center put:
Raisins
Chopped nuts
Sugar, brown and white
Cinnamon
Dot of margarine
Wrap tightly and twist the top. Bake 30-45 min. depending on size.

FOILED APPLES
(Serves 4)
4 apples, peeled and cored
4 tbls. crushed pineapple
Cinnamon sugar
Raisins (optional)
Place each apple on a doubled square of heavy foil. Fill apple centers with crushed pineapple (and raisins). Sprinkle generously with cinnamon sugar. Fold foil around each apple and seal tightly. Place in glowing coals and bake 20-40 min. depending on size.

CHAPTER THIRTEEN

Nature's Bounty

To be a real One-Burner Gourmet you should be able to identify several wild plants to add to your provisions. Get a well-illustrated book and read the text thoroughly. Euell Gibbons or Bradford Angier can give you enough clues to make your identification positive.

What is acceptable food for some persons could cause allergic reactions to others, so try new wild foods sparingly at first. *Eat Only What You Can Positively Identify.* Most animals and birds eat plants which human digestive systems cannot accept, so *do not* use them as a guide.

There is no need to go on an extensive wilderness outing to acquaint yourself with wild edibles. A great variety of wild foods grow profusely around vacant buildings and old farms, along the edges of fields, fences and walls, across open hillsides, in marshes, ponds, lakes and streams, in burned-over areas, along country roads and in your own favorite flower bed. *One word of caution:* If you use pesticides in your yard, don't eat any edible weeds which might appear. Also, be absolutely certain that wild foods you find elsewhere have not been contaminated by bug sprays or weed killers. Stay away from large cultivated agricultural areas.

Books often are too bulky to carry on a long wilderness trip. Look for pamphlets in local museums or the college extension service.

Two pamphlets that I particularly like (probably because they deal with an area I am familiar with) are:

"Guide To Common Edible Plants Of British Columbia"
    by A. F. Szczawinski and G. A. Hardy
British Columbia Provincial Museaum, Victoria, Canada, and "Wild, Edible and Poisonous Plants Of Alaska"
    Division of Statewide Services
    Cooperative Extension Service
    University of Alaska
    College, Alaska

There also is a series of booklets from Life Support Technology, Inc., Manning, Oregon 97125 that include titles on edible and poisonous plants.

Pamphlets can include only a few of the edible plants in a given area, so you need the more comprehensive books for better information.

WILD WATERCRESS looks just like that found in the supermarket. Some streams can become almost choked with it at low water. It needs fresh, moving, cold water to grow well. We have found watercress in the bottom of the Grand Canyon, along the California coast near Morro Bay, and at a roadside rest in southeastern Washington State.

Its pungent taste makes an ordinary bologna sandwich an epicurean delight. To gather watercress, pinch off just the top couple of inches, and do not disturb the rest of the plant. Wash (yes, wash!) in lots of clean water to remove attached water bugs and mosquito larvae. If you are still squeamish, soak it in heavily salted cold water for 10-15 minutes, making sure it is completely immersed.

Snip into green salads, lay on sandwiches, or use as a cooked vegetable, simmering in a small amount of salted water. It also is good cooked with other milder greens.

EGG N' WATERCRESS SALAD
(Serves 4)
Combine:
¼ tsp. salt
1 tbls. lemon juice (fresh or bottled)
1 small can shoestring beets, drained
4 hard-cooked eggs, chopped

Wash watercress, drain and place on individual plates. Spoon egg and beet combination over cress.

CRESS N' COTTAGE CHEESE

Chop several sprigs of watercress with scissors and add to a carton of cottage cheese.

Serve on a bed of watercress and lettuce with tomato wedges and salad dressing.

Wilderness Way: Reconstitute freeze-dried cottage cheese, add chopped cress and use drained canned tomatoes.

WILD MUSTARD is a relative of cabbages and radishes. Unless you gather mustard leaves from very young plants, the greens are bitter and nasty tasting. Use only the finely toothed lower leaves that are deeply indented. The young plant goes well with fish and meat.

Blossoms of wild mustard can be cooked into a broccoli type dish. They also add a nice fresh garnish for cooked vegetables. Decorate with the whole bright yellow flower. It is nippy, so be careful.

Gather a cup full of wild mustard seeds. Spread out on a piece of foil to dry in the sun, stirring occasionally. Store in a tightly closed bottle and use sprinkled in salads, in barbeque sauces, or as an addition to pickle making. Prepare your own table mustard by grinding the seeds between two smooth stones or in the food chopper. Add water and vinegar to make a paste.

DANDELIONS . . . Maybe you would like to have your first wild food experience with those detested dandelions in your yard . . . kind of a way of getting even. Perhaps you will enjoy eating them so much that the once obnoxious weed will become a cultivated, favorite flower.

Tender young dandelion greens can be cooked by simmering in a small amount of salted water, or try a tasty recipe:

Steam washed leaves for 5 min. over low heat.
Add:
1 tbls. margarine
1 tbls. flour
Dash or two of salt
Enough hot water to make a thick sauce
Add sour cream to taste
Stop right there and eat.

DANDY GREENS
Wash leaves and discard wilted or brown leaves. Barely cover the pot bottom with lightly salted water.

Simmer leaves, covered, 5-10 min. or until just tender.

Serve with butter, salt and pepper or French dressing or vinegar.

DANDELION ROOT
Scrape and boil like carrots. Serve with margarine, salt and pepper.

Dry slowly in the oven or on foil in the sun until they snap easily. Pulverize and add to soups or stews or use for a coffee extender.

DANDY BLOSSOMS
Wash full open blossoms and shake the water from them. Dip in seasoned scrambled egg batter and fry in margarine.

OR: cut the washed blossoms into quarters and add to scrambled eggs for a vitamin treat. Unopened blossoms can also be used.

GREENS will be best when they first appear as juicy new shoots. Older leaves are usually bitter and unpalatable. This does not mean that new "weeds" can't be enjoyed in August. We found *chickweed* in Alberta and *sorrel* on Vancouver Island that couldn't have been better.

YELLOW OXALIS, or sour grass, grows in cultivated gardens, usually as a pretty border, but it also has escaped to grow wild. All parts of the plant are good to eat. The yellow flowers, placed whole in a green salad, make an unusual addition.

Both red and white CLOVER are valuable sources of food. The young leaves and flowers are good raw, or cooked in a small amount of salted water. The dried blossoms can be rubbed between the hands into small particles and brewed for tea. Seeds and dried blossoms can be added to bread doughs for valuable nutrition.

MINER'S LETTUCE and SHEEP SORREL both have distinctive leaf characteristics. Miner's lettuce has leaves that grow together part way up some of the stems to form a "saucer" through which the stem continues occasionally several times to terminate in a loose bunch of white or pinkish edible flowers. Base leaves are triangular or kidney shaped. The leaves and blossoms can be simmered in a small amount of salted water until wilted, or made into a succulent salad, especially when mixed with SHEEP SORREL.

Sheep Sorrel has leaves which are lobed at the base like an arrow, and contain a sour juice. The leaves are refreshing when used raw and also can be used as a seasoning for fresh caught fish in place of lemon juice.

WATERCRESS also can be added to your combination salad.

SORREL 'N EGGS
(Serves 3)

Wash and sort a 4 quart container of sorrel leaves.

Cut up and cook in a small amount of salted water in a covered frying pan for 2-3 min.

Drain if necessary and gently stir in margarine, salt and pepper to coat the leaves.

Level and make a hollow with the back of a spoon to make a cup for 3 eggs.

Sprinkle each egg with sharp cheese or grated parmesan cheese.

Cover tightly and cook over *low* heat until eggs are set.

Any greens can be used for this recipe. Try miner's lettuce or spinach.

ASPARAGUS: Wild asparagus is found wherever it has escaped from cultivation. It is edible only in the spring. Look for dead brown stalks from the year before. New tips appear in the midst of the old stalks. New tips can be added raw to that wild salad. To cook, cut below ground level, snap off the tough ends, tie in a bunch using twisted grass blades or a cord, and sit upright in the coffee pot in 1/2" of salted boiling water. Cover and steam NO LONGER than 10 min. Pour the cooking water over buttered toast or bread and lay the cooked stalks on top.

FIREWEED is a member of the willow family (note the leaf shape), and is one of the first plants to invade a burned area. It likes full sun and well-drained soil. It can be found from sea level to timberline. The blossoms are four-petaled, rose-colored and appear in a spike-shaped cluster. Young shoots appear in March and April and look like small willow trees. They rise from the base of last year's dead stalks and grow to six feet.

Cook the young leaves and shoots as greens. They are bitter when eaten raw. The unopened flower buds also can be cooked. Sun or oven-dried leaves make an excellent hot tea.

JERUSALEM (GROUND) ARTICHOKE: Before the early settlers arrived, this wild sunflower was cultivated for its tubers by Indians. The stalk can grow 10' to 12' tall. The blossoms are 2" to 3" across and have a pale center that lacks any seeds to harvest.

When you see the plants in the summer, make a mental note of the exact spot. By the last of October (later if possible) after the plants have died, you can dig a delicious harvest of knobby tubers that resemble ginger root. When digging, start at least 2' away from the dead central stalk. You can easily fill a 5 gallon bucket if the plant is large.

The tubers are sold in Southern California markets. Choose firm ones to take home, but don't cook them all. Plant 2-3 as you would potatoes. You can have your own back yard harvest in the fall. Since they store best right in the ground, dig only as many as you can use at one time and fill in the hole until next time.

Jerusalem artichokes cook quicker than potatoes. They can be boiled, baked, added to stew, pot roast, or chicken, deep fried, hash fried and even substituted for pumpkin in a chiffon pie. To cook, scrub thoroughly with a stiff brush, but do not peel. Break off knobs to get all the dirt. Simmer in a small amount of salted water 5-10 min., depending on size. The remaining liquid will become gelatinous on cooling. Add it to soups and stews.

To eat them raw (my favorite way) remove the peeling with a sharp knife by scraping. Slice or dice to add to a salad. Drop tubers into a lemon or vinegar water solution to keep white for eating whole.

SAUTÉED JERUSALEM ARTICHOKES

Scrub thoroughly with a stiff brush and cut into thin slices.

In a heavy skillet melt 2 tbls. margarine and add slices. Sauté, stirring often. Sprinkle lightly with salt. When about half cooked, sprinkle with crumbled basil. Cook until crisp-tender. DO NOT OVERCOOK.

Variation: Sauté bacon, ham slices, Spam, sausages, etc., at the same time for a complete one-pot dish.

PRICKLY PEAR CACTUS: Members of the Opuntia family of cactus such as Prickly Pear and the Tunas, are a valuable food source. New leaf pads taste like green beans when de-spined, sliced and cooked, and are especially tasty when simmered with bacon and tomatoes.

Choose new, limber pads, cut from the plant at the base of the pad. If you hold the pad at the cut end you will avoid most of the spines. Cut the spines out with the tip of a sharp knife. Slice the pad diagonally into strips the size of whole green beans. A whole cactus pad is called a nopales; sliced or diced it is nopolitos.

FRENCH FRIED NOPOLITOS

Make a thick batter from pancake or biscuit mix. Add a little Worcestershire sauce. Pat the sliced cactus pad dry with paper towels, dip into batter, then fry in deep fat until browned, 3-5 min. on each side. Serve with catsup or chili salsa.

To boil: Sauté pieces of bacon or salt pork in a sauce pan. Add cactus and sauté quickly. Add a small amount of water to barely cover the pan to ¼". Salt and cover, simmer about 15 min. Drain and serve as a hot vegetable, or rinse several times to remove the gelatinous water and use the cooked cactus pieces in soups, chowders, salads or scrambled eggs.

NOPOLITO OMELET
(Serves 3-4)

5-6 slices bacon (or salt pork) diced
½ cup cooked, diced cactus pad (or use a small jar of nopolitos, drained. See Mexican section of food market).
1 small green pepper, diced
1 small onion, diced
1 medium solid tomato, cut up.

Fry bacon with green pepper, onion and tomato. Add nopolitos and simmer until all is tender.

Add 6 beaten eggs, salt and pepper to taste. Stir often until eggs are set. Serve in or with warmed tortillas.

CACTUS SCRAMBLE
(Serves 2-3)

4 eggs, lightly beaten
1 cup nopolitos (canned or fresh cooked)
½ cup shredded cabbage
1 tsp. minced dry onion
1 small can, or ½ cup fresh tomatoes, chopped
1 tbls. margarine
Chili salsa

Place margarine in a skillet, heat and add other ingredients, except eggs. Toss vegetables gently and blend. Heat through. Add beaten eggs and cook until they are done.

Serve topped with a tsp. of chili salsa on each portion.

Chef's secrets:
- *Use your tongue to feel for cactus spines "misplaced" in your fingers. Pull them with your teeth.*
- *The juice from cactus pads stops bleeding and is said to settle muddy water.*

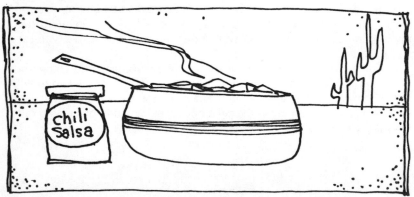

THE VERSATILE CATTAIL: Cattails can be a veritable super market unsurpassed for the variety of food and useful items derived from them.

The plant's long, tough leaves can be woven into matting, baskets and straps, and mixed with mud as a building material. Mature cattail fluff was used by Indians for padding of cradle boards and stuffing sleeping bags. It can be used as a filling for pillows, too. During the Second World War the cattail fluff was used for stuffing toys and life preservers, and for padding on tanks and airplanes. The current use of the plant is for woven rush seating and baskets.

One of its almost unknown features is its usefulness as food:

Roots: The tangled root system usually lies just a few inches below the soil. A square yard of cattail swamp can yield enough material for several pounds of flour.

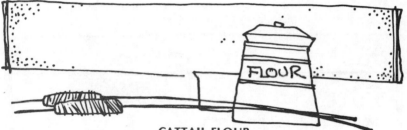

CATTAIL FLOUR

Dig the roots. Wash and peel, exposing the white core which is about 1/2" thick. Separate into fibers in a large container of cool water. Work the juice out of the fibers, remove and let the water settle. When the starch has settled to the bottom, pour off the water and replace with fresh cold water. Stir up the starch and repeat the settling. The "flour" will be a white, fine material. Use it wet for best results. Use half cattail flour with regular flour in breads, cookies and other baked products.

Root Buds: The bud-like sprouts, located on growing ends of the rootstock, have a sweet taste when peeled, boiled and served with butter or cooked with meat.

Shoots: Collect when about 2' high. Grab the inside leaves and give a sharp tug. The tender inside shoot should break loose from the roots. Peel off the leaves to expose the inside white section. This can be eaten raw or cooked with salt and butter added for flavor.

Pollen: In the spring when the spikes turn yellow with pollen, bend the heads over a bucket and rub the pollen off. Put it through a fine mesh sieve. The pollen powder is as fine as talcum. It can be used half and half with regular flour for pancakes, muffins or biscuits. The finished product has a golden color and a pleasant taste.

Green Bloom Spikes: Cut just before they break through the sheath that covers them. Husk like corn and boil a few minutes in salted water. Serve with melted butter (they tend to be dry). Eat as you would an ear of corn.

POND LILY: The roots of common yellow pond lilies can be cooked as a starchy vegetable. The ripe seeds may be roasted or ground into flour. Popped like corn, they are very nutritious and palatable.

POND LILY POP CORN

Pound the pods to loosen the seeds. Parch (heat and shake or stir in a frying pan) to separate the kernel from the shell. Winnow away the shell, then parch the kernels which will swell. Salt as you would popcorn.

THISTLE: Has alternate, toothed leaves and fuzzy flowers, both covered with sharp spines. The roots can be eaten raw or boiled. The stems also are edible when peeled. Cut the spiked leaves off the stalk before harvesting to avoid becoming a pin cushion.

The dry seed head makes good tinder for making a fire.

According to Indian lore, the most highly favored help for a stiff neck was a poultice of mashed thistle leaves.

WILD FLOWER BOUNTY

Be certain that the flowers are non-toxic. Questionable flowers can be checked out with the county agricultural agent or local botanical garden. Don't use any flowers that might have been sprayed.

WILD FLOWER SYRUP

Fill a glass jar with washed blossoms, not too firmly packed.

Cover with boiling water, put on a lid, and let stand 24 hrs. (Add more boiling water in about an hour if necessary to cover).

Open and strain the liquid, squeezing the flowers by hand until "dry". Discard blossoms.

To each half cup of extract, add 1 cup sugar and 1 tsp. lemon juice. Bring to a boil, pour into sterilized jar and cap. Keep in refrigerator if not to be used in a few days.

Chef's secrets:
- *Clover blossoms and seeds can be dried and used for making breads.*
- *Milkweed blossoms are rich in nectar and can be used as brown sugar.*
- *Yucca and Joshua Tree blossoms are rich in sugar, and the fat pulpy fruit is good to eat raw, roasted or dried for later use.*

WILD BERRIES
THERE ARE NO KNOWN VARIETIES OF
EDIBLE *WHITE* BERRIES

Wild blackberries come in several varieties. Tiny vine blackberries stay close to the ground and creep across the trail to trip you up and leave a bloody scratch across the back of your ankle. The evergreen blackberry, which grows along roadsides and fences in dense thickets, has deeply notched leaves and firm berries. The flatter-leafed Himalayan blackberry also has trailing stems growing into thickets and the fruit is more fragile.

Huckleberries can be large and blue, or smaller and red. Both are tart and refreshing. The bush is "picking high" with berries of the familiar smooth blueberry shape. They are of the Vaccinium family.

Raspberries, thimbleberries and salmonberries are all of the RUBUS family with red berries composed of many seeds. Salmonberries can grow in such dense thickets that you can't see more than a foot or two in any direction. You can also find bushes growing side by side with dark red berries and yellow-orange berries, each with a distinctive taste. They are all delicious when washed in cold mountain water and eaten on the spot.

Wild strawberries often are found with wild raspberries in the northern parts of Canada. Though tedious to pick, the flavor is outstanding.

Huckleberries need to be pulled off the shrub, but the other wild berries are ripe when they fall into your hand at a touch.

WILD BERRY JAM NO. 1
(Makes 1¼ cups)
Combine in a large kettle:
1 cup tart berries (mix different kinds as you wish)
⅔ cup sugar
1 tbls. lemon juice, fresh or bottled
1 whole cinnamon stick (optional)
Boil rapidly until thick as desired.

WILD BERRY JAM NO. 2
2 cups berries
1½ cups sugar
Wash and sort berries. Crush, then measure berries and juice. Bring to a boil, add sugar and cook rapidly, stirring frequently, until thick.

BERRY SYRUP

Combine:
2 cups berries
1 cup sugar
½ cup water
  Boil until berries are soft.

BERRY SAUCE

4 cups fresh berries
1 cup sugar
½ tsp. cinnamon
5 tbls. flour
1 tbls. margarine
  Crush berries in a large saucepan.
  Combine sugar, cinnamon and flour and add, stirring constantly. Boil until thickened.
  Add margarine and stir to melt and combine.

BERRY COOLER

  Crush fresh washed berries and add 7-Up (or substitute water and lemon juice).

WILD BERRY GOOP

2 cups fresh, cleaned berries
1 cup dry milk
  Crush the berries and mix thoroughly with the dry milk. Add honey to taste.
  Use for a topping on a Dutch oven cake.

At-Home Recipe . . .
WILD BERRY SYRUP

3 cups berries, washed and drained
¼ cup honey
  Whirl the berries in a blender until smooth. Leave the seeds for good nutrition.
  Add honey and mix well.
  Use immediately, or keep refrigerated.

HUCKLEBERRY PANCAKES

Wash and sort berries. Add to pancake batter, with a little extra sugar. The berries will "pop" like fresh cranberries when cooking.

Any wild berry can be added to pancake batter. Top with berry syrup or sauce.

BERRY BREAD
(10-12 biscuits)

2 cups biscuit mix
⅔ cup milk
1 cup fresh berries, washed and sorted
½ cup sugar
Margarine for frying

Combine biscuit mix, milk, berries and sugar. Spoon onto hot, greased skillet and flatten with a spatula. Fry until brown on one side, turn, brown other side.

Cook about 5 min. per side.

Chef's secret: A couple of yards of washed cheesecloth can be used for:
Covering wild leaves and flower petals left in the sun to dry for tea.
Squeezing rose hip pulp to separate from seeds and skin.
Straining seeds from cooked wild berries for jelly.
Making a container to hold foods and beverages in a cold stream. Double or triple the fabric. Tie to the nearest root, log, or rock.

WILD ROSE HIPS: (the seed pod of wild roses) Red rose hips are loaded with Vitamin C. Three hips have as much as an orange. They cling to the bushes throughout the winter and so are available when other wild food is covered with snow. They can be cut up into a salad, baked in cakes or bread or boiled into jam, jelly or syrup. Green hips are tasteless. Use only the mature red ones. Plain *dried* hips can be munched like raisins. They are rather tasteless raw, but the vitamin content could be very important on a long wilderness trip. To prepare them, cut off the bud end, cut in half, remove the seeds and eat as is, or dry in a frying pan over very low heat, stirring often. Don't over-do; they'll become too hard.

SYRUP NO. 1

Combine in a saucepan:
2 cups red rose hips, budded, washed and seeded
1 cup water
Boil, covered, 20 min. Add 1 cup sugar and boil 5 min.

SYRUP NO. 2

(Delicious on pancakes, ice cream or vanilla pudding.)
Snip the bud ends of rose hips, wash, place fruit in a large saucepan. Cover with water and boil rapidly until soft. Strain off the juice and save.

Return the pulp to the kettle, add more water to cover and make a second extraction. For every 2 cups of juice, add 1 cup sugar and 1 tbls. lemon juice.

Boil until thickened.

ROSE PETALS: The flowers from wild roses make a delicious fragrant tea. Snip off the bitter green or white base of the petal. Dark red roses have the strongest flavor; light pinks have the most delicate flavor.

Use 1 heaping teaspoon of dried petals or 2 heaping teaspoons of fresh.

Add 1 cup of boiling water. Steep 5 min. Add honey or sugar to bring out the fragrance.

ROSE PETAL SANDWICHES: Add wild rose petals (with bitter base removed) to your peanut butter sandwich for a taste experience.

Chef's secrets:
• *The seeds from rose hips can be ground and added to flour, and are reported to be rich in Vitamin E.*
• *Rose leaves can be dried and used to make tea.*

FISH: Cooking methods are varied according to the fatness of the species. Chunky fish such as trout, salmon and whitefish bake well in a reflector oven, Dutch oven or foil. The Indians of northwestern Washington state fasten large salmon, split, on a heavy plank with wire mesh. The plank is set upright with a driftwood fire placed between it and the beach. The onshore breeze forces the heat from the fire toward the fish, and the fish bastes in its own fat.

Leaner catches such as pike, perch, pickerel and grayling lend themselves to poaching or steaming, because the flesh is more firm.

All fish can be fried. The most important thing to remember is not to overcook it. When it flakes, it is done. You can also test as you would a cake, by piercing with a toothpick.

If catfish can be kept alive until all the food has been digested (12-14 hrs.) the flesh is said to be sweeter.

The strong flavor of pickerel and pike can be improved if the cleaned fish is simmered in salted water to which 3 tbls. of vinegar or lemon juice has been added.

Chunks of filleted and skinned fish can be dropped into boiling salted water. Add a slice of onion and simmer for a few minutes.

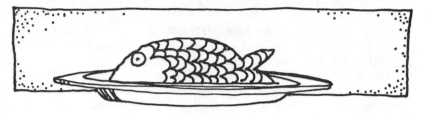

CLAY-BAKED FISH

Any fresh caught fish may be used, but neither clean nor scale it.

Pack the fish in a blanket of fine sticky clay about an inch thick, completely covering the whole fish. Allow the clay to dry near the campfire for a few minutes.

Bury the fish in hot coals and ashes, baking until the clay is hard. Allow about 15 min. per pound.

When ready, rake it from the fire, break open with a rock or stout stick.

The cooked fish splits easily and the bones can be lifted out. The intestines will have shrunk into a firm ball. The scales stick to the clay along with the fins and tail.

Sprinkle with salt and lemon juice.

Variation: Split and clean the fish. Fill the cavity with lemon slices, then wrap in the clay blanket.

Chef's secret: Various coatings can be used to crisp-fry pan sized fish. Try biscuit mix, chicken coating mix, pancake mix, cornflake crumbs, fine seasoned bread crumbs.

PAN-FRIED TROUT

Wipe fish dry. Dip in canned milk, then roll in a mixture of half flour and half cornmeal, well seasoned with salt and pepper.

Use enough oil to keep them from sticking. When oil is hot, gently lay the trout in the pan. Fry quickly until crisp and brown. Turn with a wide spatula or tongs to the other side. Don't let the oil burn.

TROUT AND VEGETABLES
(Serves 2)

Thin slice 1 large onion, 2 stalks celery and 2 small carrots.

Melt 1/4 cup margarine in a saucepan. Stir in 1/4 tsp. each salt and thyme.

Dip 2 cleaned trout into batter mixture turning to coat both sides; remove and set aside. Stir vegetables into the butter mixture and lay the fish on top. Cover and cook over low heat about 15 min. or until fish is flaky.

FISH CHOWDER
Sauté bacon cut into small pieces with thin sliced onion.
Add water and diced potatoes, salt and pepper. Simmer until almost done.
Add cleaned fish cut into pieces, and cook until flaky.
Stir in some powdered milk and a spoonful of margarine.

POACHED FISH
Fill a large frying pan 1½" deep with water or bouillon broth.
Add a thin sliced onion, carrot, celery stalk.
Add salt and pepper and a pinch of basil.
When liquid is simmering, add small cleaned trout and cook gently, uncovered until fish flakes when poked with a sharp twig or toothpick.

FISH CAKES
Combine cooked, de-boned fish, prepared mashed potatoes, dry onion flakes, little flour, 1 egg, beaten. Shape into patties and fry, browning both sides.

SMOKED FISH
Clean and fillet fish. Rub well with salt and pepper and bacon fat.
Lay on a grate over a smoldering fire. Dry birch or aspen work well.
Baste occasionally with bacon fat if pike or perch or non-fat fish. Trout are fat enough.
Turn occasionally. Bank the coals with ashes so they won't flame. Move the grate a little higher and leave for the night.

CRAWFISH
(Crayfish)
Look for crawfish under rocks in a stream, or dangle a piece of meat in the hole behind a rock or below a riffle. When the crawfish grabs the meat, lead him to a net.
Bring a kettle of salted water (½ cup salt to a gallon of water) to a fast boil. Add the crawfish and simmer until they turn deep red.
After shucking, dip the tails in melted lemon-butter and enjoy.

CLAM FRITTERS
2 cups biscuit mix
⅔ cup milk
1 egg
2 cups minced, drained clams
Combine biscuit mix, milk and egg. Add drained clams.
Spoon onto hot, well-greased griddle and frv like pancakes.

FRIED FROG LEGS
(Serves 3-4)
8 large frog legs
Salt and pepper, egg and bread crumbs
Frying fat
Use only the hind legs. Cut from the body, wash thoroughly, turn back the skin like a glove and peel off.

Pat legs dry with paper towels. Roll in seasoned bread crumbs, then in beaten egg, and again in crumbs.

Fry until golden brown, about 3 minutes on each side. Drain on paper towels.

SALT WATER CLAMS: To rid clams of sand, cover them with clean ocean water to which you have added one cup of corn meal. Let stand 3-4 hours and the clams will cleanse themselves.

Be sure the clams close when you handle them. Discard any that remain open. Scrub the shells with a vegetable brush and rinse well.

STEAMED CLAMS
(Use the small varieties)
Place the cleaned clams over a trivet in a deep kettle with about 1" of water. Cover. Bring to a boil and steam the clams until the shells open, 10-15 min. Dig the meat out with a fork, dip it in melted butter with a few drops of lemon juice added. Plan about 2 dozen clams per serving.

SEAFOOD BUTTERS
To ½ cup butter (1 cube) add:
3 tbls. lemon juice
¼ cup ground almonds and 1 tsp. lemon juice
Melt butter, allow salt to settle, pour off oil into small cups.
Brown butter and add ⅓ tsp. Worcestershire sauce with 3 tbls. lemon juice.
Add 1 tsp. salt, ¼ tsp. pepper, 5 tbls. minced parsley, 2 tbls. lemon juice.
3-4 tbls. finely chopped watercress.

CLAM SCRAMBLE
(Serves 2-3)
3 slices bacon, cut up
½ cup minced clams, drained
6 eggs
3 tbls. milk
Fry bacon until almost crisp. Drain fat and reserve 2 tbls. Reduce heat. Beat eggs and milk together. Add clams.

Cook and stir until eggs are set.

CLAM PUFFS

2 cups ground clams (put through food chopper)
1¾ cups flour
3 tsp. baking powder
½ tsp. salt, dash of pepper
½ cup milk
2 tbls. melted margarine
1 egg, slightly beaten

Combine the dry ingredients. Add margarine, milk and egg.

Add clams and mix gently. Drop by spoonfuls onto hot greased skillet and fry until browned on both sides.

If the clams are too juicy, increase the flour and reduce milk.

CLAM CHOWDER

Shuck the scrubbed and rinsed clams with a heavy knife. Rinse the clam meat in fresh water, then put through the food grinder.

In a large kettle, sauté a small chopped onion with several strips of bacon cut into small pieces. Add peeled, diced potatoes with enough water to cover. Add any juice drained from the chopped clams and simmer until potatoes are done. Add chopped clams and canned milk (small or large depending on how many clams), salt and pepper. Reheat until the mixture barely simmers. DO NOT BOIL.

Chef's secrets:
- *Chopped celery, parsley and green pepper (fresh or dried) may be added with the potatoes.*
- *The chowder base can be made up ahead of time and transported to the beach in cartons from milk. Add the clam juice, clams and milk at the beach.*

TOMATO CLAM CHOWDER
(Serves 2-3)

3 cups water and drained clam juice
1 tbls. minced dry onion flakes
1 can potatoes, drained, rinsed and diced
1 pkg. tomato-vegetable soup mix
1 cup chopped clams, drained
Salt and pepper to taste

Combine water, clam juice, onion, potato and soup mix. Simmer 10 min.

Add drained clams, salt and pepper. Reheat, do not boil.

POOR LUCK CLAM CHOWDER

1 can (6½ oz.) chopped clams, drained
2-3 cups water
1 pkg. Wyler's Potato Soup with Leek
½" of bacon bar, crumbled
1 tbls. each dry onion, celery flakes, green pepper flakes, parsley flakes
½ bag Idahoan hash potato shreds

Combine water, clam juice, potato soup, bacon bar and vegetable flakes. Simmer until potatoes are done, 10-15 min.

Combine ¾ cup dry milk and ¼ cup coffee lightener in small amount of water, just to moisten (or use small can evaporated milk).

Add milk mixture and chopped clams and reheat. Do not boil.

Add salt and pepper to taste.

½ pkg. freeze dried corn can be substituted for clams.

OYSTERS

Be sure the shell is tightly closed to insure freshness. Scrub the shells thoroughly and rinse in cold water. To shuck, pry the shell apart at the hinge to slip a knife inside to cut the muscle that clamps the shell shut. To cook unshucked, place on a grill over hot coals. When the shells open, pry them apart, remove the meat with a fork, dip the oyster into melted Seafood Butter and eat.

CAMPFIRE OYSTERS

Rinse the shucked oysters and drain.

Wrap each one in a half slice of bacon and slide onto a skewer.

Broil over hot coals, turning often until bacon is crisp and the edges of the oyster is ruffled.

Squeeze lemon juice over and serve immediately.

FRIED OYSTERS

Combine egg with a little milk. Dip oysters in egg, then seasoned crumbs, and fry in hot fat about 2 min. until browned.

FRIZZLED OYSTERS

Fry bacon strips until crisp and place on paper towel to drain.

Drain fat from frying pan.

Place shucked, washed and drained oysters in a very hot frying pan without liquid.

Shake the pan while the oysters are cooking until the edges curl.

Add salt and pepper and margarine.

Serve on buttered toast with bacon strips.

Garnish with parsley, watercress, sorrel or alfalfa sprouts.

OYSTER STEW
(Serves 4)

6 cups milk
1 qt. oysters
¼ cup margarine (½ stick)
1½ tsp. salt, dash of pepper
2 tsp. celery salt

Scald milk. Set aside. Heat oysters in their own liquid for about 5 min., until edges begin to curl. Add margarine and seasonings and hot milk. Serve immediately.

TEAS

Dry your own herb teas. Choose young tender leaves, wash, pat dry and spread out on a cookie sheet. Place in an unlit gas oven. The pilot light will provide sufficient heat to dry them. Or, place on the shiny side of foil and cover with a layer of cheesecloth. Leave in the hot sun to dry.

All of the following can be used to make acceptable, vitamin-rich beverages: Alfalfa, mint, nettle, parsley, celery.

Strawberry tea: To 1 quart of boiling water add 2 large handfuls of fresh washed leaves. Steep 5 min.

Clover: Take fully dried blossoms and rub into small particles. Use one teaspoonful for each cup of boiling water.

Raspberries: Use young twigs or tender leaves.

Blackberries: Add two to three tsp. of crushed dry leaves to a cup of boiling water.

Willow: Young leaves are rich in Vitamin C. A tea made by boiling the inner bark, twigs, leaves or roots is the next best thing to an aspirin. Willow contains salicin, closely related to acetylsalicylic acid.

Juniper: Boil a handful of juniper twigs (no berries) in a quart of water. Cover and simmer 10 min. Remove from heat and let stand a few minutes. Strain and serve. Indians used this for stomach upset.

WILD MINT SAUCE
(Makes 1¾ cups)

¼ cup vinegar
1 cup water
½ cup chopped mint leaves
¼ cup lemon juice
1½ tbls. sugar
½ tsp. salt

Heat vinegar and ½ cup water to boiling and pour over *half* the mint leaves. Let stand 15 min. Strain.

Add the remaining water, lemon juice, sugar and salt. Chill.

Add the remaining mint leaves, stir to blend.

Serve with lamb.

CHAPTER FOURTEEN

Consumer Buying Guide:
How To Pick A One-Burner Stove

Dry, dead fire wood is practically non-existent in some of the popular high mountains such as the Sierras. Blackened rock rings are a blot on the landscape, especially when adorned with a necklace of burned tin cans. There is an awakening to the new ecological awareness and new outdoor compact stoves seem to be jumping out from behind every tree and rock.

The advantages of a light-weight, one-burner stove far outweight the esthetics of a campfire for cooking. The extra weight is worth it when you are too tired to hunt firewood, and too hungry to wait for cooking coals to burn down.

I much prefer washing up shiny pots rather than fire-blackened ones, and I was never smart enough to figure out where to wash off the soot-covered liquid soap and keep my hands unsullied. Surely not in a clean stream!

We own three one-burner stoves: an American Coleman Sportster, a Swedish Optimus 99 lightweight and a German alcohol stove called a Turm-Sport. The Coleman holds enough fuel for a weekend canoe trip with plenty of fuel left over. The Optimus is lightweight and hot, but the silence is welcome when the stove is turned off. The alcohol stove requires frequent fill-ups, but it is lightweight and easy to fill. It is not very hot so is slower to cook on. However, we like it for heating water for freeze-dried foods and hot drinks.

Wind causes the big difficulty in lighting a stove, and a wind-blown flame will not concentrate heat to the pot. An adequate shield of rocks, logs or a folding screen of aluminum or asbestos will help get that pot boiling much quicker and easier.

If you set the stove on a cold spot such as snow or rock, the stove base may be cooled to the point that it may go out even after it has been burning well. A small piece of Ensolite under the stove will prevent this problem. Moss, twigs or leaves also could be used in an emergency.

Colin Fletcher, in his excellent book, THE COMPLETE WALKER, discusses various stoves in detail. The JOY OF CAMPING by Richard Langer also compares good points and draw backs of various camping stoves. However, I found several concise tips and good information about stoves in general in the Recreational Equipment catalog for 1974:

"A small stove is becoming more and more a camping necessity. Several factors must be considered when choosing a stove. Not only must the stove weight be considered, but also the weight of the fuel and fuel containers. Other important factors are compactness, ease of operation, fire hazard, stability for cooking, heat output, burning time and cost of operation.

The type of fuel used in a stove will determine the limitations and ease of operation. Kerosene is the least volatile of the fuels used in camp stoves. Kerosene vapors will not ignite at normal room temperatures; therefore the stove must be preheated or primed before the fuel will burn properly. A disadvantage of kerosene stoves is that a separate priming fuel, usually alcohol, must be carried.

White gas is the most commonly used fuel. Being quite volatile even at low temperatures, white gas stoves should not be filled inside a tent. The high volatility of white gas eliminates the need for a pump except in extremely cold weather. White gas stoves need preheating but a small amount of fuel from the stove will usually be adequate for the job.

Butane stoves are the simplest to operate. Just turn on the valve while holding a lighted match at the burner and the stove is ready to start cooking. Since the fuel is in cartridges there is no danger from spilled fuel. The convenience of the butane stove is offset by the higher cost of fuel, and the heavier containers that must be carried out when empty. Butane stoves can be used at high altitudes and low temperatures IF the fuel cartridge is kept above freezing.

Before attempting to operate a new stove, read the instructions carefully. Use only clean fuel of the type indicated in the instructions. Try the stove to see that it operates properly before taking it on a trip."

Liquified-Petroleum Gas: L. P. gas includes two distinct types of fuel — butane and propane — and they are NOT interchangeable. The type used in most light weight stoves, BUTANE, liquifies at a lower pressure, allowing it to be stored in a thin-walled, lighterweight cartridge. PROPANE is commonly used for multi-burner stoves used in campers and trailers. CAUTION: L. P. gas on your skin can cause frost bite.

Tip: To gauge the amount of L. P. gas left in the tank, place your hand on the botton of the tank and move your hand slowly upward until you reach a warm level. (L.P. gas makes metal cold to the touch.)

White Gas: White gas still is the most commonly used fuel. It is quite volatile, even at low temperatures, and so no pump is needed except in extremely cold weaather. White gas stoves need preheating, but a small amount of fuel from the stove usually will be all that is needed.

Remember these safety tips when operating white gas stoves:

Fuel spilled on hot equipment can start a fire.

Don't open the fuel tank while the stove is operating.

Always turn off the fuel supply before extinguishing the stove. This permits residual vapor to burn off and prevents flare-up the next time it is used

A blue flame is ideal. Yellow flames mean lack of air. A sharp flame that burns over the top of the burner means an excess of air.

Refill your stove on a level surface. This will prevent flooding and flare-up.

Use soapy water or commercial testing solution to find leaks. Use linseed oil in cold weather. NEVER test with a match.

General Safety Tips For Camp Stoves

Before trying to operate your new stove, read all instructions carefully.

Use only clean fuel of the type requested in the directions. Try the stove at home to see that it operates properly before packing for a trip.

Never start or generate a stove inside a tent or building, unless weather conditions are impossible. Provide ample ventilation when in a confined area.

Refuel the stove only when it is cool. Do not attempt to replace fuel cartridge on Gaz stove until the cartridge is empty.

Keep your stove clean. Empty the stove at the end of the season.

If the burner plate is loose on the top of your gas stove, bend the tabs to fasten it securely. A lost burner plate makes the stove inoperable.

Alcohol is recommended for priming because it burns clean, but it cannot be used as a fuel in the gas stove. An eyedropper can be used to place the fuel in the priming cup.

A piece of nylon stocking makes a good emergency gasoline filter.

Keep your stove closed against rain. It is difficult to light when wet.

A folding aluminum grease splatter shield placed around a single burner stove will concentrate heat to the pot. However, you must have an ample "cushion" of air around the stove so the fuel tank will not get overheated.

Matches are important to the operation of your stove. Make wooden matches waterproof by dipping the heads in nail polish or melted paraffin. Untreated matches soak up the night dampness. Keep them inside a waterproof container. A plastic pill bottle with a snap-on lid works well. To keep several matches, put them in a metal can with a plastic lid such as nuts or coffee come in, or use a metal bandage box. Tape a section of abrasive (such as fine sandpaper) inside the lid for striking.

INFORMATION ON VARIOUS STOVES

COLEMAN SPORTSTER — Uses white gas or Coleman fuel. One filling cooks several meals. Cooks simple meals fast and quietly. Lights easily at 0 degrees or below. Weight: 3 lbs. 2 oz. full of fuel. Size: 5¼" diameter, 5¾" high. Lightweight aluminum cookset case carries stove. Bottom unpacks to become 2 qt. saucepan, top becomes 6" square frying pan. (Optional) $13.50-$14.25 (1974 catalogs).

Personal Opinion: This stove has a solid wide cooking surface for a larger pot. It is not easily tipped over. It holds enough fuel for a weekend trip if simple meals are prepared. This eliminates the necessity of carrying extra fuel containers. The flame can be regulated, but the handle gets hot if the pot or fry pan is wider than the stove top. NOT a back-pack stove, but great for canoe or car camping. No one that I interviewed had an unkind word about this stove.

PRIMUS 8R — Swedish made. Uses white gas. Capacity: 1/3 pint. Comes with brass carrying case, 5 3/4" by 3 3/4", serves as wind screen and cooking grid. Tank folds forward for easy filling. Self-priming and starts fast. Built-in cleaning device, no pumping required. Valve knob detaches. Weight 1 lb. 9 oz. or 1 lb. 4 oz. depending on catalog consulted. $13.95-$14.50 ppd. (1974 catalogs)

Opinion: Man interviewed said his Primus 8R gives out a lot of heat for its size and he feels it is very efficient. Because of the low profile it is very stable. It is also very compact. However, it is extremely noisy and he had some trouble with it at 8,000'.

PRIMUS 71L — Made in Sweden. Uses white gas. Capacity: 1/2 pint. Burns approximately 1 1/2 hrs. Comes in metal container. Is reliable and efficient. Container is the wind screen. Cleaning needle and valve key included. No pumping required. Weight 1 lb. 3 oz. Folded size: 3 1/4" by 5 1/2". $13.95 (1974 catalogs)

Opinion: Person interviewed is happy with his Primus 71L. It works well at all altitudes but the stove will not light unless it is cool. He has dunked the top of his stove in water to cool it before relighting for 20 years, and it still is his favorite one burner stove. Like the Primus 8R, it is very noisy.

PRIMUS "RANGER" mini-stove — Uses butane cartridge. Burns up to four hours. Tripod stand makes a sturdy base on difficult terrain. Broad burner can handle larger pots. Weight of stove only 15 oz. Folded size: 12 1/2" by 3" by 3". $15.00, stove only. $5.00, 4 to a box cartridges. Wt. 2 lbs. 11 oz.

Opinion: One owner considered this one hard to start in cold weather. He also felt it was more stable than some small stoves. Man interviewed felt this model was the best for the weight. It is small enough to fit in a pack sack pocket. However, pots must be kept small. The flame will not heat the sides of a larger pot.

OPTIMUS 8R — Made in Sweden. Uses white gas. 1/3 pint burns approx. 1 1/4 hrs. Smaller version of 111B. Develops very hot flame. Self-pressure system. Self-cleaning device built in. Must insulate from snow and cold to maintain pressure. Folds into its own carrying case. Easy fill tank pops out front when open. Weight, 1 3/4 lb. Size: 5" by 5" x 3". $15.00-$17.50 (1974 catalogs).

OPTIMUS 111B — Burns white gas. 1 pint burns up to 2 hrs., full flame

Larger than 8R model. Lights fast and heats "like a blow torch". Enlarged burner provides extra heat. Stove is wide and low to give a stable base for pots. Regulating burner with self-cleaning device. Polished brass 1 pint tank has a built-in pressure pump. Tank has a safety valve. Opens to form wind screen to insure best performance. Weight: 3½ lbs. Folded case: 7" by 7" by 4½" $27.00-$29.00 (1974 catalogs).

Opinion: Person interviewed recommends this stove for its reliability, fast heat, low profile, compactness, and construction. However, he did NOT consider it a backpack stove. Another interviewee stressed the fact that this stove was excellent for winter camping. He found it worked well at 11,000 feet on a backpack trip.

The National Outdoor Leadership School in Lander, Wyoming, has tried various stoves, but "we have decided for our purposes — expeditions of quite a duration — that the Optimus 111B performs best and is most reliable although its weight is considerably more than most stoves."

OPTIMUS 99 — Burns white gas. Uses ¼ pint fuel per hour. Capacity: ⅓ pint. Compact two-piece pack stove. Top doubles as cook pot. Comes with wind screen and handle. Uses same burner and tank assembly as the 8R version, but comes with aluminum case to reduce weight. Folds easily. Must insulate from cold and snow to keep pressure. Has regulating burner, requires no pumping. Has self-pricking jet and safety valve. Weight: 1 lb. 5 oz. Folded case: 5" by 5" by 3⅛". Weight full of fuel: 1 lb. 10 oz. $16.25-$17.95 (1974 catalogs).

Opinion: (my husband) He thinks it is tempermental in starting. Once it is going it works fine. It is reasonably easy to fill. The wire pot rack should have a catch spot so it doesn't fold up when moving a pot.

My opinion of Optimus 99: I don't like it for cooking. The pot rack is too small and there is nothing to keep the pot from sliding off if it is on any kind of a tilt. The wind screen is very ineffective and a gimmick. It can't work at all if you use a pot bigger than a cook kit coffee pot. If the wind screen was the same height as the pot rack it could be used to steady larger pots.

OPTIMUS 100 — Uses kerosene. A larger (than 99 model) collapsible stove with a silent burner and wide burner plate. Also has a roarer burner to spread the flame. Weight 2½ lbs. Size: 8" high by 8½" diameter. $14.95 (1974 catalogs).

OPTIMUS 80 — Uses white gas. 1/2 pint burns about 1 1/2 hours. Requires no pumping. Comes in metal box which serves as wind screen/cooking stand. Weight: 1 1/4 lb. Box size: 3 1/4" by 5 1/2" by 5". $12.50-$13.00 (1974 catalogs).

OPTIMUS 00L — Burns white gas or kerosene. Tank holds 1 pint. Burns about 2 hrs. Has pressure pump and roarer burner. Fuel can be carried in tank when stove is dismantled. Comes with priming fuel storage can, wrench, cleaning pins. Weight: Approx. 2 lbs. Folds to 5 1/2" by 7" by 3 1/2". $16.25-$17.00 (1974 catalogs).

Opinion: This stove is reasonably stable. A large pot only bubbles in the center even though the roarer burner spreads the flame to cover more surface. The stove is quite noisy. This owner felt the kerosene stove was hotter than gas and much hotter than propane.

OPTIMUS 48 — Burns kerosene. Large stove with silent burner and wide burner plate. Larger tank size. Fuel can be carried in tank when stove is dismantled. Weight: 2 1/2 lbs. Size: 8" high by 8 1/2" diameter. $17.00 (1974 catalogs).

OPTIMUS 77A — Burns alcohol. Uses .35 pints per hour. Explosion proof and safe. Stove lights instantly. No priming. Very little heat lost when cooking in pots and pans designed for set. Performance not affected by wind, cold, high elevations. Weight complete with cook set: 28 oz. 4 1/4" high by 8" diameter. $16.95.

OPTIMUS 731 — "Mousetrap" — Butane cartridge. Burns 2 hours or more at normal output. Compact, stable, collapsible. Performs exceptionally well in strong winds, high altitudes, sub-freezing weather. Self-sealing butane cartridge is removable and can be reused without leakage. Exclusive gas preheating system permits stove to reach maximum output quickly. Upright cartridge avoids flare-ups. All the gas is used. Weight, stove only: 11 1/2 oz. Wt. full cartridge: 9 1/2 oz. Folded stove dimensions: 4 3/4" by 7 3/16" by 1 3/16" $13.00-$12.95 stove only. Cartridge only $1.00.

PHOEBUS 625 — Uses white gas. Burns 1 1/2 hrs. on one pint of fuel. Ideal for high altitude use. Compact, reliable in all temperatures. Good for winter use. Large capacity and heavy duty construction. Very powerful for its weight. Must be primed. Has pump, silent burner, self-cleaning device built in. Spare parts included. Comes with light weight carrying cannister: 5 1/2" diameter by 7 1/2" high. Stove weight: 2 lbs. 6 oz. With cannister: 2 lbs. 14 oz. $19.50-$21.50 (1974 catalogs).

Opinion: Person interviewed feels the stove is very fast and uses fuel efficiently, but it is narrow and high so it is not as stable as other stoves. He doesn't like the fact that the paint gets burned off the top of the fuel tank.

BI EUET — Made in France. Uses disposabl: butane cartridges Purns 2½-4 hrs. at full flame. Regulating valve controls flame. No filling, priming, pre-heating, or pumping. Cartridge snaps into place and is immediately ready to use. Easiest of stoves to use. It is clean, efficient, less noisy. Base removes and pot support folds for packing. Wind screen sold separately. Increases efficiency greatly under adverse conditions. Cleaning needle 5¢ extra. Weight of stove with cartridge: 1 lb. 9 oz. Extra cartridge: 10 oz. $7.00-$10.00, stove and one cartridge. (1974 catalogs).

Opinion: 1st owner: Found his Bleuet did not work at high altitude and, with disposable containers, it is an ecological detriment.

2nd owner: A world wide mountain climber give the Bleuet a thumbs down in cold weather. He says it loses pressure and won't light. However, under better conditions it works efficiently and can be regulated to simmer well.

3rd owner: Has two Bleuets and likes to take both on long canoe trips. He finds the cartridges expensive and the high profile of the stove make it quite unstable, but the stove is light weight, fast and easy to regulate.

4th owner: Warns that care is necessary in attaching the cartridge. If it is not lined up straight the fuel spurts out.

5th owner: "Turn it on and it goes. It has never leaded gas. It tends to be tippy, so I don't use the base that comes with it. I dig a shallow hole and pack dirt around the base to keep it steady, only about an inch up the side."

6th owner: Did not have a wind screen on his stove and he felt the stove was not efficient without it. If the pot was kept small the flame covered to cook well.

No. 303 MINI-STOVE — Burns white gas (From Eddie Bauer, Seattle, Wash.) Lightweight compact design permits it to be taken apart to fit inside its own unit. Pressurized, adjustable flame. Baked enamel steel case contains cooking grill, pre-heater, pressure pump, flame adjusting handle, wrench, cleaning needle. spare parts kit. Total weight: Approx. 24 oz. Size: 4" by 5½" by 2¾". $22.95 (1974 catalog).

Lady interviewed . . . "I don't like to carry the cans. They are very expensive, and a can lasts only about three hours. The stove is instant hot and easy for ladies to work, but the wind screen is heavy and awkward to install."

SVEA 123 — Burns white gas. Capacity: ⅓ pint burns 1 hr. High efficiency and light weight. Reliable. Requires no pumping. Safety valve, built-in wind screen also serve as pot stand. Works well at high altitude. Must be insulated from snow or cold to maintain pressure. Comes with small pot. which inverts to form cover. Includes pot, lifter, cleaning needle, and valve key. Fits into smallest Sigg pot. Weight: 1 lb. 2 oz. Size: 5" high by 3¾" diameter. $12.50-$15.50 (1974 catalogs).

Opinion: 1st owner: Similar to Primus 71L. Best stove for one person. It is an excellent backpack stove.

2nd owner (female): "It is hot. I have no trouble keeping it lit. I have cooked for 5 people with enough fuel to cook 2 or meals with one filling. Since you can't build up pressure it takes a little longer to get going. It is stable if the right stand is used. I find it hard to start if cold, and the pot tends to get off center when moving it. The stove is noisy."

POCKET STOVE — Uses fuel cans. 4 oz. of fuel good for 3 hrs. of simmering. Light, compact, safe. Fits in palm of hand or pocket. All parts precision engineered. Nickel-plated tripod designed for stability. Holds common sizes of cookware. Good for one person. Weight 9 oz. including fuel can. $8.75, stove only. $1.95 two 4 oz. cans.

SIEVERT POCKET STOVE — The catalog says: Burns any type of gasoline without pumping. Lid converts to a small pan for cooking. Stove made completely of brass. Weight: 1⅛ lb. 5" high by 3¾" diameter. $14.95 (1973 catalog).

GERRY MINI-MARK 2 STOVES—Removable butane cartridge. Burns more than 2 hrs. at full flame. Cartridge attaches by needle valve. Gas self-sealing valve gasket. Cartridge can be removed from stove before empty and replaced for further use. Fits into its own self-contained unit. Stable base, broad top. Burner and valve unit screw into bottom half of container unit. Top half becomes wind screen and grid. Weight, stove only: 7 oz. Weight, cartridge: 10 oz. Folded: 1½" high by 4½" diameter. 5" high when assembled Stove, $10.45-$14.95 (1974 catalogs). Cartridges: 95¢-99¢.

Opinion: No problems though it is hard to light if the cartridge is cold. The tank helps to stabilize the stove.

GAZ S 200—French made. Butane cartridge. Burns up to 3½ hrs. DO NOT REMOVE CARTRIDGE UNTIL COMPLETELY EXPELLED. Easy to operate. Not recommended for extreme cold unless cartridge can be kept above freezing. No priming or pumping necessary to start or maintain flame. Weight of stove: ⅞ lb. Weight of cartridge: 10 oz. $7.45, stove only. 86¢ for cartridge. Uses Gaz C 200 only.

Opinion: Owner found it bulky and not very stable.

FOLDING CANNED HEAT STOVE—Uses Sterno fuel. Folds flat. Weight 13 oz. Size: 6½" square. 4" high when open. Stove only: 88¢ Fuel—One 2⅝ oz. can burns 50 min. . .24¢. One 7 oz. can burns 1 hr. 40 min. 43¢.

Opinion: Neat, compact, handy. Good for a one night trip. One can of fuel is adequate for one or two meals. The big problem on a long trip is carrying enough cans of fuel.

ALCOHOL BURNER—Uses denatured alcohol for fuel. Easy to start, good for emergency cooking, lightweight. Pocket-sized brass stove. Gives hot, clean, smokeless flame. Weight stove: 4 oz. $2.50.

STOVE COMPARISON TABLE

Stove	Fuel	Capacity	Burning Time (Full Flame)
Svea 123	White gas	1/3 pint	1 hour
Optimus 80	White gas	1/2 pint	1 1/2 hours
Optimus 8R, 99	White gas	1/3 pint	1 1/4 hours
Phoebus 625	White gas	1 pint	1 1/2 hours
Optimus 111B	White gas	1 pint	2 hours
Optimus 00L	White gas		
	Kerosene	1 pint	2 hours
Optimus 48	Kerosene	1 3/4 pint	4 hours
Gaz S 200	Butane	Cartridge	3 hours
Alcohol Burner	Alcohol	.38 pint	25 min.
Bleuet	Butane	Cartridge	3 hrs.

FUEL COMPARISONS
(From Rec. Equip. Catalog)

WHITE GAS: *Advantages*
    Light weight stove.
    Spilled fuel evaporates readily.
    Stove fuel used for priming.
    Fuel readily available in U.S.

KEROSENE:
    Spilled fuel will not ignite readily.
    Stove can be set directly on snow.
    Low cost fuel.
    Fuel available throughout world.

BUTANE:
    No priming required.
    No fuel to spill.
    Immediate maximum heat output.

Disadvantages
    Priming required.
    Spilled fuel very flammable.
    Self-pressurizing stoves must be
      insulated from cold and snow.
    Difficult to start in wind.
    Priming required.
    Spilled fuel does not evaporate
      readily.
    Difficult to start in wind.
    Higher cost fuel.
    Empty cartridge disposal a
      problem.
    Fuel must be kept above freezing
      for effective operation.
    Bleuet cartridges cannot be
      changed until empty.
    Lower heat output.

PROBLEMS AND POSSIBLE SOLUTIONS
(From Rec. Equip. Catalog)

PROBLEM	POSSIBLE CAUSE	SOLUTION
Failure to operate	Fuel tank empty	Refill tank per instruction.
	Burner plate missing	Bend tabs on burner plate to hold securely.
	Orifice clogged	Remove nipple. Run cleaning pin through orifice. Blow out loose particles. Invert stove to remove particles from top of vaporizer. Replace nipple. (Self-cleaning models only require operation of built-in cleaner, according to directions.)
	Pressure leak	Check filler cap. Replace gasket and/or relief valve if necessary. Retighten.
	Inadequate preheating	Fill priming cup and relight. Protect from wind.
Weak flame	Orifice clogged	(See above)
	Pressure leak	(See above)
	Charred wick	Replace wick.
	Low vapor pressure	Insulate stove from snow or cold
	Improper fuel	Use only the type of fuel recommended by manufacturer.
	Internal cleaning pin improperly set	Reset cleaning pin per instructions.
Unable to turn off fuel	Internal cleaning pin improperly set	Reset cleaning pin per inst.
	Vaporizer bent	Replace vaporizer (Use wrench on hex only when turning vaporizer)
Pump fails to build up pressure.	Leather dried out	Remove pump rod, oil and carefully spread leather. Replace leather if hardened.
	Edge of leather turned under	Straighten leather. Install carefully
	Check valve leaks	Replace (Special tool needed)

Flame at spindle	Packing nut loose	Tighten
	Packing worn	Replace
	Spindle damaged	Replace
Flame at filler cap	Cap loose	Tighten
	Gasket hardened	Replace
	Relief valve leaks	Replace cap
	Threads damaged or filled with braze metal.	Chase threads (Special tool needed)

FUEL FLASKS

Don't forget a small funnel for filling and an eyedropper for priming the stove.

Metal gas cans: Slender, reusable, easily stored. Durable container for white gas storage. Look for built-in filtering mesh screens over filler cap and pouring spout.

Flat type: Many are considered leakproof and are of non-corrosive metal. Some people feel the flat ones are a little more sturdy. Some containers are made of German tinned steel, others are of tin alloy.

Aluminum Bottles: Also considered leakproof and non-corrosive. There are no solder seams and the cap will not corrode. One owner dropped a full aluminum bottle. It now leaks, but it is impossible to see where. Aluminum bottles are not recommended for alcohol or acid liquids.

Plastic Gas Cans: Tough container. Look for a spout which turns inside the top for transport. It fits into the opening for pouring. Be sure it is of an approved design.

ON OBTAINING FUEL: When traveling overseas be sure you have a stove that uses available fuel. Mexico, Africa, and Nepal do not have white gas except occasionally. Kerosene is a good choice for those countries.

White gas is usually available in Europe, but it may be called benzine or petrol.

Bleuet cartridges can be found in *some* European countries with good French relations.

OUTDOOR CATALOGS
(Partial List)

GERRY, 5450 No. Valley Hwy., Denver, Colorado 80216

SIERRA DESIGNS, 4th and Addison St., Berkeley, Calif. 94710

THE SKI HUT, 1615 University Ave., Berkeley, Calif. 94703

NORTH FACE, P.O. Box 2399, Station A, Berkeley, Calif. 94702

EDDIE BAUER, P.O. Box 3700, Seattle, Wash. 98124

KELTY, 1801 Victory Blvd., Glendale, Calif. 91201

KLINEBURGER, JONAS BROS. OF SEATTLE, 1527 12th Ave., Seattle, Wash. 98122

FAMOUS DEPARTMENT STORE, 530 So. Main St., Los Angeles, Calif. 90013

GANDER MOUNTAIN, INC., P.O. Box 248, Wilmot, Wisc. 53192

GREAT WORLD, 250 Farms Village Rd., Box 250, West Simsbury, Conn. 06092

WATERS, INC. 111 East Sheridan St., Ely, Minn. 55731

LAACKE AND JOYS CO., 1432 N. Water St., Milwaukee, Wisc. 53202

HANCOCK VILLAGE OUTFITTERS, INC., Hancock, New Hampshire 03449

RECREATIONAL EQUIPMENT, INC., 1524 11th Ave., Seattle, Wash. 98122
(Membership Fee . . . $2.00)